A History of the Garda Síochána

A Social History of the Force 1922–52,
with an Overview for the Years 1952–97

Liam McNiffe

WOLFHOUND PRESS

First published in 1997 by
Wolfhound Press Ltd
68 Mountjoy Square
Dublin 1, Ireland

Reprinted 1999

© 1997 Liam McNiffe

British Library Cataloguing in Publication Data
A catalogue record for this book is available from the British Library.

ISBN 0-86327-581-8

Front cover photograph: Garda Jeremiah Murphy (motor cyclist) and Garda
                           Culhane (side car)

All photographs in this book are reproduced by kind permission of the Garda Museum with the exception of the following:

Section 1
Page 7, (bottom) by kind permission of Nuala Doyle
Page 11, by kind permission of Dorothy Archer

Section 2
Page 1, (bottom) by kind permission of Eda Sagarra
Page 7, (bottom) by kind permission of Anna McCabe

Cover Design: Slick Fish Design
Typesetting: Wolfhound Press
Printed and bound in Great Britain by MPG Books Ltd, Bodmin, Cornwall

Contents

*To my wife Mary, and to our children
Aisling, Ruairí and Shane,
as well as to the memory of my father,
Willie McNiffe.*

Acknowledgements

This book grew out of a PhD which I completed in 1994 at St Patrick's College, Maynooth, under the supervision of Professor Vincent Comerford. His help, encouragement and advice, from the very beginning of the undertaking until its completion as a book, have been immense. His willingness to help at all times despite the pressures of his own commitments was deeply appreciated. I am grateful to the staffs of the National Archives of Ireland, Maynooth College Library, the Archives Department at University College Dublin and the Franciscan Institute of Celtic Studies in Dublin. A special word of thanks is due to those people whom I interviewed. They were invariably unfailing in their courtesy, willing in their answers and encouraging in their comments. Four of them have since died: John Heffron, W. J. McConville, Dick Hearns and Mary Shaw. Requiescant in pace. Retired Sergeant Gregory Allen, former curator of the Garda Museum, has been very unselfish in his help. The present curator/archivist, Sergeant John Duffy, has facilitated the researching of this book in every possible way. As well as making available almost all the illustrations that appear, his help and support over the past few years have been inestimable. Dr Adrian Kelly and Dr Raymond Gillespie of St Patrick's College Maynooth rendered very professional assistance in the computerisation of data relating to the guards. Seán Fegan helped in the presentation of some statistical charts. I owe a great debt of gratitude to the typist Jennifer Reilly, who assiduously attended to the numerous redraftings. Thanks are also due to Nuala Doyle, Professor Eda Sagarra, Dorothy Archer, J. B. Murphy and Anna McCabe for photographs which they kindly provided.

Seamus Cashman and Emer Ryan of Wolfhound Press have been a pleasure to work with in the production of this book.

On a personal note, my wife Mary has been unfailing in her support, both moral and practical. She has acted as a sounding board, a proofreader and an interpreter of my hieroglyphics. The disruption of family life in the past six years has been significant owing to my obsession with the guards. Mary has borne this stoically and I thank her most sincerely. Finally I thank our children, Aisling, Ruairí and Shane, who will be very glad to see this book completed.

Liam McNiffe
Kells, 1996

Abbreviations

BA	British army
DJ	Department of Justice
DMD	Dublin metropolitan division
DMP	Dublin Metropolitan Police
DT	Department of the Taoiseach
GM	Garda Museum
G. Rev.	*Garda Review*
GS	Garda Síochána
IRA	Irish Republican Army
IRP	Irish Republican Police
NA	National army
NAI	National Archives of Ireland
NCO	Non-commissioned officer
RIC	Royal Irish Constabulary
RUC	Royal Ulster Constabulary
UCDA	University College Dublin, Archives Department

Ranks of Garda Síochána

Gd	Guard
Sgt	Sergeant
St sgt	Station sergeant
Insp	Inspector
Sup	Superintendent
Ch sup	Chief superintendent
Ass comm	Assistant commissioner
Dep comm	Deputy commissioner
Comm	Commissioner

Introduction

This book is a social history of the Garda Síochána for the period 1922–52, with a chapter covering the years 1952–97. The focus is primarily on the experience of being a policeman. Administrative and political considerations are dealt with where they impinge on the social history of the force. While the overall structure of the book is thematic, a chronological sequence is followed within the confines of each individual chapter. Much of the archival material relating to the post-1952 period has not yet been released to the researcher, making it impossible to treat the years 1952–97 using the methodology followed for the 1922–52 period. Chapter 13 then is quite different from the remainder of the book. It is divided into sections, each dealing with a decade and highlighting the major developments in the Garda Síochána in that decade.

In the mid-1980s a wealth of previously inaccessible archival material relating to the Garda Síochána was made available for research. The Department of the Taoiseach S files and the Department of Justice H series and 4 series in the National Archives, Dublin, cover every conceivable aspect of the force in minute detail. In 1987 a Garda Museum was officially opened at Garda headquarters in Dublin. This meant that historical material previously in the possession of private individuals scattered throughout the country was now more easily accessible in one location, as well as official garda archival material. The Garda Museum was in its infancy when this work was being researched and consequently the material had not been catalogued or indexed. A number of registers in the museum record the particulars of every man who joined the guards in the 1922–31 period. A computerised analysis of this data (augmented by a registry of candidates for the 1931–52 period, which is in private hands) forms an integral part of the research behind this book. In 1977 retired Sergeant John Shaw asked surviving members to send their detailed reminiscences of the 1922 period to him. Over sixty did so. In 1992 his widow, Mary, very generously gave me unlimited access to this treasure trove. In the course of my research I interviewed retired members from all ranks of the force, the majority of whom had joined in the 1922–24 period. I also interviewed the spouses of a number of members.

Very little has been written on the history of the Garda Síochána and what has been written tends to be political in emphasis. Conor Brady's pioneering work, *Guardians of the Peace*, was published in 1974. The core of Brady's book concerns itself with the force and with political developments in the 1922–35 period. Its emphasis is on government decisions and dealings with the entire force, rather than on the experience of being a guard. Seamus Breathnach's *The Irish Police, From Earliest Times to the Present Day* was also published in 1974. Only a few chapters deal with the Garda Síochána, and the emphasis is on police and politics. A slim volume entitled *Salute to the Gardaí*, by Denis O'Kelly, which was published in 1959, gives a brief history of the force. In 1985 *Lugs: The Life and Times of Jim Branigan* by Bernard Neary was published. This gives a flavour of garda life in Dublin in the 1930–70 period. In 1969 *De Réir Uimhreacha*, a semi-autobiographical novel, was published. Its author, Pádraig Ua Maoileoin, had spent thirty years in the force. Numerous articles relating to the history of the Garda Síochána have appeared over the years in the garda magazine, the *Garda Review*, as well as in *An Síothadóir* (later renamed *Síochán*), the publication of the Garda Pensioners' Association.

1

Policing in Ireland before Independence

A regular police system began to emerge in Ireland only about 200 years ago. At various times from as early as the fourteenth century, the Anglo-Normans had established constables or watchmen in different parts of the country. However, such policing was very limited in scope and members of the watch were easily bribed and intimidated.[1] There was no great change in policing in Ireland until the last quarter of the eighteenth century when a number of acts were introduced to improve the situation. In 1787 the Lord Lieutenant was empowered to appoint a chief constable to each barony, and grand juries were empowered to appoint sixteen sub-constables to each district. In practice, however, constables tended to be undisciplined and ineffectual. An act of 1792 allowed grand juries to appoint additional 'baronial' constables to each district. Although thirteen counties were exempted from its operation this act pushed the traditional constable into the role of the modern policeman. In 1814, Sir Robert Peel introduced a new act, which set up the Peace Preservation Force. It provided an important link between the traditional idea of the old constabulary and watch systems and the modern concept of a civil police force.[2] This allowed the Lord Lieutenant to proclaim any area to be in a 'state of disturbance', in which case he could appoint a chief magistrate, a chief constable and fifty sub-constables to such an area. The Peace Preservation Force was to operate as a flexible and mobile instrument, which would be drafted into troubled areas once they were proclaimed 'troubled' under the new act.[3] The

Irish Constables Act, 1822, set up four provincial police forces, each under the supervision of an inspector general. The new force grew to over 303 chief constables and over 5,000 constables. The men, who were armed and uniformed, were given three months' training. The force was of a paramilitary character. The Irish Constables Act created a permanent police establishment throughout the country. The force was to be known as the County Constabulary, and in practice was administered at county level by the magistrates and chief constables.

Dublin, like London, was always treated as a separate entity as far as policing was concerned. For the purpose of a watch system, the city had been divided into twenty-one parishes, each of which contained fifteen watchmen who were supervised by a constable appointed by the churchwarden. These watchmen were frequently elderly men who 'patrolled the streets at night as best they could in pretentious uniforms of blue and gold'.[4] There were no day patrols. In 1786 a new act set up the Dublin metropolitan district (DMD), which was divided into four divisions with a chief constable and ten petty constables in each. Dublin had now, for the first time, regular policemen, charged with patrolling the streets of the city by day and by night. Watchmen were also appointed under this act, as well as additional constables to supervise them. By 1820 there were five police forces in Ireland: the Dublin Police, the County Constabulary, the Peace Preservation Force, the watchmen in all corporate towns, and the embryonic Revenue Police. The latter's main function was the suppression of illicit distillation. Although the Irish Constables Act of 1822 rationalised the position by bringing most of the country under the discipline of four provincial police forces, it did not affect the Dublin police.

RIC

The Constabulary (Ireland) Act of 1836 overhauled the administration of policing in Ireland and created a new centralised police force called the Irish Constabulary. The first national police force to exist in Ireland, with only the cities of Dublin, Derry and Belfast remaining outside its jurisdiction, it had a uniform standard of clothing, and a set of rules and regulations that applied to all policemen, no matter where they served. The inspector general was in charge of the entire force.[5] The vast majority of the rank and file of the old County Constabulary and most of the officers were accepted into the new force.[6] From 1840 onwards, recruits were trained at one central training depot in the Phoenix Park, Dublin.

The rank and file of the Irish Constabulary comprised mainly the sons of small farmers. The majority of promotions to the officer class came via the cadet system, with only a minority of the ranks being promoted to that class. Most officer positions were reserved for men of high social standing and good education. Before 1836 the old County Constabulary was perceived by most peasants as a sectarian force. By 1841 over 51 per cent of the rank and file of the new Irish Constabulary were Roman Catholic, and by 1914 this had risen to almost 81 per cent. In 1911 the Roman Catholic proportion of the general population was approximately 74 per cent.[7] By the outbreak of the First World War, however, Protestants still occupied a disproportionately high number of officer positions in the police force.

From its inception in 1836 until its disbandment in 1922 the Irish Constabulary was responsible for policing all of Ireland, with the exception of the cities of Dublin, Belfast and Derry. In 1865 the Belfast borough police was abolished, and in 1870 Derry's local police was similarly abolished. Henceforth, both cities were policed by the Irish Constabulary. In the late 1860s the Irish Constabulary received the additional appellation of 'Royal', in recognition of its work in helping to suppress the 1867 Fenian rebellion. For most of its life the RIC operated with five or six members stationed in small barracks dotted all over the country. By 1914 there were 1,129 RIC barracks and eighty-three temporary huts in all of Ireland.[8] As well as their general duty of preventing and detecting crime, members did foot and bicycle patrols, enforced the licensing laws, attempted to suppress the distillation of illicit liquor, and collected agricultural statistics. Although the RIC was officially an armed force, rural day-time patrols and beats in towns were performed by pairs of policemen who carried no firearms. Firearms were usually carried only if there was a disturbance or the threat of one.

The RIC was a native Irish police force, loyal to the government and enforcing the law of the land. Throughout most of the nineteenth and early twentieth century its members enjoyed fairly good relations with the general Irish public. At times of political, social or economic crisis, relations between the police and the public tended to deteriorate. The tithe war of the 1830s, the Young Ireland rebellion of the 1840s, the Fenian rebellion of the 1860s and the land war of the 1880s were all times of crisis. The land war was by far the most trying time for the force during the nineteenth century in that 'for the first time the RIC was viewed with hostility by a large section of the community'.[9] By the late 1890s, however, the constabulary was as popular with the rural community as it had been before the land war. As individuals, members of the RIC were generally personally popular.

DMP

In 1818 there were seventy-two chief constables and peace officers, twenty-six watch constables and 493 watchmen in Dublin. The force was regarded as fairly efficient. However, by 1837 many of the watchmen were old and decrepit. The city's police was reformed in 1838. The watch was abolished and the existing day police force was enlarged and reformed. The new force was modelled on the London Metropolitan Police. Most Dublin Metropolitan Police (DMP) recruits came from rural Ireland — many were agricultural labourers. They were trained at Kevin Street training depot. Towards the end of the nineteenth century the authorities recruited an increasing number of tall recruits. Between 1895 and 1914 two-thirds of all DMP recruits were over 6 feet tall. As there was no cadet system, practically all the officer positions in the Dublin Metropolitan Police were filled by men who had been promoted from the ranks. In 1857 there were 1,092 officers and men in the Dublin police. Approximately 88 per cent of these were Roman Catholic and 12 per cent were Protestant.[10] Protestants, however, were over-represented in the officer class. The DMP was an unarmed force scattered in small to medium-sized groups in barracks throughout the metropolitan area. Its members tended to be busier than their rural counterparts in the RIC, as the city's number of indictable crimes was out of proportion to its population. Throughout the nineteenth and early twentieth centuries there was fairly widespread hostility towards the DMP in the lower-class areas of the capital. The confrontations between the DMP and the public during the 1913 Lock Out merely exacerbated the situation.

At the outbreak of the First World War in 1914, Ireland had two police forces. The RIC policed the entire country with the exception of Dublin. Although it was armed on occasion, there was no widespread antagonism towards the force. The DMP, although unarmed and generally respected by the higher social classes of Dublin, experienced hostility from some of the lower social classes. The political role of the RIC and DMP has been emphasised quite frequently but in reality the vast majority of these policemen spent most of their time performing mundane, non-political tasks.[11] This situation was to be radically altered by the events of 1919–21.

POLICE AND THE POLITICAL SITUATION, 1919–21

On 21 January 1919 the first Dáil met at the Mansion House in Dublin to proclaim Irish independence from Britain. This assembly was made up of Sinn Féin members (excluding those who were in jail) who had been elected in the 1918 general election, but who refused to take their seats in Westminster. By this policy of abstention and non-co-operation, Sinn Féin hoped to render inoperative British administration in Ireland and force the British government to recognise Irish independence. This was the political wing in the struggle for independence. The military arm of the fight for independence was the IRA who engaged in guerrilla warfare against any forces in Ireland loyal to Britain.

The IRA's military campaign began in January 1919 and lasted two and a half years until the truce of July 1921. In January 1919 two locally based RIC men were escorting a cartload of explosives to a quarry at Soloheadbeg in County Tipperary. They were ambushed by an IRA brigade, which included Sean Treacy and Dan Breen. In the ensuing confusion the constables were killed. On 31 January *An t-Óglách*, the official organ of the Irish Volunteers or IRA, stated that every volunteer was entitled to use 'all legitimate methods of warfare against the soldiers and policemen of the English usurper, and to slay them if it is necessary to overcome their resistance'.[12] RIC members were an attractive target for the IRA for a number of reasons. Their location in isolated barracks in many parts of Ireland left them vulnerable to attack. Successful attacks by the IRA had a two-fold benefit: they disarmed the RIC, and they augmented the IRA's own very scarce arsenal of weapons. Furthermore, continued attacks on isolated RIC barracks forced their evacuation, thereby leaving many areas of the country outside the control of British administration.

The first phase of the War of Independence lasted from January 1919 to March 1920 and mainly involved the IRA against the RIC. The second phase of the war was from March 1920 until July 1921. This was by far the more brutal and grim period. Refusing to recognise the disturbance in Ireland as war, British Prime Minister Lloyd George reinforced the police rather than the army. In the spring of 1920 new English recruits were enlisted as a reinforcement for the RIC. Very soon they were nicknamed the Black and Tans because of the colour of their uniform. A second group of specially recruited Englishmen began to arrive in Ireland in the summer of 1920. Officially known as the Auxiliary Division of the RIC, these were soon called the 'Auxies'. The activities of some Black and Tans caused widespread revulsion in Ireland, and the commanding officer of the Auxiliaries, Brigadier General E. F. Crozier, eventually resigned his post rather than go on leading what he described as a drunken and insubordinate body of men. Terror and counter terror shocked the country at this time. In July 1921 the IRA and the British Government agreed a truce.

The 1912 Home Rule Bill had a somewhat detrimental effect on the

RIC, as members anticipated the eventual disbandment of the force when Home Rule would become a reality. The prospect of a permanent career in the police seemed unlikely and this had an adverse effect on recruitment, as had the government's emphasis on army recruitment after the outbreak of war in 1914. The rampant inflation of the war years seriously eroded the standard of living of RIC men. Consequently, by 1918, morale among many members was not very high. This situation was greatly aggravated by the War of Independence. In many parts of the country RIC men were ostracised, threatened, shot at and sometimes killed. One estimate puts the number of RIC men killed at 425 with 725 wounded, in the period January 1919 to July 1921.[13] By the beginning of 1920 there were approximately 1,500 vacancies in the ranks of the regular RIC.[14] During that year, hundreds resigned from the force. The experience of individual RIC men during the War of Independence varied a great deal, depending on where they were stationed. Some areas remained relatively calm, with ordinary life by and large continuing as it had done before 1919. Other areas experienced an almost total breakdown in law and order and became virtual war zones. All RIC men were expected to do a stint in 'troubled counties' during the War of Independence. The son of one RIC man recalls that 'Families of policemen were not treated as outcasts by their neighbours'.[15] However, William Dunne, a Catholic who joined the RIC in 1917, had a very different experience of the years 1919–21. Stationed in County Kerry for the entire period 1917–22, he talks of RIC and former British army men being shot dead, of roads and bridges being blocked or blown up, of ambushes, and of RIC men being met by a crowd of people who told them that they were not welcome.[16] On their own, the RIC men were not able to restore law and order. Furthermore, the war situation made it impossible for many of them to discharge their duties as a civil police.

The Dublin Metropolitan Police was unarmed except for the detective division or 'G men' as they were called. During the early twentieth century, the force had maintained a strength of about 1,200. Like that of the RIC, DMP morale had been damaged by the 1912 Home Rule Bill, the emphasis on army recruiting in 1914 and the fall in living standards owing to the inflation caused by the War. The DMP had also experienced the unhappy events of the Dublin Lock Out of 1913. However, unlike the RIC, the DMP was not usually in the frontline in the war against the IRA in the 1919–21 period. This may have been in part because it was unarmed. Of course, the G division of the DMP, which dealt specifically with political crime, waged an all-out war on the IRA. Michael Collins retaliated with his squad of hit men, which killed many of these detectives. The ordinary DMP constable reported as normal for duty, but ensured his own safety and longevity by keeping a very low profile. Many resigned and plenty looked the other way where rebel activity was concerned.[17] The attitude of the DMP members themselves, coupled with the activities of the IRA, meant that many ordinary civilian-type police duties were not performed in the 1919–21 period in Dublin.

During the War of Independence, Dáil Éireann attempted to undermine British authority in Ireland, by persuading the Irish public to transfer its allegiance to the indigenous parliament. The successful Sinn Féin courts, which were established in many parts of the country, were a central plank in this strategy. The Dáil's Ministry of Home Affairs called into being a republican police force. This body's function was to enforce the orders of Sinn Féin's courts and to carry out ordinary police duties. Most, though not all, of these police were members of the IRA. They operated under very difficult circumstances. By and large, the members were an untrained, unpaid and un-uniformed body of volunteers. The more able-bodied and energetic IRA men tended to be deployed on active service rather than to be engaged in police work. There was also a general breakdown of law and order in many parts of the country during this period. Perhaps the greatest difficulty for the Irish Republican Police (IRP) was the fact that they themselves were on the run from the British army, the DMP and the RIC, as well as the Auxiliaries and the Black and Tans. Some parts of the country had no republican police at all, and others had only a token force. In August 1922 General Richard Mulcahy (Minister for Defence in the Irish Provisional Government, which had been set up when England began to evacuate) wrote to Michael Collins and referred to 'the wretched Irish Republican Police system and the awful personnel that was attracted to its ranks'.[18] Individual groups of republican police did have some striking successes in apprehending criminals. However, the near anarchy of the 1919–21 period meant that, at best, the force could hope for only limited success.

While hostilities decreased dramatically in the period July–December 1921 (from the truce to the Treaty), the confusion over the administration of law and order, if anything, increased. In the twenty-six counties which were to become the Irish Free State, there were the British army and two police forces, the DMP and the RIC. The latter was reinforced by the Black and Tans and the Auxiliaries. All of those forces owed their allegiances to the British Crown. The IRA and the republican police were on the opposing side, owing their allegiance to Dáil Éireann. A few urban centres had developed their own police force or vigilante groups at this time. In addition to all of these, Michael Collins had set up a small plain-clothes unit of police, commonly known as the Oriel House squad, which combined protection and detective work. Despite the presence of all these law-enforcing agencies, the country was not policed at all effectively. There was great uncertainty as the whole country awaited the outcome of the Treaty negotiations. The RIC anticipated disbandment at an early date. The republican police became more confident and visible, with many of its members now wearing a distinctive armband. While the republican police and the RIC co-operated on occasion in the pursuit of ordinary criminals, there were also many instances of clashes between these two forces.[19] The same applied in relations between the IRP and the DMP.

On 6 December 1921 the Irish delegation led by Arthur Griffith signed the Anglo-Irish Treaty with Great Britain. On 7 January 1922 the Dáil by a slender majority accepted the Treaty. De Valera and his followers withdrew from the Dáil. Griffith replaced De Valera as President of the Dáil but the Treaty did not recognise that assembly. Therefore Collins was appointed chairman of a Provisional Government whose function it was to oversee the transfer of power from Britain. Signs of a split in the IRA began to appear only days after the crucial Dáil vote. The British almost immediately began the process of withdrawal. British troops began to leave the country, and the Black and Tans and Auxiliaries were sent home. It was decided to retain the DMP for the present, but the disbandment of the RIC was set in motion. Although it took a number of months before the last remaining RIC members were formally disbanded, the force ceased to be operational from early in 1922. Most of its members remained in barracks until they were ordered to vacate them. They usually marched to the local train station and from there to a designated military camp such as Gormanstown, County Meath, where they were formally disbanded. The situation can best be summarised by the words of Patrick Shea, himself the son of an RIC man: 'For the first few months of the new regime there was a police force which had been stripped of its authority; for many months afterwards there was none.'[20]

By the end of January 1922 the new Irish Free State was beginning to emerge amid growing division and confusion. It was against this background of unprecedented change that a new police force, the Civic Guard, was about to be born.

2

GENESIS 1922

ORGANISING COMMITTEE

The Provisional Government of the Irish Free State set up a committee to organise a new police force. The committee first met in the Gresham Hotel, Dublin, on Thursday, 9 February 1922. Those in attendance included politicians, policemen and ex-policemen.* Among those present were Eamonn Duggan, Minister for Home Affairs; Richard Mulcahy, Minister for Defence; Eoin O'Duffy, chief of staff National army; and Alderman Michael Staines, TD. Michael Collins was also there but did not take an active part in the proceedings. The police were mostly RIC men, with just two DMP among them. Duggan addressed the committee and appointed Staines as chairman.

Michael Staines was born in Newport, County Mayo, in 1885. A member of the Gaelic League and Sinn Féin, he joined the Irish Volunteers in 1914, becoming quartermaster general, and was part of the GPO garrison in 1916. He served on Dublin Corporation and was elected to Dáil Éireann in 1918. He subsequently lost his seat in 1923.

After this initial meeting it appears as if the politicians, with the

---

* Some had resigned or had been dismissed from the RIC while others were still in the force that was in the process of being disbanded, hence the reference to policemen and ex-policemen; all subsequent references to RIC and British army personnel imply that such men were former members of those forces.

exception of Staines (himself the son of an RIC man), left the detailed work of organising in the hands of the policemen. Three sub-committees were formed and they met frequently during February.[1]

Staines sent the committee's report and recommendations to the Provisional Government on 27 February. The name suggested by the committee for the new force was 'The People's Guard'. By the end of February, however, the Provisional Government was referring to it as the 'Civic Guard', by which name it was soon popularly and officially to become known. The policing of the city of Dublin was to be left un-touched for the moment, remaining as it was under the control of the DMP. (In 1925, it was amalgamated with the Garda Síochána — as the Civic Guard was to become known.[2]) The new force was to be armed with Webley revolvers, waist belts, truncheons and whistles — all such articles to be found at the RIC depot in Phoenix Park, Dublin. The committee recommended that the Desborough commission's scales of pay and pensions, as applied in Great Britain, should be adopted by the new police.

The committee's report also advocated that promotion be made from the ranks by competitive examination, except for the post of commis-sioner, which could be filled from outside the force. Temporary recruiting centres were to be established in each county headquarters. Recruiting staff for each county would include one medical examiner, one person with police experience and one representative from the army for that county.[3] The Civic Guard was to be drawn from the fol-lowing classes:

(a)   IRA as well as Irish Republican Police;

(b)   men dismissed or resigned from the RIC or DMP because of con-scientious or patriotic motives;

(c)   the civilian population; and

(d)   disbanded RIC and DMP members.

The new policeman had to take an oath in which he would swear among other things not to join any political party or secret society, a list of which included the Free Masons.[4]

The Provisional Government under Collins was preoccupied with the transfer of power from Britain, the crisis in the army over the long-promised holding of a convention, and the inexorable slide towards further division and possible civil war. Consequently, Staines' organis-ing committee's recommendations appear to have been accepted without question. The Civic Guard was influenced to a great extent by its predecessor, the RIC. The entire work of the organising committee was carried out by the three sub-committees, which consisted exclusively of RIC and DMP policemen. Staines, the only true civilian, appears to have played a primarily co-ordinating role among the sub-committees. The ranking structure of the Civic Guard basically resembled that of the RIC, with some minor modifications. Former members of the RIC wishing to join the new force were to be credited with their previous service when considering rank, pay and pension. The appointments officers in each county were informed by the organising committee that resigned and dismissed RIC men (where found suitable) were to be called first. Where possible, the new policemen were to occupy the old RIC barracks. Practical considerations dictated that anything — from attestation forms to barracks bedding — that had belonged to the former police force would now be used by the new one.

Pragmatism, rather than any conspiracy to hijack the new force, accounted for the RIC virtual monopoly of positions on the organising committee. Many of these men had been tried and trusted by Collins in the War of Independence. Who better to set up a police force than policemen themselves? Their recommendations naturally relied heavily on the RIC system, which had worked reasonably effectively for quite some time. This seminal group drew up a comprehensive and detailed blueprint for the establishment of a new police force. The vast bulk of its proposals stood the test of time, forming the basis of the administration and organisation of the Garda Síochána for the next fifty years. To achieve this work in the space of two and a half weeks was no mean feat. However, there were to be some problems. The committee suggested that the force be armed with service rifles and Webley revolvers. The unsettled conditions in the newly emerging state, the lack of time, and the fact that so many of those involved had been part of a semi-military police force contributed to the decision to arm the Civic Guard. It was a decision that was to lead to an early crisis for the force.

RECRUITMENT

The cornerstone of the entire recruitment system was the temporary recruiting centre in each county. Candidates meeting the required height and chest measurements were to make written applications to the county recruiting officer, and include a birth certificate along with recommendations from the local IRA divisional commandant and from a minister of religion. Each candidate underwent a medical examination and sat a simple educational examination. All candidates found to be fully qualified were to be attested on a temporary basis, given their train fare and sent to the training depot in Dublin. The local recruiting authority carried out a preliminary vetting of candidates, with the final decision being taken at the depot in Dublin.

Despite the turmoil in which the country found itself, recruitment for the Civic Guard took place in a relatively organised fashion. The overwhelming majority of recruits in the first year came from the ranks of the pro-Treaty IRA, with a sprinkling of RIC, IRP and others. Local pro-Treaty IRA officers contacted their men, directing them to apply for admission to the emerging force. The case of Tom Boland is typical.

A native of County Clare, born in 1902, Tom Boland was an active member of the Volunteers. He recalled:

> I applied to join at Ennis Court House in early March 1922. I was measured and directed to get a medical cert from Surgeon McClancy. I did the exam at the Christian Brothers School on 17 March 1922. About nine others did it on the same day.[5]

One week later he received confirmation by post that he was to report the next day at the showgrounds of the Royal Dublin Society (RDS), which were being used as a temporary training centre.

Patrick McGonagle of Moville, County Donegal, had become a member of the local IRA in 1920. When the RIC was disbanded in Moville he and another IRA member took responsibility for policing the area. He sat the examination for the Civic Guard in Letterkenny. In late May 1922 he and thirty-four other successful young men headed for the training depot, which was now in Kildare. They had to go via Sligo because of the interruption of the rail service in Northern Ireland. On their overnight sojourn in Sligo, they were accommodated in the cells of the local jail.[6] While some individuals who intended to join were threatened, and a few even temporarily abducted, there does not appear to have been widespread intimidation of prospective recruits.

Of course there were plenty of exceptions to the orderly process of recruitment envisaged by Staines and his committee. Patrick Lawlor left Portlaoise military barracks, in charge of 150 members of the IRA, on 21 February 1922. They travelled by train to the RDS and presented themselves, with a view to joining the new force. Staines received them there. At this stage the organising committee had not even completed its report. There were at least six ex-RIC men there who had been appointed instructors in drill and police duties. Patrick Walsh, former district inspector of the RIC and member of the committee for organising the Civic Guard, was also there.

Quite a number of individuals, on their own initiative and without any letters of recommendation, began to present themselves at the RDS gates, seeking admission to the Civic Guard. Walsh, with over thirty years of RIC service behind him, insisted that they procure the necessary documentation.

RDS

The Royal Dublin Society had given the use of its Ballsbridge grounds to the Civic Guard on condition that they be vacated in time for the annual Spring Show in early May. From about the middle of February until then, young men poured into this temporary training centre at the rate of approximately 100 per week. The first recruit was officially attested on 21 February 1922, and he had been joined by ninety-eight others by the end of that month. There is some confusion as to who was the very first recruit. A County Cavan man, Patrick McAvinia, had helped the IRA while serving in the RIC. As clerk of the Sinn Féin arbitration courts in Galway, he met Staines who brought him to the RDS to start the Civic Guard. He helped to drill and discipline the incoming recruits. An RIC sergeant, P. J. Kerrigan of Westport, County Mayo, was already in the depot when McAvinia arrived, but had not yet been recognised as a member of the Civic Guard. McAvinia was given registration No. 1. After a few days, however, all recruits were lined up and numbering commenced from the first man in line, who happened to be Kerrigan. McAvinia became No. 2. Kerrigan emigrated to the US within a matter of months. McAvinia retired as a sergeant after twenty-five years' service.[7]

The following account by William Mitchell from County Sligo epitomises what awaited the new recruit on arrival in Ballsbridge:

> We were given our registration number and marched to the canteen where we were advised to purchase a large enamel plate, knife, fork, spoon and mug. We were then taken to the mess room where we got two cups of tea from a galvanised bucket and two slices of bread and butter. Then we were marched to a large store where we were given free a large bag or mattress cover, four blankets, four sheets, one pillow with pillow-case, three nine-by-one inch thick boards that were six foot long as well as two trestles. We were then led to the stalls where we packed straw into the bag for bedding.[8]

The daily programme of instruction was haphazard because of a shortage of instructors and inadequate facilities. The day usually began with reveille at 7 a.m. and the recruits had one hour to dress, shave and make their beds, before breakfast at 8. Parade was at 8.45 a.m., followed by drill on the square. Dinner was at 1 p.m. and tea at 5. The recruits were free in the evening from 6 o'clock but had to be back for roll call at

10. The emphasis was on physical training and many men received few, if any, police duty classes while at the RDS. Irish classes were conducted intermittently and recruits also received some firearms training. Sentry duty was an integral part of daily life, with recruits on guard armed with rifles, on a twenty-four-hour roster of two hours on, four hours off — the latter being spent in the guard room. In the very early stages shots were fired at guards and they had to be withdrawn temporarily.

Conditions for the growing number of recruits in Ballsbridge were primitive, even by the standards of the time. Initially, the men were billeted in the central exhibition hall but, as numbers increased, recourse was had to the balconies. The bedding was so cramped in these areas that most recruits had to dress while standing on their own bed. The trestle-type bedding made of timber laths was obviously quite hard and many members tried to compensate by stuffing extra straw into their mattress, only to discover that this caused them to roll off their small bed in the middle of the night. The stars could be seen through the glass roof of the RDS building. Washing facilities were equally inadequate, with no hot water and few mirrors, and with most men using cut-throat razors, blood inevitably flowed quite frequently. The food was basic but adequate, one consolation being that there were no machines to cut the bread, which consequently was quite thick. On 11 March, Michael Staines had been appointed by the Provisional Government as commissioner of the new force. In early April, he pleaded with the government to procure the RIC depot in Phoenix Park and the adjoining Marlborough barracks for training recruits. Three days later, he threatened to resign if something was not done to alleviate the situation.[9]

Of the thousand or so recruits who came to the RDS, a small minority left soon after arriving. Others were rejected on medical grounds, while some were found unsuitable owing to their poor educational standard. The vast majority of recruits, however, stayed on, despite the terrible conditions, and made the best of it. These very conditions gave rise to humour on many occasions. A young recruit on parade upon being reprimanded for not shaving is supposed to have given the excuse that as eight of them were using the one mirror, he obviously shaved the wrong man.[10] The energy and exuberance of such large numbers of men manifested itself in pranks on fellow recruits, as well as the occasional jump from a moving train in order to be back for roll-call at night. The month of March appears to have witnessed a holding operation, with training in drill being almost the only instruction given, which meant that the recruits spent much of the day lounging about with little to do.

Most of the men were totally unused to any great discipline and found it difficult to adjust to life in the depot. Infringements such as being slovenly in dress, smoking on parade, having hands in pockets, talking to lady friends in the vicinity of the depot, visiting the pubs in Ballsbridge during the day and breaking out at night were quite common. As April progressed, discipline was tightened up. Punishment fines replaced confinement to barracks. However, the authorities still had difficulty preventing a number from slipping out to the pubs in Ballsbridge during day-time duty hours.[11] Many were keenly involved in football and hurling, and matches were frequently played in the grounds in Ballsbridge. A match was arranged against the Dublin Junior team and the recruits also played a few games in Croke Park.

The men in Ballsbridge were divided into companies, each with its own company officer and orderly. These positions were usually filled by senior IRA officers. The police instructors were almost exclusively RIC men hand-picked by Collins himself. A potentially explosive situation was brewing. Hundreds of young IRA men, including many who had seen active service, were herded together under RIC men whose War of Independence credentials, while apparent to Collins, were certainly not so clear to their fellow recruits. Nothing of any significance occurred in the RDS to ignite this powder keg, but events in Kildare were to prove decisive in a few weeks' time.

KILDARE MUTINY

On 25 April 1922 the Civic Guard vacated the RDS showgrounds in time for the Spring Show. Staines led his eight or nine hundred men by train to new headquarters in Kildare town where they were to occupy the recently vacated military barracks as well as the local RIC barracks. Things were not at all in order as the train loads of men arrived. The absence of bulbs in the lights did not greatly assist matters, as many of the recruits found themselves trying to locate beds in the dark. They got nothing to eat from 4 a.m. until late that evening when they received bully beef, bread and butter, but no tea. Some of the blankets were wet as it had poured rain during the journey. Despite the initial hardship, conditions in Kildare were much better than those endured in Ballsbridge. The accommodation consisted of British army corrugated iron huts with hand basins. Once inside the hut door, the recruit felt free and relaxed, unlike the RDS where there was barely standing room.[12] Training consisted of drill, police duty classes and some instruction in the Irish language. Football matches took place and even a sports day was held. Recruits continued to flock in at an average rate of about 130 a week, so that by mid-May the former military barracks was home to about 1,300 recruits.

Over 6.5 per cent of recruits in Kildare were RIC men.[13] They comprised two categories: those who had resigned or had been dismissed for patriotic reasons (about half of the 6.5 per cent had been in the IRA), and those who had been disbanded. The disbanded group of about forty-five included rank-and-file civic guards, police instructors who were looked upon by many as civilians, and a number of key officers. With the notable exception of Patrick Brennan and one or two others, Staines appointed RIC men to almost all the influential positions in the Civic Guard. District Inspector Patrick Walsh became deputy commissioner. The handful of superintendents and chief superintendents included six RIC men appointed in February and March. The barrack master, accounts officer and his assistant, the chief of stores and Staines' private secretary were all RIC men as were many others. There had been some discontent in Ballsbridge in mid-March when a group of recruits complained of the presence of RIC men in influential positions. Brennan had promised them that it was only a temporary arrangement and that they would soon be dispensed with.[14] However, the trend was accelerated in Kildare. The rest of the recruits who were almost exclusively IRA volunteers did not object to the presence of RIC men as ordinary members of the Civic Guard. They did object, however, to the RIC men being given commissions in the new force, as they felt that the two or three IRA men on headquarters staff were greatly outnumbered by the RIC men.[15]

Rumours multiplied, fuelled by individuals and groups who had a vested interest in spreading discontent. Matters came to a head on 15 May when five RIC men were given commissioned ranks. The presence of Deputy Commissioner Kearney, an RIC district inspector present when Roger Casement was arrested, caused great resentment among the rank and file. In fact, Kearney had befriended Casement, and an IRA intelligence officer had written to Desmond Fitzgerald praising Kearney's work during the War of Independence.[16] But of course these facts were not known at the time.

A committee formed among the rank and file sent an ultimatum to the commissioner, demanding the expulsion of certain officers holding high command and who had formerly been connected with the RIC. Staines immediately summoned a general parade in barrack square and, having read out the names of the signatories, ordered them to fall out. When he asked those loyal to him to stand on one side, only a dozen or so complied.[17] The commissioner, flanked by most of his senior officers withdrew to his offices. Shortly afterwards they all slipped out quietly and headed for Dublin where Staines informed the government of the garda mutiny. He proffered his resignation but it was not accepted.

The following day was filled with action and drama. Selected delegates from the men's committee travelled to Dublin for what proved to be an inconclusive meeting with the Minister for Home Affairs. On the same day, an armoured car was sent to the depot by Staines to get possession of the arms in the armoury, as he had received information which led him to believe that they were likely to fall into the hands of the anti-Treaty forces. At this stage, the IRA had split, the Four Courts were occupied and civil war seemed even closer. Free State troops in an armoured car and two Lancia trucks pulled up at the front gate of the depot in Kildare. A potentially lethal situation had developed.[18] The soldiers were heavily armed, as were the civic guards within. A few months earlier, lorry loads of RIC rifles had been delivered to Ballsbridge, and subsequently transferred to Kildare. Deputy Commandt Sean Liddy, TD for his native County Clare and superintendent in the Civic Guard, went to the front gate but refused the army's request to open it. After a brief consultation in which he assured the army officer that the civic guards had not gone over to the anti-Treaty forces, the army withdrew back to Dublin. A bloodbath had been averted.

On that same day, the men's committee assumed complete control of the camp and took over the armoury. It appointed replacements to the positions vacated by Staines and those loyal to him. Assistant Commissioner Brennan became the new commissioner. Colonel Patrick Brennan played a key role in the Kildare mutiny. A native of County Clare as well as TD for it, he was also an IRA volunteer and had been acting commandant in Ballsbridge. As assistant commissioner he had responsibility for recruiting and was particularly successful in his own sphere of influence — the counties of Clare, Galway, and Limerick. In fact, 28 per cent of the members of the new force at this stage came from these three counties. He had immense influence with the rank-and-file men. There was a strong element of the Clare clique among those who took charge in Kildare. The committee made a declaration of loyalty to the Provisional Government. Its members were at pains to point out that they were not in arms against the government but protesting against RIC appointments.

On 26 May, General Michael Collins visited Kildare, and advised the mutineers to withdraw the offending document and resume their discipline. He promised that the government for its part would hold an immediate enquiry.[19] Stalemate persisted. On 7 June the chairman of the committee, accompanied by one other member, travelled to Dublin to ask Collins when the enquiry was to begin. It was decided that

Commissioner Staines and his party would go to Kildare and take stock of the situation there. Two days later, Staines arrived at the depot gates but was refused admittance. On that same day, two sergeants, Byrne and McAvinia, arrived at the depot on Staines' instructions. They were chased not only from the depot but also from Kildare town 'pursued by a mob containing many members of the Civic Guard and had to run for their lives and take shelter . . . in the house of the parish priest for the night'.[20] At this stage, Newbridge military barracks was also being used as a training depot for the civic guards. The government viewed the recruits in both Newbridge and Kildare as mutineers. Having abandoned any plans for military action after the failure of the army to secure the arms in the Kildare depot, the government adopted a policy of isolation and deprivation. Rival headquarters and a recruiting centre were set up in Dublin and all pay was cut off from Kildare for the duration of the mutiny.

When the mutiny had broken out on 15 May, Staines and most of his senior officers, mainly RIC men, had headed for Dublin. They were joined within a few days by about eighty men from the Kildare depot. There was a strong Mayo representation among those who left for Dublin. The decision by Commandt Joe Ring, a native of Westport and senior IRA officer, to follow Staines, another Mayo man, appears to have influenced a number of Mayo recruits.[21] Having first set up headquarters and a recruitment centre in the Clarence Hotel, Wellington Quay, Staines and his party then moved to an unused warehouse in Denmark Street, off Henry Street in the centre of the city. The Civic Guard had now got rival depots, rival commissioners, rival headquarters staff and rival recruitment centres. This unusual situation existed throughout the summer of 1922. Although deprived of pay, many new recruits continued to arrive at the Kildare depot because of anti-RIC feeling, while others presented themselves to Commandt Joe Ring in Henry Street. By the end of May there were 200 recruits in the cramped and totally unsuitable warehouse. It was impossible to carry on extensive training in such conditions. Because of the increasing possibility of civil war breaking out, a number of recruits were moved to the College of Science. Around the middle of June, Clonskeagh Castle was used to accommodate the overflow from Henry Street, and seventy-five recruits were sent there first. After the Free State army attack on the anti-Treaty garrison in the Four Courts, the castle was sandbagged, rifles issued to each man and twenty-four-hour guard duty mounted. There was no regular instruction in police duties until August.

Approximately 340 new recruits came to the Kildare depot during the six weeks of the mutiny.[22] The men's committee had handed over complete control of the depot to Brennan on 23 May. He attempted to run the camp as if nothing had happened. Some restrictions, however, had to be imposed because of the unusual situation that existed. The recruits were not allowed go to the races at the Curragh and all leave, except special cases, was cancelled. Morale among the men was deteriorating. Some left, taking their rifles with them, and joined the anti-Treaty forces; others simply went home. Those who remained included a minority not enthusiastic about the action of the committee.[23] The majority of the men, while in favour of the committee, were finding the going increasingly difficult as the weeks passed and no pay arrived. They relied on money from home and the credit which local traders appeared quite willing to give. Discipline was bound to suffer under such adverse conditions. Civic guards were held responsible for breaking and entering a local hotel. Nevertheless, the Kildare depot operated reasonably successfully, while professing allegiance to a government that refused to recognise its legitimacy. An event was soon to transform the situation.

On the night of 17 June, Thomas Daly, president of the men's committee, left for Dublin with a number of well-armed men, on the pretext of collecting some men who were on guard duty at government buildings in College Street. He rendezvoused with anti-Treaty leaders Rory O'Connor, Ernie O'Malley and Tom Barry. O'Connor told the civic guards that he had issued an ultimatum against England for 21 June, and asked them to join him, promising that they would be paid next day. A few joined and the rest were kept prisoner. These few returned with O'Connor to the depot in Kildare. Using the password given by Daly, O'Connor gained entry, cleared out the armoury and headed back to the Four Courts. Three members of the committee, Daly, O'Brien and Ryan, were with him.[24] This incident acted as a catalyst in settling the dispute. President Arthur Griffith and Eamonn Duggan arrived at the depot on 24 June with the following proposals:

- The men were to be paid all money due to them for past services;

- an enquiry was to be held immediately; and

- in the meantime all men were suspended.

These proposals were accepted and the mutiny was over.[25]

On 27 June, Staines officially resumed charge of Kildare although he merely visited it on occasion thereafter. Arrangements were made so that the men could be paid. A short time later, the money arrived and the men made up for six frustrating weeks of deprivation. Much drinking and revelry took place, including firing revolvers. One tragic result was the accidental shooting dead in the public street in Newbridge of a young Leitrim recruit, Farrell Liddy, by another recruit who was his neighbour and friend. For the next eight weeks the men existed in a type of limbo. They had been paid but were suspended from duty. They stayed on in the Kildare and Newbridge depots and life carried on somewhat as before. Commandt Ring resumed duties in Kildare and there was some tightening of discipline. All rifles, revolvers and ammunition in the possession of the officers and men had to be handed in.

MUTINY ENQUIRY

The government commission of enquiry into the mutiny began work in the Kildare depot on 13 July. It was carried out by two senior civil servants, Kevin O'Shiel and Michael McAuliffe. It had three main aims: to discover the origin of the mutiny, to suggest disciplinary action if necessary, and to make recommendations for the future governing of the Civic Guard. Witnesses were heard for the commissioner's side and for the men's side, and by mid-August the commission had reached its conclusions. It believed that a small band of politically motivated anti-Treaty sympathisers, hoping to get arms and possibly to disrupt the formation of the force, had orchestrated the mutiny. The vast majority of the force who were annoyed and resentful at the prominent positions occupied by the RIC men had been manipulated by this small band of men. The enquiry supported its assertions by pointing out that the president of the men's committee and five of its fourteen members had joined the Four Courts' garrison. Furthermore, officers and men who were never in the RIC were driven from the camp during the mutiny.

The men's committee had as its secretary an RIC man and there were many others in prominent positions in the camp during the mutiny. While there is no doubt that the mutiny was the work of a cabal of anti-Treaty sympathisers, the government had made a number of serious miscalculations. It heavily armed the new Civic Guard, largely composed of young IRA men whose recent experience of solving disputes was to resort to force. Collins, personally convinced of the War of Independence credentials of his RIC appointments, failed to understand the depth of antipathy towards them among the IRA rank-and-file guards. Staines, an honourable gentleman by all accounts, was not in touch with popular sentiment. His deputy commissioner, Patrick Brennan, who was fully aware of the situation, did not inform Staines and eventually sided with the men.

The commission of enquiry also made a number of wide-ranging and detailed recommendations concerning the administration of the force. The Civic Guard was to be technically disbanded and reformed with selective re-enrolment. Influenced no doubt by the events in Kildare, the commission decided that the vast majority of the men were to be unarmed, even personal weapons not being allowed. In future, politicians were not to serve in the force. Consequently, on 18 August Staines resigned as commissioner. The government decided that Commandt Sean Ó Muirthile should replace him. Ó Muirthuile declined the position, which was officially accepted by General Eoin O'Duffy in early September. O'Duffy had been commanding officer in the IRA in his native County Monaghan and was chief of staff of the National army. The government also decided that the Civic Guard should be technically disbanded but not dispersed, remaining in Kildare and Newbridge until arrangements could be made for selective re-enrolment. Although the vast majority of the men were re-enrolled, a significant number felt that they were subsequently victimised as a result of their part in the mutiny.[26]

The commission of enquiry carried out a radical reassessment of the role of the Civic Guard, the proximate cause being the mutiny, the underlying cause being the shortcomings of the work of the original organising committee. It mapped out a role for the new force, which was at variance with that of its predecessor, the RIC. The Civic Guard was to be the servant of the people, not militaristic or coercive. The commission envisaged a greatly enhanced civilian role for the new police force. The old RIC system of stationing men in barracks doing political and military duties as well as police duties, while only assisting in a minor way with civilian administrative tasks, was to be a thing of the past. Of course, disarming the guards was central to this concept of their new role. The Civic Guard had inherited the entire RIC arsenal. Recruits had been trained in weaponry in the RDS and Kildare, and the early members already out on duty were heavily armed. Furthermore, quite a high proportion of the guards had either used firearms themselves or been in the company of those who had used them during the War of Independence. Considering that the country was in the throes of a bitter civil war, the decision to disarm the Civic Guard called for great strength of purpose. While it would take a few months to implement this proposal fully, the principle of an unarmed police force was clearly established. In the future, individual guards might be armed in response to particular events, but this was seen as an aberration of the accepted norm.

In retrospect, it can be seen that the organising committee in February did precisely what it was established to do — it attended to the nuts and bolts of organising a new police force. The task of devising some sort of elementary philosophy or ethos fell to the members of the commission of enquiry almost six months later. The government's acceptance of the commission's recommendation that the Civic Guard be unarmed set the force firmly on course as a civilian police force rather than a semi-military force, as its predecessor, the RIC, had been. The government off-loading of numerous administrative duties on to the Garda Síochána in the coming years added to the civilian complexion of the force.

To the rank-and-file members of the Civic Guard in Kildare, it was the appointment of RIC men to positions of authority that caused the mutiny. Yet these very men retained their positions of authority in the higher echelons of the guards. In the aftermath of the mutiny, Deputy Commissioner Patrick Walsh (ex RIC) offered his resignation to the government. This was accepted but he was retained as a police advisor. In August 1923 he was appointed assistant commissioner. By 1925 many RIC men had been promoted even further. It appears as if the raid on the armoury by the anti-Treaty forces catapulted the government into resolving the crisis but discredited the men in Kildare and considerably lessened their ability to force the government to dismiss RIC men already holding officer rank. It is true, however, that very few RIC men were recruited to the Civic Guard after the mutiny.

DUBLIN CASTLE, COLLINSTOWN AND PHOENIX PARK

On 17 August 1922, three small companies of the Civic Guard from Newbridge took a special train to Kingsbridge from where they marched to Dame Street and halted in front of the gates of Dublin Castle. Led by Collins and Staines, they marched in, and the last of the British army and the RIC marched out. The Castle and Ship Street barracks which adjoined it became the new depot. In the next two months most of the Kildare and Denmark Street men were moved there, although apparently not the Clonskeagh group. Training was not on a regular basis. The new men just fell into the ordinary routine of everyone else, and this usually included sentry duty on the castle and guard duty on Dublin banks. On one occasion a bomb was thrown over the wall and exploded in the yard, for which the anti-Treaty forces later apologised.[27]

Collinstown British military barracks and aerodrome (later to become Dublin airport) was taken over by the Civic Guard in late October 1922. All those in Ship Street were transferred out to it. The area contained a few wooden huts and green fields. Fifty to sixty men were allocated to each of these. With bare cement floors, broken windows and two small stoves per hut, it was a very cold place in November

1922.[28] On wet days, squad drill was held in the hangars. Police duty and Irish classes were also conducted. In mid-November Kevin O'Higgins and Eoin O'Duffy addressed about 600 recruits there.

Towards the end of December, the British evacuated the Phoenix Park depot, which had been the RIC headquarters and training centre. All remaining Civic Guard training centres were vacated and recruits moved to the Phoenix Park depot or to the adjoining Marlborough barracks (renamed McKee). There were about 1,250 recruits in training at the end of 1922.[29] In the course of ten and a half months, the new force had moved to at least eight different headquarters.

ARMING AND DISARMING

The first steps to set up the Civic Guard took place in the midst of the British authorities transferring power to the Irish Provisional Government under Collins. By the time that the commission of enquiry's report was received by the government, Griffith was dead. Collins was killed a few days later. The orderly process of a recruit being attested, trained for a period in the depot, and then released to a station, was frequently interrupted. Many IRA men, upon being accepted into the Civic Guard, were immediately sent, in civilian clothes and without any formal training, on dangerous guard duty. They were usually heavily armed and fulfilled a semi-military role. They were sent out on an ad-hoc basis, reacting to the most pressing need of the moment, rather than following an overall plan. From as early as March 1922 new Civic Guard recruits were put on armed protection duty of government buildings used by Collins in College Street, where they remained until June. Numerous recruits were engaged in armed duty protection of city banks, and this function increased considerably as the Civil War progressed. Eight guards were detailed to protect Arthur Griffith during his last illness at Leeson Street hospital. A number of civic guards formed a guard of honour at his funeral in Dublin in August. One uniformed raw recruit from Kildare who was to participate in the guard of honour had no idea as to where to go as it was his first time in Dublin. A kindly DMP man who had never before seen a civic guard in uniform directed him on his way.[30] Ten days later a larger number of uniformed guards formed another guard of honour at Collins' funeral. Leinster House was guarded by the new force from October 1922. Recruits armed with rifles and revolvers frequently escorted ministers.

On 15 July, General Richard Mulcahy, Minister for Defence and commander-in-chief of the Free State army had requested assistance from the civic guards. He wanted armed parties of them to be organised as a type of mobile unit on guard duty in the Kildare region and to liaise with the military. Anti-Treaty forces were disrupting lines of communication and it was to be the guards' job to prevent this. By 11 o'clock the following night, forty men from the Kildare depot had volunteered for this duty and were posted in groups at the railway stations in Newbridge, Kildare and Monasterevin, as well as in Monasterevin town. They were heavily armed, had no uniform and were under the control of Assistant Commissioner Brennan. These men did not see their role as purely defensive and were soon engaged in military-type activity, acting like a flying column, seeking out the enemy rather than merely reacting to an attack. Mulcahy was not pleased that they were departing from their original police duty role.[31] As a result, Staines instructed Brennan to withdraw the rifles from the men, allowing them to retain their revolvers. The disarming of the guards had begun. The history of these Kildare outposts gives a very interesting insight into the evolution of the Civic Guard from a semi-military to a civilian force. The first groups sent out to guard key installations were heavily armed, roamed the area seeking out the enemy, had no set station and referred to themselves as 'flying columns' — a distinctly military term.[32] By the end of August there was a much more civilian complexion on the force. Many of the stations had been issued with station diary and patrol book. Queries were coming from station parties as to what the procedure was regarding permits for motor cars. The duties performed, while still including duties such as the guarding of railways, also included patrolling the towns of Newbridge, Portarlington, Athy and Rathangan, and ensuring that the licensing laws were enforced.

Disarming the emerging force was perhaps the most significant contribution to ensuring that it became a civilian rather than a semi-military body. The transition to a civilian-type police force can be seen to have begun in Staines' instructions to the men being sent out to the country at the beginning of September 1922. On that occasion he gave the force its famous guidelines when he said: 'The Civic Guard will succeed not by force of arms, or numbers, but on their moral authority as servants of the people.'[33] At this stage the guards were being sent out to the country without rifles or carbines, but they were allowed a small .38 revolver for their own personal protection while on duty. In early October, shortly after his appointment as commissioner, O'Duffy issued guidelines to the force that all members were to be unarmed. By January 1923 the Civic Guard was an unarmed police force.

The Civil War raged from the end of June 1922 until the following May. By and large, the guards did not become involved in the conflict. Most of the intense fighting had taken place in the summer of 1922 when the main body of the force had not yet been sent out to the country. The fact that the anti-Treaty forces did not generally set out to kill civic guards obviously helped. The decision to send out the guards unarmed was also crucial. By the time that the civic guards had been distributed throughout the entire country and were beginning to function, the Civil War was petering out. Furthermore, the government and the members themselves came to see the Civic Guard's role as purely a policing one, and left the fighting to the army. The usual procedure was to send in the guards only when the area had returned to a degree of normality that would allow the police to take over. The force, however, did not escape unscathed from the Civil War. Civic Guard Thomas Bolton was accidentally shot dead in September while on armed duty on the railway bridge in Rathangan, while the unarmed Harry Phelan was the first guard to be murdered. He had gone into a shop in Mullinahone, County Tipperary on 14 November 1922 to purchase a sliotar, when he was set upon and shot dead. One theory about his death is that he was mistaken for his brother who had been in the RIC.

In the period from 1 November 1922 to 31 March 1923 (from when the guards were beginning to occupy numerous stations dotted across the country until just before hostilities ceased) sixty Civic Guard barracks and nineteen Civic Guard patrols were attacked.[34] In general, the armed raiding parties did one or all of the following: burned furniture, bedding and record books; stole great coats, uniforms and bicycles; and partially or fully burned the barracks. Occasionally, the guards were made prisoners for a short while, and frequently they were given stern warnings to leave. Usually they were not harmed. Attacks on patrols usually entailed the guards' bicycles or possessions being stolen.

SENDING OUT OF THE CIVIC GUARD

While groups of guards were sent to the Kildare-Newbridge area on semi-military-type duty as early as mid-July 1922, it was over a month later before the first civilian-type police stations began to be opened. In late August a temporary station was opened in Cornelscourt, Dublin, using the old hall, as the RIC barracks had been burned down.[35] September witnessed the opening of a number of permanent, civilian Civic Guard stations. On 8 September, Skerries was opened.[36] Three days later, Dundrum old RIC barracks was opened. Lucan barracks was opened on the following day. An unexpected visit by Assistant Commissioner Coogan, however, resulted in the transfer of the entire party, bar one, back to the depot for further training.[37]

There was no general issue of uniforms to the civic guards until the closing months of 1922. For the first six months of its existence the Civic Guard usually appeared in public in civilian clothes with some small distinguishing mark such as the black RIC leather belt or blue cap. On important occasions, such as Collins' or Griffith's funeral, a number of civic guards appeared in full uniform, but this was the exception. Towards the end of August there was an improvement in the situation, and one of the first appearances of the guards, in uniform and unarmed, doing purely police work, was at Bellewstown races.

From the end of September until 31 October 1922 about 1,700 men had been sent out to the country. The Civil War was still in progress and the situation varied from near normality in some counties to near anarchy in others.[38] The military situation and the level of crime were reported to be unsatisfactory or very unsatisfactory in about fifteen of the twenty-six counties of the Free State. All the Munster and Connacht counties (with the exceptions of Waterford, Limerick and Galway), as well as Monaghan, Kilkenny, Longford, Westmeath, Wicklow, Wexford and County Dublin, were in this category. By and large, the general public was well disposed to the arrival of the guards. The government was inundated with requests from numerous communities throughout the country for civic guards to be sent to them as quickly as possible. In many towns and villages the local priest publicly and warmly welcomed the new civic guards.[39]

Small bands of armed anti-Treaty men or just common criminals could, however, make life quite unpleasant for the new policemen. What happened on 13 October 1922 in Carrigallen, County Leitrim, was not untypical.[40] An unarmed group of one sergeant and six guards arrived by train in civvies from Dublin to Killeshandra, County Cavan. Having hired a small lorry with solid tyres, they loaded on to it their iron beds, straw mattresses, wooden tables and benches, as well as sheets and blankets, and headed for Carrigallen. Having no accommodation arranged, they disembarked on the public street with all their belongings, and aroused much curiosity among the local population. The national teacher of the town was very friendly and helpful and secured them accommodation in a small house, as well as ensuring that they got something to eat. They were well received by the people who were very friendly, many coming out to shake hands with them. In fact, the locals had requested that civic guards be sent to their town. Very soon, however, they were raided by a band of armed men from Arigna, a district ten miles distant. This repeatedly happened and what belongings were not taken were burned.

Very occasionally, the civic guards encountered from the public opposition that had nothing to do with politics. A small party of civic guards arrived to Carracastle, County Mayo, to open a station there. Believing that temporary accommodation was to be found for them in the local hall, they approached the somewhat dismal-looking structure, only to be refused admittance by the hall committee. The guards subsequently broke down the door and took occupation of the hall. The forthcoming dance for that night was postponed for one week, and a hostile, though not violent, crowd gathered around the premises, where they booed and protested at the turn of events.[41]

A much more serious incident of opposition to the Civic Guard, which had everything to do with politics, occurred at Pettigo, County Donegal. In the early summer of 1922, anti-Treaty forces and B Specials began sniping at each other across the border. A confrontation arose between the nationalist and loyalist sections of the community, and the British army entered the town from Northern Ireland. Many prominent nationalists left. On 28 October a party of civic guards (all Catholics) was dispatched to Pettigo. It had been hoped that the guards would carry out police duties until the situation should return to normal, and then the British army would withdraw. However, the men were threatened by some loyalists and were arrested for their own safety by the British military who put them on the train back to Ballyshannon. In mid-December, a second group of civic guards was sent to Pettigo. This group included four Roman Catholics, one Presbyterian and one Church of Ireland member. After initial suspicion on the part of the British military and the local loyalist population, tension gradually eased and things returned to normal, with the British military evacuating early in the new year.[42]

By the close of the year 1922, civic guards were beginning to appear in numerous districts throughout the new Free State. These early members encountered many obstacles. Their accommodation was almost invariably substandard, inadequate and unhealthy. Many of them had received little or no training, and outside Dublin there was no proper chain of command for country stations for a few months. Inexperienced young guards without even uniforms found themselves arriving at their new post, bereft of files and local knowledge, and armed only with a timber baton, a pencil and a notebook.[43] These men were expected to perform their duties in a country that had experienced the War of Independence and in which a Civil War was still raging in some parts — a country that had not experienced normal policing for almost four years. They were not armed, their only weapon of defence being a rudimentary belief that their power depended on moral authority. The recommendations of the commission of enquiry into the Kildare mutiny,

Staines' valedictory instructions to the force, and the statements of their new commissioner, O'Duffy, all combined to help to define the role of the new civic guards. They were to be unarmed and strictly non-political, their duty being to the whole people. They were to play a preventive rather than repressive role. By orderly habits, strict sobriety, clean living, courtesy to and respect for the public, as well as the impartial discharge of their duties, they were to win the respect and acceptance of the population.[44] As O'Duffy told them in Collinstown in November 1922: 'The Civic Guard is now on trial.'[45]

3

WHO JOINED THE GUARDS?

On 31 July 1923 Cathal O'Shannon of the Labour party moved an amendment in the Dáil that the name of the force be changed to the 'Garda Síochána', which translated into English as 'Guardians of the Peace'. The amendment was accepted. Between 1922 and 1952, 10,135 men joined the Garda Síochána. This chapter looks at the backgrounds of the men, whether military, police or civilian, county of origin, religion, and occupations or trades prior to joining the force. All statistics relating to military or police background, such as the IRA, National army, RIC and DMP, are based on an analysis of the Garda Síochána temporary register. This records the particulars of all recruits who presented themselves at the depot.[1] All statistics and charts in this chapter relating to recruitment, county of origin, trade and religion are based upon a computerised analysis of the data for the 1922–52 period. These data were taken from the Garda Síochána general register and from the Registry of candidates, both of which record only those who were fully attested.[2]

Recruitment to the force tended to be in waves rather than a consistent annual intake, as Figure 3.1 illustrates. The first and major wave of recruits came in the 1922–6 period and was the direct result of independence and the consequent need to establish a new police force. This had almost totally spent itself by 1928 when the Garda Síochána had reached its authorised strength. In 1931 recruitment received a fillip because of the need to replace gardaí who were transferred to supplement the detective branch. In the ten years from independence to the

1932 general election, 8,230 men joined the guards. They are analysed as one group in this chapter as they were the 'early men', with 87 per cent of them having joined in the first four years of the force. They constituted the overwhelming majority of the guards for the next thirty years. The accession to power of De Valera in 1932 was followed by an increase in recruitment over the next three years. Political considerations played a major role in this wave of recruitment, and so it is treated as a separate group also. The outbreak of war in Europe in September 1939 catapulted the government into setting up a temporary police force of nearly 300 men. It was called Taca, and as the background, education and condition of service of these men set them apart somewhat from previous members, they are treated as a third group. Recruitment began once again in 1943 and continued on a fairly regular basis until 1948. This last group of recruits is treated under the heading 'the forties men'. Throughout the period 1922–52 a small percentage of men who had left

Figure 3.1: Recruitment to the Garda Síochána, 1922–52[3]

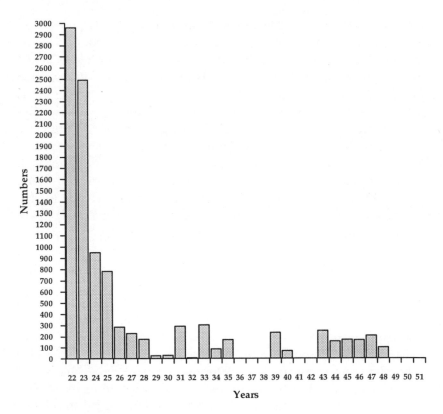

Sources: General register; registry of candidates.

the force and applied to rejoin were allowed to do so. These included the novelist Muiris Ó Súilleabháin of *Fiche Bliain ag Fás* fame, who left the force in 1934 and rejoined in 1950, only to drown in that year.

THE EARLY MEN, 1922–32

Almost 1,500 men joined the Civic Guard in the pre-mutiny period — February 1922 until the end of May. Many of these had previous military or police experience, such as membership of the IRA, National army (NA), British army (BA), RIC, DMP, Irish Republican Police (IRP). A number of men had served in more than one such group. For example, some RIC men who had left that force, subsequently joined the IRA and then joined the guards. Table 3.1 shows the military/police background of the pre-mutiny group.

Table 3.1: Military/Police Background of Pre-mutiny Civic Guard, February–May 1922

Background	%
IRA only	86.1
IRP[4]	4.9
RIC only	3.0
RIC and IRA	3.6
BA only	0.4
BA and IRA	1.0
Civilians (including a few DMP)	1.0
Total	100.0

Source: Temporary register.

Approximately 96 per cent of the first 1,500 civic guards had been in the IRA. This high number was a result of policy and pragmatism. The organising committee had specified the IRA as the first group from which to draw when recruiting. These were mainly young men who had joined the IRA some time before the Treaty was signed in December 1921. Some would have been actively involved in the War of Independence, others would have had a more passive role and some would have joined in the latter half of 1921. It is impossible to ascertain the precise level of involvement of all these men in the IRA in the 1919–21 period. The practical problem of finding so many suitable recruits at short notice was solved by relying on pro-Treaty IRA officers to send suitable men up to Dublin. The vast majority of the new civic guards were civilians who had joined the IRA. Over 6 per cent of the pre-mutiny civic guards were RIC men. Slightly more than half of these had also been in the IRA. Approximately two dozen former British army members had joined the guards by May 1922, two-thirds of these having been in the IRA.

From June to December 1922, approximately 1,500 more men were recruited into the force. The military/police/civilian background of these 1922 post-mutiny men by and large reflected that of the pre-mutiny men. During the year 1923, almost 2,500 men were attested to the Garda Síochána. Over 85 per cent of these recruits had been in the IRA. However, the National army now began to feature as a significant source of recruitment for the guards. The Civil War ended in May 1923 and the government instructed the garda authorities to give preference to army men (many of whom were being demobilised) with regard to recruitment. The army provided 23 per cent of the garda intake for the year 1923. The overwhelming majority of these (96 per cent) had also been in the IRA. In the eight-year period 1924–32, almost 3,000 men joined the guards. Over 25 per cent of the recruits to the Garda Síochána during this time came from the army and 84 per cent of these had been in the IRA.

In the ten-year period from February 1922 to February 1932, 8,230 men joined the gardaí. The military/police/civilian background is shown in Table 3.2:

Table 3.2: Military/Police/Civilian Background of Garda Síochána, 1922–32[5]

Background	%
IRA only	55.1
Civilians	23.0
NA only	1.0
IRA and NA	15.0
IRP	1.0
BA only	1.0
BA and IRA	2.0
RIC only	0.9
RIC and IRA	1.0
Total	100.0

Source: Temporary register.

In this period, three out of every four men who joined the guards had been in the IRA. It was not until 1925 that non-IRA recruits began to outnumber IRA recruits. In the 1922–32 period, approximately 16 per cent of garda recruits were former National army men, the overwhelming majority of these having previously been in the IRA.[6] In the ten years from 1922 to 1932 less than a quarter of the recruits had been civilians with no previous military or police experience when they joined. Approximately 3 per cent of gardaí in this period were former British army men. Two-thirds of these had also been in the IRA. Many Irish men had served in the British army during the First World War, and so had military training and were used to a disciplined regime. The garda authorities appear to have welcomed such experience in the first two years of the new force's existence. This trend of accepting British army men into the Garda Síochána continued (albeit at a reduced level after 1924).

Approximately 1.9 per cent of the guards recruited in the first ten years of independence were RIC men. These included men who resigned or were dismissed from the force for patriotic reasons, as well as men who were disbanded in 1922. Slightly more than half of the RIC men in the gardaí had been in the IRA. The garda authorities valued the experience of former policemen. The presence of such men in positions of authority was central to the Kildare mutiny in May–June 1922. However, RIC men were still recruited into the gardaí (albeit in reduced numbers) for the rest of 1922. (By February 1923 over 67 per cent of Northern Ireland's Royal Ulster Constabulary was made up of RIC veterans.[7]) An embargo was placed by O'Higgins on RIC recruitment to the Garda Síochána in 1923, as a committee of enquiry into resignations and dismissals from the RIC had been set up by the government. This committee was to arbitrate on the validity of claims made by resigned and dismissed RIC men that their actions had been politically motivated.[8] By 1924 the committee had produced a list of 300 RIC men suitable for the Garda Síochána. Over the next eight years, however, only a handful applied and were accepted. O'Duffy complained that these 300 included many undesirables.[9] In the spring of 1922 many RIC men had joined the Civic Guard and were very quickly promoted to high-ranking positions. By 1924, however, the need of the garda authorities for such police experience was not so acute.

There were 1,488 guards recruited in the first four months of the force's existence. Table 3.3 shows the number of guards from each county as a percentage of the total force and as a percentage of the total county population.

Table 3.3: County of Origin of Pre-mutiny Civic Guard, February–May 1922[10]

Native County	No. of Recruits	% of Total Force	% of Total County Population in 1926
Clare	179	12.0	0.19
Galway	121	8.0	0.07
Limerick	121	8.0	0.08
Leitrim	94	6.5	0.17
Mayo	92	6.4	0.05
Tipperary	87	6.0	0.06
Longford	86	6.0	0.22
Laois	75	5.0	0.15
Kilkenny	75	5.0	0.10
Wexford	66	4.4	0.06
Sligo	60	4.0	0.08
Roscommon	57	3.8	0.06
Cork	50	3.3	0.01
Kerry	45	3.0	0.03
Carlow	40	2.8	0.12
Dublin	39	2.7	0.008
Westmeath	30	2.0	0.05
Kildare	29	1.9	0.05
Offaly	25	1.6	0.05
Monaghan	24	1.6	0.03
Donegal	22	1.5	0.01
Wicklow	19	1.2	0.03
Waterford	14	0.9	0.01
Cavan	12	0.8	0.01
Armagh	6	0.4	0.005
Tyrone	5	0.3	0.003
Derry	4	0.3	0.002
Louth	4	0.3	0.006
Fermanagh	3	0.2	0.005
Meath	3	0.2	0.005
Down	1	0.06	0.0005
Antrim	1	0.06	0.0005

Source: General register.

Entry to the Civic Guard was confined almost exclusively to IRA members. As a result, there was a tendency for the areas in the west and south of the country, which had highest IRA membership, to produce more recruits for the new force. However, the actual number recruited depended to a large extent on the efficiency and zeal of the individual recruiting or appointment officers for each county. Thus, Assistant Commissioner Patrick Brennan, who had overall responsibility for recruitment, managed to deliver an exceptionally large number of men from his native Clare and the surrounding counties of Limerick and Galway. Louth, which had been active in the War of Independence under Frank Aiken, did not have such organisation and consequently only four recruits came from there. Cork, the largest Irish county, sent only fifty men to the guards, partly as a result of difficulty in getting recruiting organised because of the increasing division over the Treaty.[11]

By the end of 1922 over 60 per cent of the force came from just ten counties in the Free State. There was a very clearly defined geographical pattern, with all of these ten counties lying to the west of a line from Leitrim to Cork. O'Duffy was alarmed at the disproportionate numbers from Clare, Limerick and Galway, so he suspended recruiting in these counties for a few months.[12] Cork and Kerry, which had witnessed considerable IRA activity during the War of Independence and had relatively large populations, during 1923 began to make a bigger impact on recruiting. This was the beginning of a trend that continued right up to the 1950s.

Table 3.4 tells the county of origin of the 8,230 men who joined the Garda Síochána in the 1922–32 period.

For political, religious and geographical reasons Northern Ireland contributed only 5.3 per cent of the force's recruits. Fourteen counties in the Free State accounted for just 30 per cent of the members of the force. There was a distinct geographical division, with the eastern part of the state providing far fewer recruits than the western part. The recruitment trends for the various counties that had emerged by May 1922 remained largely unchanged for the next ten, indeed for the next thirty, years. Such large numbers were being recruited in those early months that a county with a high proportion of recruits in 1922 tended to retain its position of prominence because of the great headstart that it got. The number of recruits from Clare in the first three months of the force's existence was more than double the intake from Louth for the subsequent thirty years. Furthermore, it began the tradition of certain counties providing a disproportionate number of men for the guards. Large numbers of recruits joining from one county encouraged others from the same area to think likewise. There was a great sense of county solidarity and loyalty among the bands of recruits in the early

Table 3.4: County of Origin of Garda Síochána, 1922–32

Native County	No. of Recruits	% of Total Force	% of Total County Population in 1926
Cork	658	8.0	0.17
Kerry	576	7.0	0.39
Mayo	576	7.0	0.33
Galway	535	6.5	0.31
Clare	526	6.4	0.55
Limerick	444	5.4	0.31
Dublin	387	4.7	0.07
Donegal	378	4.6	0.25
Roscommon	376	4.6	0.45
Tipperary	370	4.5	0.26
Leitrim	334	4.0	0.59
Sligo	325	3.9	0.45
Monaghan	301	3.6	0.46
Westmeath	252	3.0	0.44
Kilkenny	244	2.9	0.34
Laois	227	2.7	0.44
Longford	226	2.7	0.56
Cavan	210	2.5	0.25
Wexford	207	2.5	0.21
Offaly	132	1.6	0.25
Carlow	107	1.3	0.31
Wicklow	107	1.3	0.18
Meath	99	1.2	0.15
Kildare	99	1.2	0.17
Fermanagh	98	1.2	0.16
Tyrone	96	1.2	0.07
Armagh	74	0.9	0.06
Waterford	72	0.9	0.09
Derry	58	0.7	0.04
Louth	58	0.7	0.09
Antrim	56	0.7	0.009
Down	50	0.6	0.02

Source: General register.

days.[13] Poorer land and worse employment prospects along the western seaboard, as well as O'Duffy's preference for farmers' sons as recruits, may have accentuated these patterns.[14] The counties in the western part of the state provided a far greater number of recruits in proportion to their population than did their eastern neighbours. The garda authorities tended to recruit members from the same counties as the RIC had done before them.[15] The two counties that caused the Cumann na nGaedheal Government the most problems with regard to law and order in the 1922–6 period were Cork and Leitrim. However, in the period 1922–32 the county that provided the greatest number of recruits was Cork, and the county with the highest number of recruits in proportion to its population was Leitrim.

Table 3.5 gives the trade of all 1922–32 recruits, prior to their joining the force.

Table 3.5: Previous Trade of Garda Síochána Recruits, 1922–32

Previous Trade	%
Farmer	40.00
Labourer	15.50
Shop Assistant	5.25
Student	4.00
Clerk	3.90
Car Driver	2.20
RIC	1.90
Railway	1.90
Teacher	1.35
Miscellaneous	5.50
Not stated	18.50
Total	100.00

Source: General register.

Farmer usually meant the son of a farmer who lived and worked on the family farm. The majority of labourers were agricultural labourers.[16] About 50 per cent of the force were either farmers or worked on the land. As O'Duffy said, 'The son of the peasant is the backbone of the force'.[17]

Over 98.5 per cent of guards who had joined the force by 1932 were Catholic. Approximately 123 men were Protestant. Of these, fifty-six belonged to the Church of Ireland, fourteen were Presbyterians and four were Methodists. The remaining forty-nine were entered in the register just as Protestant.[18] There is a strong probability, however, that they were Church of Ireland members. In 1926, approximately 7.5 per cent of the Free State's population was Protestant, yet only 1.5 per cent of the Garda Síochána was Protestant. The fact that Protestants accounted for a disproportionately large section of the higher social classes in the country may account for the small number of them wishing to join the guards. There was no discrimination on the part of the garda authorities. In fact O'Duffy stated in 1931 that, 'owing to the small number of non-Catholics in the force, I have consistently given preference to such applications (Protestant)'.[19] Protestant members of the force are not known to have suffered any adverse discrimination from the authorities or from fellow members, or to have received any special advantages.[20]

Most of the guards recruited in the 1922–32 period came from an agricultural background, were Catholic and from the western half of the new state, and had been in the IRA. They were young, in good health, over 5 feet 9" in height and had a fairly basic primary education.

SPECIAL BRANCH, 1925

A Criminal Investigation Department operated in 1922 from headquarters at Oriel House, Westland Row, Dublin (referred to as Oriel House by contemporaries). It had begun as part of Collins' military intelligence operation and had been directly under his control. It consisted of about eighty armed men in plain clothes. Their position was unclear after independence. They operated as detectives in the fight against crime both by criminals and political opponents of the state, and yet they were not officially attested as members of the Garda Síochána. They did not have to comply with the educational and physical standards of the ordinary recruit and were not trained as policemen. By May 1923 they were pressing to have their position regularised by the government.[21] O'Higgins, however, realised that while Oriel House had given loyal service in very trying times (three of its members having died in the execution of their duty), its tactics and personnel were not suited to the changed situation that existed by the summer of 1923.[22] He disbanded this group in October 1923 and transferred those suitable for detective work to the G division of the DMP. All thirty-one of these had been in the IRA, most of them holding officer rank. The G division was the detective branch of the DMP. Augmented by the former Oriel House men, it now numbered fifty-five. For the next two years it operated in the Dublin region, combating armed crime, both ordinary and political.

In 1925 it was decided to augment the G division further and divide it into two sections, one to deal with ordinary non-political crime and the other to deal with special or political crime. The latter, which became known as the Special Branch, was armed and under central control from Dublin Castle. It was made up of members of the G division (including the former Oriel House men), the general body of the gardaí, and officers in the National army. All its members had been in the IRA, many having held officer rank in the National army, most of them having been lieutenants.[23] Detectives wore plain clothes and were usually armed. In the various divisions they dealt with political and ordinary crime. The Special Branch dealt with political crime, not only within the Dublin area but throughout the country, although remaining under central control from Dublin Castle.

DE VALERA'S MEN, 1932–35

Commissioner O'Duffy was a very able, extremely energetic and impartial administrator of the Garda Síochána from his appointment in September 1922. He liked to get things done and greatly resented any bureaucratic meddling as he saw it, whether from the Department of Home Affairs, the Department of Finance or the Executive Council. This was apparent from the earliest days. In December 1922 in a highly indignant letter to Home Affairs he threatened to resign because the Department of Finance rapped him over the knuckles for sanctioning an appointment and retrospectively seeking payment.[24] In 1923, O'Duffy wanted to have administrative control of the finances of the force. The Department of Finance refused and the tone of the exchanges between the commissioner and this department became increasingly acerbic.[25] Throughout the 1920s, O'Duffy clashed with the Department of Home Affairs/Justice,[26] the Department of Finance and the Executive Council over numerous issues such as his 1926 proposal for authorisation to arm the general body of the guards.[27] By the late 1920s the government was showing growing irritation with the commissioner's approach.[28] In 1930–31 the Department of Finance and O'Duffy clashed over the former's belief that recruiting should remain closed, promotions to vacancies be suspended and a cautious policy be adopted with regard to building new stations in rural areas.[29] In the early days of the new state O'Duffy had been given a relatively free hand in setting up the new police force. By 1931, however, various officials and ministers with whom O'Duffy came into contact, appeared to be tiring somewhat of his behaviour.

After De Valera's victory in the February 1932 election, many of his supporters assumed that he would remove many prominent Cumann na nGaedheal appointees, including O'Duffy, but De Valera did not want to be pushed into acting immediately.[30] In the June 1932 issue of the *Garda Review*, O'Duffy appeared very angry and resentful in an interview regarding his personal salary and a proposed pay cut.[31] In July, O'Duffy and the new Minister for Justice, James Geoghegan, clashed over who had authority regarding the internal workings of the force. In November, O'Duffy sanctioned a collection for two dismissed detectives who were found by a public enquiry to have exceeded the law when dealing with Republicans in Clare.[32] The Executive Council told O'Duffy that they regarded as 'a grave indiscretion his action in sanctioning the collection'.[33] O'Duffy was deeply hurt and upset.[34] In January 1933, De Valera improved his political position by winning an overall majority in a snap general election. On 22 February he removed O'Duffy from office. The former commissioner was offered a civil service job at a similar salary, which he refused. He was then given a pension of 40 per cent of his salary, although he had served for only ten years. Nobody doubted O'Duffy's efficiency or integrity, qualities acknowledged by the Minister for Justice, P. J. Ruttledge, who, however, went on to state in the Dáil that, 'the man who was fitted in 1923 or '24, after a civil war, may not be the best fitted, although competent in 1933'.[35] De Valera bluntly stated that O'Duffy was removed because the Executive Council did not have full confidence in him. It wanted to appoint someone who had not been chief of police for ten years under the previous administration. De Valera wanted all sections of the community to accept the police commissioner, so the government did not appoint one of its own party members to the job.[36]

The new garda commissioner was Colonel Eamon Broy. He had joined the RIC in August 1910, only to resign from it three weeks later. He joined the DMP in 1911. As a member of its G division, he acted as a double agent for Collins in the 1919–21 period. He was arrested by the British military in 1921 and imprisoned in Arbour Hill until the Truce. After the Treaty he was appointed secretary to the Department of Civil Aviation and then adjutant to the Free State Air Force. In 1925, after the amalgamation of the DMP and the Garda Síochána, he was made chief superintendent of the new Dublin metropolitan division.[37] In 1929 he was transferred to the depot as commandant. By early February 1933 he was head of the detective division of the Garda Síochána.

Broy wanted the government to reopen recruiting, but in April 1933 it refused his request. By August, however, the situation had changed. The Army Comrades Association had been established to resist anticipated dismissals from the army by De Valera. More commonly known as the Blueshirts, it attracted many Cumann na nGaedheal supporters who saw it as a bulwark against a Fianna Fáil government and a seemingly revitalised IRA. O'Duffy was now leader of the Blueshirts, which was renamed the National Guard. He planned a mass march on 13 August to Glasnevin cemetery on a route past Leinster House, to commemorate the deaths of Griffith, Collins and O'Higgins. De Valera and his government feared a Mussolini-type coup and hurriedly decided to recruit new and politically totally dependable policemen. On 5 August 1933, forty-two men were attested to the Garda Síochána and appointed as detectives to the Special Branch on the same day.[38] On 9 August, another eighteen men were similarly attested and appointed on the one day to the Special Branch. These were all loyal Fianna Fáil supporters who were drafted into the force before O'Duffy's proposed march. They were armed, in plain clothes, and assigned to Dublin Castle detective section. On the day of the march they were posted along the route and at key government buildings. The government had banned the meeting and O'Duffy complied with the order. One month later another nineteen men were recruited in a similar manner and also assigned to the Special Branch. Government detractors soon termed these new guards 'Broy Harriers' — a reference to a famous pack of hounds, the Bray Harriers. This was also implying an analogy between them and the infamous Black and Tans who had augmented the RIC in the War of Independence and had been nicknamed after another hunting pack. The appellation stuck and was sometimes used to describe not only these seventy-nine recruits but all men attested from 1933 to 1935.[39]

These seventy-nine recruits were unusual in many respects and merit closer inspection. They received no formal training, being assigned to operational duty as detectives on the actual day of attestation. Approximately 80 per cent were over the required entry age of 27, 62 per cent were under standard height and 43 per cent were married (recruits were supposed to be single). Overall, only 10 per cent of these men actually complied with all three standard entry stipulations. Approximately three-quarters of these new guards had been members of the IRA. They had opposed the Treaty and subsequently followed De Valera into Fianna Fáil. It was the first real influx of anti-Treaty men into the force, apart from the minority who had orchestrated the mutiny in 1922. All seventy-nine recruits were living in Dublin, the result no doubt of having to recruit, attest, arm and assign men in an extremely short space of time. Over 80 per cent of them were natives of the city. The trades of these new recruits reflected their life in the city and were in complete contrast to the profile of the bulk of the pre-1932 men, with not one farmer among them. The breakdown of trades was as illustrated in Table 3.6.

By the end of 1934, another 310 men had been recruited and assigned to ordinary garda duties after a period of training. Over 56 per cent of these recruits were over age, 32 per cent were below the required height and 25 per cent were married. In the first three months of 1935

Table 3.6: Previous Trade of Broy Harriers, 1933

Previous Trade	%
Accountant, clerk, insurance agent, sales assistant	27
Car, van, lorry, bus driver or mechanic	22
Machinist, engineer, railway, fitter, printer, electrician	22
Labourer, gardener, blacksmith	18
Miscellaneous (including egg testing!)	11
Total	100

Source: Registry of candidates.

(after which recruiting was effectively closed until the outbreak of World War II) a further 170 men were attested. Quite a number of these did not fulfil all of the entry requirements. The desire of the government to promote the Irish language in and through the Garda Síochána was reflected in the increase in the number of recruits from Gaeltacht areas.[40]

A total of 570 men (including a small number of re-joiners) joined the force in the 1932–5 period under the Fianna Fáil government. Most of these came from Dublin, Cork, Kerry, Mayo, Clare, Donegal and Galway. The main trades of the newly attested guards were as shown in Table 3.7.

Table 3.7: Previous Trade of Garda Síochána, 1932–5

Previous Trade	%
Farmer	26.0
Labourer	16.5
Car Driver	10.5
Clerk	7.2
Student	6.3
Car Mechanic	3.6
Miscellaneous	29.9
Total	100.0

Source: Registry of candidates.

There were four Church of Ireland members in the 570 recruits, two were in the Broy Harriers and two in the remainder. The rest were Catholic.

The vast majority of the guards recruited in the 1933–5 period were loyal Fianna Fáil supporters. The government believed that the force needed an injection of Fianna Fáil blood to redress the imbalance of the 1920s when the great majority of the members came from the pro-Treaty side of the political division.[41] Initially the Broy Harriers were treated with suspicion and distrust by the pre-1932 men, but in time both learned to live with each other. The remaining 1933–5 recruits blended in well with the existing members of the force quite quickly. The injection of Fianna Fáil blood had an important political effect. It made the Garda Síochána acceptable to the anti-Treaty side of the political division and helped it to identify with the new state. Allowing for the aberration of the Broy Harriers who were recruited under exceptional political circumstances, the vast majority of the 1933–5 recruits were not unlike the 1920s men. They came predominately from the western half of the country, were mostly farmers and labourers, and were overwhelmingly Catholic. The difference was that they were 'Dev's men'.

TACA, 1939–42

Commissioner Broy retired in June 1938. He was replaced by Michael J. Kinnane LLB, who had been educated at Blackrock College, Dublin, before joining the British Civil Service in London in 1908. In June 1922 he became principal officer at the Department of Home Affairs in the Irish Free State. He was a civil servant, not a policeman and this caused some resentment among the force, although he had been associated with garda administration from the government side for a number of years.[42]

On 2 September 1939, the day after Hitler invaded Poland, the Department of Justice insisted that recruitment of a new paid force was absolutely necessary. By the end of September, it had been decided to recruit 400 men to a temporary police force called Taca. The term Taca comes from the Irish, meaning 'prop or support'. The usual entry stipulations applied. Service in Taca was on a temporary basis and was non-pensionable. Pay was non-incremental and the right to annual paid leave was not guaranteed to members until August 1940. In September 1939, 233 Taca members were attested and trained in the depot in Phoenix Park, followed by another seventy the following March. The entry requirements pertaining to height, marital status and age were rigorously applied. None of these men had been in the IRA as they were too young to have served in the organisation when it was respectable in the eyes of the establishment. As had become the familiar pattern, two-thirds of the recruits came from the western half of the country, with

Kerry and Cork providing over 25 per cent of the total. While farmers continued to form the back bone of the recruits who joined (39 per cent), there was an increase in the number of clerks and sales assistants and a decrease in the number of labourers. Occupations such as commercial traveller, shopkeeper, insurance agent and agricultural instructor showed an increase, whereas traditional backgrounds such as railway employee, mason, mechanic, plasterer, carpenter and fitter accounted for only 5 per cent of Taca members. All members of the temporary force were Catholic.

The Taca members represented a new generation of policemen. They were well-educated men in their early twenties, while the overwhelming majority of the members of the Garda Síochána were heading into their forties. Unlike the recruitment of men in the early 1920s or in the early 1930s, the recruitment of these Taca members was not based on political considerations whose origins were to be found in the Civil War divide. However, a great number of them still came from the western half of the country and were farmers. When training was completed, all of these Taca members were sent out on uniform duty to the city of Dublin. Although constituted as a temporary force, they were actually indistinguishable from ordinary gardaí in the duties that they performed, while their conditions of service remained less favourable. In April 1942 the 281 remaining Taca members (the others had resigned or died) were fully attested as members of the Garda Síochána.

THE 1940s MEN

Recruitment for the ordinary force was re-opened in 1942, with the first new men being attested in January 1943. It continued on a regular basis up to April 1948. Until February 1947 only those who had served in the National army or auxiliary defence forces could join the guards. Of the 1,052 men attested in the 1943–8 period the military background was as illustrated in Table 3.8.

Almost two-thirds of the total number of recruits came from eight counties in the western portion of the state, with Cork and Kerry taking the lion's share. Farmers and farm labourers accounted for almost half of the new recruits. Students and clerks accounted for a quarter of the total. Five of the 1,052 recruits were Church of Ireland members, the remainder were Catholic.

By 1948 almost 15 per cent of the members of the Garda Síochána had been recruited in the previous five years. They were a new generation compared to the men of the early 1920s and early 1930s. While many of them had military experience, it did not originate in their politics or attitude to the Civil War. In general, they were better educated than the previous generation of recruits. However, the bulk of them came from the west of the country and were farmers just like the men of the 1920s and early 1930s.

Table 3.8: Military Background of 1943–8 Garda Síochána

Background	%
LDF/LSF[43]	63.5
NA	25.0
FCA	6.5
Civilians	5.0
Total	100.0

Source: Temporary register.

1922–52

Almost two-thirds of the 10,135 men who joined the Garda Síochána in the 1922–52 period had been in the IRA. One-fifth of these had also served in the National army. Most of the IRA men had joined the guards in the early 1920s. Army personnel dominated recruitment to the Garda Síochána in the 1923–7 and 1943–7 periods, when over half of garda recruits joined the force. The LDF, LSF and FCA appeared in the 1940s and were a major source of recruitment at that time. Slightly over 1.5 per cent of the force had been in the RIC, with half of these having served in the IRA. Practically all of these RIC men had joined in 1922. During the first ten years of the state's existence less than a quarter of the force's recruits were civilians. In the early 1930s, less than half were civilians and in the 1940s this dwindled to a mere 5 per cent. The only time in which civilians dominated recruitment was in the 1939–40 period, when 303 Taca members were attested as a temporary police force.

Table 3.9 shows the county of origin of the members of the Garda Síochána in the 1922–52 period.

Throughout the thirty-year period under review the western sea board counties of Kerry, Clare, Galway and Mayo, as well as Cork, provided nearly 40 per cent of the force's members. These five counties provided the most recruits, irrespective of whether it was pro-Treaty

Table 3.9: County of Origin of Garda Síochána, 1922–52

Native County	No of Guards	% of Total Force	% of Total County Population in 1926
Cork	952	9.40	.26
Kerry	861	8.50	.57
Mayo	768	7.58	.44
Galway	712	7.03	.42
Clare	567	5.60	.60
Dublin[44]	559	5.52	.11
Limerick	526	5.19	.37
Roscommon	475	4.69	.56
Tipperary	422	4.17	.30
Donegal	421	4.16	.27
Sligo	363	3.58	.50
Leitrim	351	3.47	.63
Kilkenny	284	2.80	.40
Monaghan	272	2.64	.41
Laois	248	2.45	.48
Wexford	245	2.42	.25
Cavan	237	2.34	.28
Longford	206	2.03	.51
Offaly	178	1.76	.34
Westmeath	162	1.60	.28
Meath	149	1.47	.23
Kildare	143	1.41	.24
Carlow	141	1.39	.41
Waterford	135	1.33	.17
Wicklow	134	1.32	.23
Fermanagh	112	1.11	.19
Tyrone	103	1.02	.07
Armagh	85	0.84	.07
Louth	78	0.77	.12
Antrim	67	0.66	.01
Derry	65	0.64	.04
Down	65	0.64	.03

Source: General register; Registry of candidates.

men who were required in the 1920s, De Valera supporters in the early 1930s, temporary policemen in the late 1930s or army/auxiliary force men in the mid-1940s. The pattern set in the first few months of the force's existence dominated and influenced subsequent recruitment. Another band of six counties still in the western half of the state contributed one quarter of the force's members. The remaining fifteen mainly eastern counties contributed only approximately 30 per cent of the force's members. Northern Ireland accounted for just under 5 per cent of the total gardaí and most of these joined in the very early years. The map in Figure 3.2 shows the distribution according to county.

When the number of recruits per county is related to that county's population, this west/east divide is reinforced. The top nine counties who produced the most guards per head of population in descending order of importance were as follows: Leitrim, Clare, Kerry, Roscommon, Longford, Sligo, Laois,[45] Mayo and Galway.

Table 3.10 shows the principal trades of the 10,135 guards before entry to the force in the period 1922–52.

Table 3.10: Previous Trade among Garda Síochána, 1922–52

Previous Trade	%
Farmer	38.10
Labourer	15.35
Student	5.26
Sales Assistant	5.25
Clerk	4.96
Car Driver	2.50
Railway	1.63
RIC	1.57
Teacher	1.21
Carpenter	1.13
Car Mechanic	1.04
Miscellaneous	22.00
Total	100.00

Source: General register; Registry of candidates.

The most common trades of the miscellaneous category of recruits were as follows: asylum assistant, businessman, commercial traveller, electrician, engineer, fitter, fisherman, ganger, gardener, insurance agent, mechanic, postman, post office, tailor and wireless operator. The farmer and labourer percentage of members remained high and fairly consistent throughout all stages of recruitment. Some change was perceptible

Figure 3.2: County of Origin of Garda Síochána Recruits, 1922–52

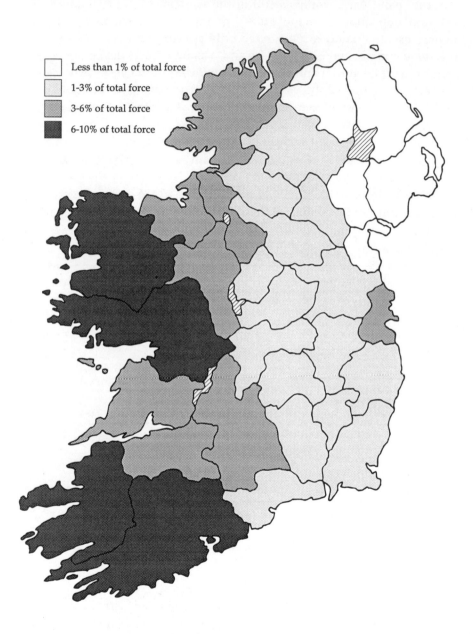

Less than 1% of total force
1-3% of total force
3-6% of total force
6-10% of total force

Source: General register; Registry of candidates.

in the occupations of recruits after 1932, with a noticeable increase in the number of students, clerks and car drivers. Other trades such as insurance agent, commercial traveller and car mechanic began to increase or appear for the first time. This trend was accelerated when Taca members were recruited, and during the 1943–8 recruitment drive. However, farming and labouring backgrounds continued to predominate. Such classes dominated recruitment from the western counties. Recruits from the east coast were far less likely to be from a farming/labouring background.

Almost 98.7 per cent of the members of the Garda Síochána were Catholic, with only 1.3 per cent Protestant. Most of the Protestants who joined the force did so in the very early years, with fewer than a dozen joining after 1932. Protestants did not join the guards in proportion to their number in the general population. Seven Protestants from Northern Ireland joined the guards in the thirty-year period under review.

All members who joined the Garda Síochána between 1922 and 1952 had to be male. Most of them came from the western part of the state, and the overwhelming majority of them were Catholic. The vast majority were 19 to 27 years of age, over 5 feet 9" tall, and unmarried. Most of them had received only primary education. By and large, they reflected the religion, occupation and education of the vast majority of the people of the state. The garda authorities tended to recruit members who were almost identical to those recruited by the RIC, with regard to age, height, marital status and county of origin.[46]

4

ENTRY, TRAINING AND ORGANISATION

ENTRY

The organising committee of February 1922 recommended that recruits be unmarried, between the ages of 19 and 27, at least 5 feet 9" in height, and with a minimum chest measurement of 36 inches or 37 inches if 5 feet 11" or taller.[1] Only men could join the guards, a stipulation so widely taken for granted that it did not even feature in any of the entry requirements. They were to be examined in reading, writing from dictation, spelling and arithmetic. They also had to write a short composition. For the first few months of the force's existence candidates were informed of recruitment either by a notice in the public press or by their local superior IRA officer. The Garda Síochána (Temporary Provisions) Act, 1923, gave a statutory basis to the new police force. The Garda Síochána Act, 1924, made the 1923 act permanent. Neither of these acts substantially changed the entry requirements for the force as laid down by the organising committee, and which were to remain almost unaltered for the next thirty years. In 1942 the upper age limit was reduced to 23 years. The entry age remained 19 to 23 throughout the 1940s although there were special concessions made for members who had served in the defence forces.

At key points in the evolution of the force, a 'rider' or extra stipulation was added to the regulations, which greatly restricted access to the guards and transformed the complexion of the force. The organising committee's suggestion that pro-Treaty IRA volunteers get preference in admission to the civic guards had profound consequences for the composition of the infant force. In August 1923 the government decided that recruitment for the Civic Guard was to be confined for the present to a number of groups that had helped the emerging state, chief among them being the IRA and the army. Civilians were allowed to join the guards even in the early days of the force. However, with such preferential treatment being given to the IRA and army, the number of ordinary citizens was very small, especially in the first year or two. However, as more settled conditions returned, the number of recruits from the general public increased steadily.

By December 1923, the situation had returned to near normal — the Civil War was over, the army was withdrawn from most areas and the Garda Síochána had been distributed throughout much of the country. There were now 5,500 guards who had been hastily recruited, ill-trained and not properly vetted before being sent out among the public. Under the Garda Síochána (Temporary Provisions) Act, 1923, every member of the guards was on probation for one year, and would be made permanent under the proposed 1924 Garda Síochána Act only if proven to be efficient. O'Duffy had serious reservations about the educational standard and general efficiency of some members of the force. In 1924 he held efficiency tests. A total of 3,597 guards had to sit the efficiency tests, as they had originally been admitted without an adequate written examination. Only a few were actually discharged as a result of this examination.

Until early 1924 the Garda Síochána authorities themselves were exclusively in charge of entry to the force. Garda personnel conducted the literary examinations and ensured that the candidate possessed the prescribed qualifications in respect of age, physique etc. In 1924 the civil service commissioners took responsibility for the literary examination (as they had done previously for the RIC) while the rest of the procedure remained in garda hands. The literary examinations were very simple and no syllabus was ever prescribed. Candidates spent one hour writing an English essay, thirty minutes on arithmetic and thirty minutes on dictation. There was no algebra, geometry, history or geography, although an oral in Irish was conducted by the Irish instructor at the depot. The general standard of the entrance examination was approximately that of third class in primary school. It remained at this level until 1938. A young man wishing to become a guard applied in writing direct to the commissioner or visited his local garda station. If approved, he underwent medical and literary examinations at district or divisional headquarters in his local area. If successful in these examinations and suitable for the job in the eyes of the chief superintendent, he was called to the depot for a final examination and another medical. If successful, he was finally attested by the commissioner himself. In effect, recruiting was carried out from depot headquarters through chief superintendents and district officers on whose recommendations the commissioner relied. The recruiting officer in each area was the local sergeant. The civil service commissioners merely conducted literary examinations.

The entry requirements of the Garda Síochána were enforced quite rigidly, with only occasional lapses, for the first ten years of the force's life. Although there was a screening of candidates at local level prior to their arrival in Dublin, approximately 30 per cent of candidates who presented themselves at the depot up to 1932 were rejected for one reason or another. Many were found to be medically unfit or under height, and others did not reach the standard of literacy required. There was also a small number who, deciding that the life of the guard was not for them, left very soon after arriving. Over 95 per cent of the guards recruited before 1932 fulfilled the stipulated height requirement. Very few married men were admitted to the force and the number exceeding the age requirement was insignificant. Numerous mothers and some fathers wrote directly to O'Duffy pleading that their sons be accepted into the guards. According to the letters, these candidates had impeccable credentials regarding education, health, references etc. They appear to have invariably been rejected by O'Duffy.[2] The greatest number of exceptions to the entry requirements occurred in the first 2,000 recruits who had joined by October 1922. Some of these left voluntarily, others left or were not re-attested after the Kildare mutiny, and the efficiency tests of 1924 weeded out some of the remainder. By December 1924, O'Duffy had ensured that the vast majority of gardaí satisfied the entry requirements and that future recruits would be rigorously vetted before attestation. Those who joined in the latter half of the 1920s included fewer exceptions to the regulations. With thousands of pleading letters arriving on the desks of the Minister for Home Affairs and the commissioner during the 1920s, the authorities could afford to be selective in whom they accepted into the guards.[3]

From De Valera's accession to power in 1932 until the end of 1935, 570 guards were recruited, including the Broy Harriers. Political expediency meant that over half of the recruits attested in this period failed to satisfy at least one of the major entry stipulations. However, the entire operation was in keeping with the letter, if not the spirit, of the Garda Síochána Act, 1924, which allowed the authorities to waive certain regulations in special circumstances.[4] The Cumann na nGaedheal government appears to have availed of this when recruiting the Special Branch in the spring of 1925 — 44 per cent of them were over the statutory age and 20 per cent were below the minimum height requirement.

In 1936, Deputy Commissioner Edward Cullen wrote to the civil service commissioners requesting a raising of the standard of the entrance examination. He claimed that the existing standard was very low indeed, the problems posed being very elementary, and that a few weeks' study was sufficient to pass. He believed that this caused serious problems later on, as very many of the men accepted were found to possess a very poor standard of education.[5] A draft syllabus was discussed by the garda authorities with the civil service commissioners and a new standard was introduced in 1937. New subjects were introduced to the examination: general knowledge, history, geography and précis writing. Irish, previously optional, was now compulsory. The new standard was slightly below what those who had finished sixth class in primary school should have attained.

Recruitment for the temporary police force, Taca, began in September 1939. Most of the candidates called to the depot for examination, medical and interview were drawn from those who had applied to join in the previous few years but could not be accepted as recruitment was closed. Approximately 20 per cent were found to be medically unfit on arrival at the depot, for reasons ranging from defective vision to inflamed acne.[6] There was a dramatic improvement in the educational standard of these new admissions. Figures available for the last batch, which was attested in February 1940, are shown in Table 4.1.

Table 4.1: Education of Taca Recruits, February 1940[7]

Level of Education	%
Primary education (5th class standard and upwards)	33
Secondary education	23
Intermediate Certificate	31
Leaving Certificate	6
Matriculated	7
Total	100

Source: Taca file (GM).

Most of the candidates with second-level education certificates were exempt from doing the literary entrance examination. It was not only in educational achievements that the Taca members differed from the earlier recruits. They were also much taller. The higher qualifications in physique and literary ability among this group can be attributed to a number of factors. There had been no recruitment at all for the previous four years, and consequently the authorities had a greater number than usual on which to draw. Of more significance, however, was the fact that for almost the first time since the establishment of the force, the government did not feel obliged to give preferential treatment to some particular group, such as the IRA, National army or De Valera supporters. With emigration to the US closed, the choice for many was Taca or England. At least one recruit, a young man from County Kerry, came to the depot for interview, with his bags packed for England should he be unsuccessful.[8] The standard of education was also, slowly but steadily, increasing in the country.

In March 1942 the government decided to reopen recruitment but confine it to members of the army or auxiliary services, such as the Local Defence Force, Local Security Force or Air Raid Precaution Service. From the thousands of applicants about 200 were selected to sit the civil service commissioners' examination in July for the 100 places available. Over half of these failed. In April 1943 the Minister for Justice, Gerard Boland, amended the appointment regulations to allow 100 members of the defence forces to be attested to the gardaí without the necessity of passing the civil service literary examination. Two batches of candidates were examined in May and October 1943, each consisting of just over 100 men. The standard of education of these recruits from the defence and auxiliary forces was well above that of the previous year's intake. Over 75 per cent had received some secondary education, with a number having passed the Intermediate Certificate, and a smaller number having been successful in the Leaving Certificate.[9]

The tide of the War had begun to change in 1942. By mid-1943 this was much more apparent and may have prompted a greater number of well-qualified defence and auxiliary force personnel to seek a permanent and secure job in the Garda Síochána. Furthermore, the commissioner seems to have selected candidates with a better level of education than previously to sit the civil service commissioners' examination, the standard of which had been lowered somewhat from 1942.

In December 1943 the age regulations for admission to the guards were relaxed somewhat to facilitate defence force members. Despite this, there was still trouble getting enough suitable recruits. The low pay for new members and the much more attractive wages to be earned in post-war Britain accounted in large measure for the shortage. In 1946 the authorities sought 200 recruits but secured only 168 suitable men. The tendency towards improved educational standards continued, with 45 per cent having attended secondary school. However, Commissioner Kinnane was not satisfied and stated that at least half of the recruits

An RIC officer. There was great continuity between the RIC and its successor, the Garda Síochána.

Armed Civic Guards, Portarlington, August 1922. Many men, upon being accepted into the new force, were immediately sent out, in civilian clothes and without any formal training.

Funeral of Frank Lawless TD, Swords, County Dublin. Earliest picture of the newly formed 'Civic Guard' at a public event in civilian clothes.

Attestation of recruit, 1930s. A place in the guards was much coveted from the earliest days of the force's existence.

School No. 7, Depot. In 1944 Comhdháil Náisiúnta na Gaedhilge urged that the Irish language be used as the medium for instructing recruits while in training. However, few instructors were capable of giving police instruction through Irish.

Footbaths in the Garda Depot washroom, 1940s. Shows the vast improvement in twenty years. For the first recruits there was no hot water, gas lamps provided the light and sanitation was in the form of dry toilets.

Bedroom, Parkgate Hall, 1950s. Recruits had to keep the dormitory in a spotless condition.

Kitchen, Depot, Phoenix Park, 1940s.

Messhall, Depot, Phoenix Park, 1940s.

Officers' Dance, 1940s.
Back L to R: Sup Breen; P. Kennedy, Assistant Secretary to Government; Chief Sup Sean Gantly;
Miss Caulfield; Mr Maurice Moynihan, Secretary to Government; Commissioner Michael Kinnane;
Chief Sup George Butler; Dep Comm W.R.E. Murphy; Chief Sup Richard Creagh; Mrs Patrick Carroll;
Sup Ryan D. District; Insp Kennedy, RUC Headquarters, Belfast; Ass Comm T. Woods.
Centre L to R: Mrs Brodie; Mrs A.H. Kennedy; Mrs P. Kennedy; Mrs Early; Mrs Kinnane; Mrs Moynihan;
Mrs Flood; Mrs Woods. **Front L to R:** Chief Sup Patrick Carroll; Miss P. Felton; Sup A. Flood;
Mr J. Murphy; Miss Joan Murphy; D/Sup George Lawlor.

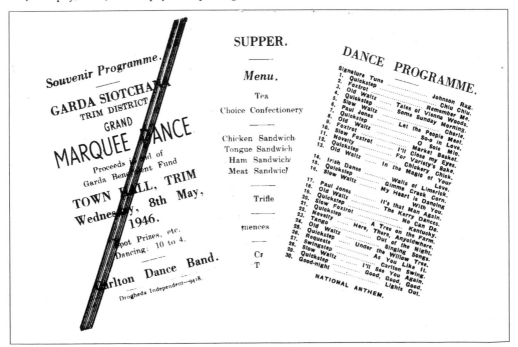

Dance ticket, 1946. From the early 1930s, Garda Síochána annual dances were held in each
division and the proceeds donated to charity.

Card playing in the station. In the 1922–51 period, the actual amount of work to be done was frequently insufficient to occupy a guard's time totally during his long hours of duty.

Sgt John and Mary Shaw, Portarlington, County Laois, 1950.

Physical education class for recruits in Kildare Depot, 1922. The first annual garda sports day was held in Kildare in September 1922.

Sgt J. Beale, drill instructor, 1920s.

Garda Síochána football team, 1947, at Croke Park.

Garda swimmers, 1940s.

Garda boxers. Members of the force had an extraordinary list of successes in boxing.

Sgt Dick Hearns, 1935. Garda boxer 1928–39; boxing and drill instructor at the Depot, 1939–64.

19 MONDAY

Sunday 18th.

Saw friend home from Dance, went in to house and had some refreshment; later attended fam. Div. service rested for some time, attended 10.30 a.m. Parade; rested until 2.30 p.m. later on the Town, met friends on main street at 4.0 p.m. went for a walk via Rly. Stn. to farm, remained here for some time; on return made the acquaintance of the Gibsons opposite Bangha Rd. To Devotion later; afterwards met friends in the street; and went to the Tivoli cinema; on duty about Town for some time later; nothing of any importance occurred or transpired the whole time. "Monday" attended fam. Parade & Police duty class until 10 a.m. On duty in the Town from 1 p.m. to 6 p.m. called to some houses on messages, remained in one with friend for some time had a good enjoyable evening; later to Devotions, had a chat re. Dance etc. with an acquaintance for some time. later met friends went to Town Hall Pictures, on duty about Town Rly. Stn. etc. for some time off duty at 10.45.

20 TUESDAY

Attended 9 a.m. Parade; and gaelic class until noon. later attended Circuit Court, their cases, met some acquaintances nothing of any importance occurred or transpired. On duty in the Town during the afternoon, called to a few houses got watch regulated at Mr. Bradshaw's, had a long conversation re matters in general, also with some people in Town. nothing of any importance occurred or transpired. called to 5 Henry Street met friends, had a long conversation re. matters in general, nothing of any importance. To Devotion at night; later met friend at Technical Gate, went for a walk on the Old Road, had a long chat re. things in general. got some rain; later called to 5 Henry Street, made an acquaintance remained for a short time. later met patrol and conversed on the street re. ...

21 WEDNESDAY

Remained on duty in the Town until 2.30 a.m. kept several houses under observation; also attended the arrival of the mail Train and escorted the mails to the Post Office; also paid a visit to the Co. ... Brewery from the rear via Rly. Stn. grounds. nothing of any importance occurred or transpired. Rested in the morning; had a conversation with J. Healy from Cappawhite re. matters in general. later met Tout who called to the station; had a chat re. wanted men etc. made arrangements to meet in Cappawhite about 25th inst. at 3 p.m. later on duty in the Town, called to see a Tout, had a chat re. some movements arranged to meet later. afterwards met friend, went for a walk out the hills, had a long conversation. To Devotions at night met friend later, went to Town Hall Pictures; remained on duty in the Town until 11 p.m. nothing of any importance occurred.

Extract from diary of Garda John Hartigan, who was stationed in Emly Station, County Tipperary. The diary, which he kept in a Browne's scribbling notebook from 1 January 1928 until 17 November 1928, is now in the Garda Museum.

Cadet class, 1923. In February 1923, Commissioner O'Duffy got government approval to recruit a cadet class.
Middle Front: Chief Sup F.J. Maguire. **Front L to R:** D.P. Comyn; T. Noonan; E. O'Riordan; J.A. O'Shea; F.J. Maguire; R. Downey; E.C. Millard; D. Connolly; M.J. Higgins. **Middle L to R:** T. Collins; G. Butler; C.B. Heron; P.M. Slavin; P.J. Carroll; T. McNeill; T. Woods; J.J. Kelleher; P.M. English.
Back L to R: A. Connor; J. McNulty; W. Quinlan; G. Flynn; M.C. Connolly; J.N. Gilroy.

Gardaí with Commissioner O'Duffy on the steps of St Peter's during the Garda pilgrimage to Rome in 1928. Almost 98.7 per cent of gardaí in the 1922–52 period were Roman Catholic.

Garda recruits at the Depot, Phoenix Park, 1943.

Taca recruits, 1939. Service in Taca Síochána was on a temporary basis — for the duration of the Emergency — and was non-pensionable. Taca members were well educated and in their early twenties.

A Garda member of the
Emergency De-contamination
Squad (*c.* 1940).

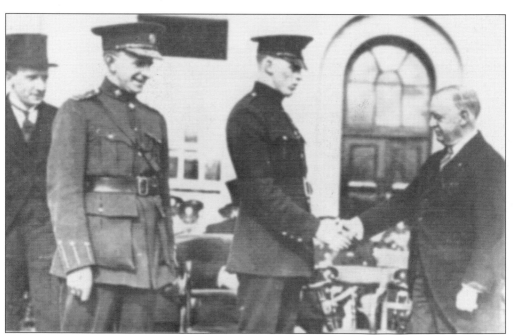

Colonel Walter Scott congratulates Garda James Mulroy, the first recipient of the
Scott medal, 1924. Also in the picture are Home Affairs Minister Kevin O'Higgins and
Commissioner Eoin O'Duffy.

were not physically and educationally first class.[10] He urged the Department of Justice to open recruitment to the general public, not just the defence forces. The government acquiesced to his demands in February 1947 but stipulated that the defence forces members be given preference regarding entry.

A place in the guards was much coveted from the earliest days of the force's existence. Any recruitment announcement was almost invariably followed by a deluge of applications. Thousands of unsuccessful applications were received throughout the 1920s, including one from the assistant superintendent of the Indian Imperial Police in Bengal seeking an equivalent position in the Garda Síochána.[11] The applications continued to pour in even when recruitment was closed. In 1933, following recruitment notices in the public press, the response was so immediate and of such magnitude that the waiting lists were almost instantly filled. In 1942 over 3,300 applied for just 100 places in the force.

There is no doubt but that people tried to exert influence or 'pull' to get their son or neighbour into the guards. As early as October 1922, O'Duffy stated in a public notice: 'Any attempt to obtain entrance other than as laid down (in the regulations) will be regarded as disqualification.'[12] Thousands upon thousands of letters were received by the Ministers for Home Affairs (later Justice) and commissioners from anxious parents, hoping that they would use influence and relax the regulations so as to allow their son entry into the force. Ministerial colleagues, TDs and other public representatives frequently wrote to the Minister for Justice with the same purpose in mind. All extant material which is accessible seems to indicate that this was rarely successful.[13] The letters received by the Minister were sent to the Garda Commissioner who decided each case on its merits, but did not relax or bend the rules. However, it is obvious that the successful application of influence to gain entry to the force would hardly be recorded in the official files. Information gleaned from various sources, including off-the-record interviews, supports the view that influence was at times successfully employed in order to gain admission to the force, but it does not appear to have been successful on a very widespread scale.

While the entrance examination to the guards in the 1920s was very elementary, it was in accord with the general standard of education received by most of the population at that time. It had to be readjusted upwards in the mid-1930s to reflect a nationally increased level of education. By the late 1940s it had gradually increased, keeping in line with improved educational standards. The garda authorities regarded the entrance examination as setting a minimum standard of education essential for all members of the force. It was not a competitive examination, in that those scoring highest were by no means assured of admission. In fact, in 1937, Deputy Commissioner Cullen, while advocating the raising of the educational standard required for entry, stated that he wished also to avoid attracting the over-educated type.[14] While many were above the basic minimum standard, quite a number hovered close to it. Other considerations such as general character and reliability, willingness to learn, good physique and appearance, as well as perfect health, were all very important. With the exception of the periods early 1922 and 1933–4, the vast majority of the recruits were well built, healthy, reliable, unmarried young men with a reasonable education for the time. This was the case despite the fact that for much of the period 1922–52 admission to the guards was tilted in favour of groups who were accorded preferential treatment.

TRAINING

The training received by the recruits in 1922 was haphazard. The lack of a sufficient number of qualified instructors, grossly inadequate facilities, and the continual transfers to yet another new depot made the task very difficult indeed. Many recruits did receive some training, but there was no uniformity in its duration, content or standard. O'Duffy's efficiency tests of 1924 necessitated that the 1922 men train and teach themselves, if they wished to be made permanent. By a combination of some training received as recruits, on-the-spot training picked up as young guards and some private study in their own time, the 1922 members were reasonably well trained.

The occupation of permanent headquarters in the Phoenix Park depot and adjoining McKee barracks in late December 1922 permitted a more organised training of subsequent recruits. Accommodation was basic but reasonably adequate with fifteen to twenty men in each dormitory or squad room. There was no hot water for shaving, gas lamps provided the light, and sanitation was in the form of dry toilets. The food, which included meat and potatoes, was not well cooked but was adequate. The recruits paid for their own messing. Training usually lasted about four months. O'Duffy relied heavily on former RIC police instructors to train the new men. Some of the instructors were former British army men.

The system of training established in 1923 remained virtually unchanged for the next thirty years. The day started at 6.30 a.m. with reveille, followed by washing in cold water and sweeping out the dormitory. A few recruits were detailed to help to make the breakfast. Roll-call was at 6.50 a.m., followed by drill for the next three-quarters of an hour. Breakfast frequently consisted of thick, gluey, solid porridge with no sugar and little milk, buckets of tea and hunks of bread.[15] The individual recruit then got ready for inspection by having the compulsory morning shave, checking uniform buttons, boots etc., as well as neatly folding his spare uniform. The dormitory had also to be in a spotless condition. The sergeant in charge of each group checked this before the morning parade at 8.45 a.m. Prior to this, each day a different group of recruits — called a fatigue party — scrubbed the floors, tables and forms of the messhalls, washed and disinfected the lavatories and cleaned out the wash-houses. Any individual failing to satisfy the company officer's inspection on parade was either cautioned or disciplined. Discipline could involve being detailed for extra drill or fatigue duties or being confined to barracks for a night or two. Drill followed immediately after the parade and lasted one hour.

The remainder of the day until 5 p.m. consisted of police duty and law classes, an Irish class, physical training in the gym or outside, with a dinner break of one hour. Recruits also received instruction in first aid, fire drill and sometimes swimming and life-saving classes. Tea was at 5.15, after which the recruits were free to leave the depot until roll call at 10 p.m. Young recruits out in the city were not supposed to loiter around, have their hands in their pockets or be seen smoking in public. Those who preferred to stay in the depot could play billiards, meet in the rest room or dry canteen (no alcoholic drink), play football or hurling or do some private study. On Saturday the recruits were free from 2 to 10 p.m., and Sunday was completely free except for the march in uniform to Aughrim Street Chapel for Catholics and St James' Parish Church for Church of Ireland members.

By the mid to late 1940s garda recruits were still being trained in the Phoenix Park depot using the same hard iron dormitory beds and keeping their few possessions on the surrounding shelves rather than wardrobes. The sanitation had improved somewhat, although washing facilities were still fairly primitive. Electric lighting had replaced the gas system. The food, while not particularly inviting, was wholesome and nourishing.[16] There were still periodic examinations during and at the conclusion of training. Training lasted six months, having fluctuated between four and six months for the previous twenty-five years, although there were some notable deviations. In 1933, the Broy Harriers received no training whatsoever. In 1938, the Taca Síochána received only six weeks' training owing to the outbreak of the Second World War.

Commissioner O'Duffy believed that, once trained, a member was basically on his own. For O'Duffy the success or failure of the force depended on the self-discipline of each individual member. He wished to inculcate in the recruit habits of implicit discipline, which would never lapse when on his own.[17] Therefore, training was conducted in a semi-military-type atmosphere in which the recruits' hours of sleeping, waking, working, eating and recreation were all scheduled precisely. This, it was hoped, would make such routine instinctive. O'Duffy's philosophy of training, which permeated the Garda Síochána for thirty or forty years, was not original. Not only did the basic training of recruits not change over the thirty-year period 1922–52, but neither did it change from that received by the RIC prior to independence. It was conducted in the same depot, frequently using the same personnel and the same manuals, and while the Garda Síochána was a less military-type body than the RIC had been, the training of the two bodies differed in degree rather than in kind.

ORGANISATION

There was no general distribution of the Civic Guard throughout the country until the closing quarter of 1922. Various random policing schemes, such as the Irish Republican Police, attempted to fill the void, though numerous districts in the country had very little or no policing whatsoever during this period. From early March 1922 the government had been inundated with requests from locally elected authorities all over the country, clergymen and the general public, requesting either permission to set up some temporary policing scheme or the sending of the Civic Guard to the locality. By mid-autumn the general situation with regard to law and order, though by no means normal, had improved. In the last week of September, O'Duffy began sending out members of the new Civic Guard, mainly to some of the larger towns. They were despatched in groups of twenty or twenty-five men to the following towns and cities:

Bruff	Roscrea	Mullingar	Ennis
Maryboro	Longford	Kilkenny	Galway
Athlone	Ballinasloe	Naas	Granard
Monaghan	Carlow	Letterkenny	Clones
Wicklow	Buncrana	Cavan	

Fifty men were sent to Limerick city. A party of twenty-one guards arrived in Galway city on 25 September. They got accommodation in the County Club in Eyre Square, a gentleman's club for the local aristocracy, as the RIC barracks in Eglinton Street had been burned down.[18] Other stations already occupied at this juncture were:

Swords	Kildare	Rathangan	Dundrum
Newbridge	Castledermot	Lucan	Clonee
Portarlington	Foxrock	Athy	

In early October 1922 smaller bands of gardaí, usually consisting of a sergeant and seven or eight guards, were sent to Counties Cavan, Monaghan, Louth, Meath, Wexford, Roscommon and Dublin, opening a further twenty-two stations.[19] This process continued, with O'Duffy sending out men to areas deemed to be free of serious disruption by anti-Treaty forces, and ready to accept normal policing. Once a larger group had become established for a few weeks in a county town, smaller parties were sent from there to open new stations in smaller nearby towns in the adjoining rural areas.

In August 1922 local merchants in Cork had set up a Civic Patrol to police the city. The government accepted financial responsibility for the patrol, which consisted of over 100 men with no uniform. Forty-five were ex-IRA, forty-seven ex-British army and twelve ex-navy men. In October the government had sent three civic guards in civilian clothes to Cork to recruit for the force. They selected those who were suitable in the Civic Patrol, allowing them to continue police work in the city. Fifty civic guards were then sent from the depot in Dublin to leaven this Civic Patrol force, and the local men were gradually withdrawn, trained and sent elsewhere. The government feared that precipitate action would result in local hurt feelings and a hostile reception for the new civic guards who were strangers to the area.[20] The new guards, including some Corkmen, travelled on 9 November by cattle boat from Dublin to Cork as the railway line had been sabotaged. They occupied the School of Music in Union Quay, and a week or two later they moved across the Lee to open a barracks in Moore's Hotel. Small groups left from Cork almost immediately to open stations in Bandon and Dunmanway.

By the end of April 1923 the Civic Guard was occupying 270 stations, chiefly in county towns and other such centres of population. By February 1924, gardaí were in occupation of 695 stations scattered throughout the country. By June 1926, when the massive recruiting drive of the previous four years was petering out, gardaí were distributed in 842 stations throughout the twenty-six counties of the Free State, excluding the Dublin metropolitan area.[21]

The organising committee of February 1922 had recommended that the new force be centrally controlled. The government appears to have been strongly in favour of a centralised police force.[22] In 1923, Kevin O'Higgins introduced the Civic Guard Bill to put the force on a permanent statutory basis. The Labour party suggested that the alternative of local control be looked into and that the Bill be passed as a temporary measure to allow this. O'Higgins agreed to make it a temporary measure, but it was made permanent in 1924 without any changes with regard to control. The 1923 and 1924 acts spelled out the details on how the force was to be organised:

- The garda commissioner was appointed by the Executive Council of the government and could be removed at any time by it. All appointments of officers such as chief superintendents, superintendents, assistant commissioners and deputy commissioners were also by government. In practice, however, these were nominated by the commissioner whose recommendation the government almost invariably accepted.

- Appointments to the lower ranks were directly the responsibility of the commissioner.

- The Minister for Home Affairs reserved the right to make regulations in the future regarding recruitment procedure, promotion and dismissals, the duties of the various ranks, training, discipline and efficiency, as well as the formation of representative bodies.

In practice, the commissioner enjoyed a great deal of freedom in the internal affairs of the Garda Síochána, but in matters of general policy such as pay and allowances, numbers to be recruited, the question of whether to arm or not, the government held the whip hand. Furthermore, the commissioner owed his position to the government who could terminate it at any time.

The headquarters of the Garda Síochána were in the Phoenix Park, which also housed the central depot. For administration and distribution purposes, the country outside Dublin was divided into areas called divisions, each under the control of a chief superintendent. The station occupied by this officer was called divisional headquarters and was situated in a principal town. In July 1924 there were twenty such divisions outside Dublin, usually coinciding with county boundaries and occasionally covering two counties. They were as shown in Table 4.2.

The area of these divisions varied considerably, with Mayo covering 1,328,000 acres, and neighbouring Roscommon covering 582,000 acres. Each division in turn was divided into districts, each of which was under the control of a superintendent. The station occupied by this officer was known as district headquarters. The number of districts per division varied but was usually five or six. The district was known by the name of its headquarters station. Each district was divided into a number of sub-districts known by the town or village in which it was located. A sergeant was in charge of each sub-district. The number of sub-districts varied between six and ten per district.

Table 4.2: Divisions of Garda Síochána, 1924[23]

Division	Divisional Headquarters	No of Stations Occupied
Carlow-Kildare	Naas	31
Cavan-Monaghan	Monaghan	38
Clare	Ennis	35
Cork East Riding	Cork	60
Cork West Riding	Bandon	38
Donegal	Letterkenny	44
Dublin-Wicklow	Bray	43
Galway	Galway	59
Kerry	Tralee	41
Kilkenny	Kilkenny	28
Leix-Offaly	Tullamore	34
Limerick	Limerick	38
Longford-Westmeath	Mullingar	36
Louth-Meath	Drogheda	35
Mayo	Castlebar	40
Roscommon	Roscommon	27
Sligo-Leitrim	Sligo	43
Tipperary	Thurles	48
Waterford	Waterford	25
Wexford	Wexford	34
20 Divisions		777 stations

Source: Commissioner Staines' file (GM).

The ranking structure of the Garda Síochána closely followed that of the its predecessor. The position of chief superintendent corresponded with that of county inspector in the RIC. The position of superintendent was similar to that of district inspector. The rank of inspector roughly corresponded with that of head constable. The lower ranks of sergeant and guard coincided with those of sergeant and constable. From September 1924, the rank of inspector was to be discontinued, but this decision was soon reversed.[24] The ranks from commissioner down to and including superintendent constituted the officers. Inspectors, sergeants and station sergeants were non-commissioned officers (NCOs). Those of garda rank were below this and were referred to as 'the men' or the ranks.

DMP

From 1838, Dublin had been policed by the reorganised Dublin Metropolitan Police. The area covered mainly Dublin county borough and the borough of Dún Laoghaire. Unlike the RIC, the DMP was not disbanded and continued to operate much as before for the first few years of the new state. The new government did intend ultimately to amalgamate the two forces, but in 1922–3 it deferred action, partly from fear of mass resignations from the DMP under the fairly generous terms of Article 10 of the Treaty. A recruitment drive in the spring of 1923 did not secure enough recruits to replace the numbers resigning and lost through natural wastage. Recruitment was confined to the National army and other such groups who had given service to the new state. By June 1924 over 50 per cent of the new recruits were National army men.[25] Most of the recruits who joined in the three years after independence were farmers' sons from rural Ireland, with a small number coming from Dublin itself.[26] In 1925 only 35 per cent of the DMP were pre-1922 men. The rest had resigned, retired or been asked to retire.

As of 3 April 1925 the Dublin Metropolitan Police ceased to exist as a separate entity, under the terms of the Police Forces Amalgamation Act, 1925. It now became another division of the Garda Síochána, known as the Dublin metropolitan division, and its commissioner, William R. E. Murphy, became a deputy commissioner of the guards. At the time of amalgamation, the DMP had approximately 1,000 constables, 200 sergeants and almost forty officers, all of whom automatically became members of the Garda Síochána. Kevin Street training depot was discontinued and all recruits were now trained in the Phoenix Park depot. Former DMP members were never transferred out of the Dublin metropolitan area unless they requested it. The metropolitan uniform with its distinctive helmet was phased out. The DMP member who had been proud to be called a constable was now a guard.[27] Many of the city stations had enjoyed wet-canteen facilities — a recreation area where off-duty members could relax and enjoy a drink. By the late 1930s these had become dry canteens, with no alcohol available. The DMP had a unique rank of station sergeant, which lay between the position of sergeant and inspector, and this was allowed to continue. The force had not been armed, so no change was necessary here. The severe dislocation in policing experienced throughout the country as a result of the War of Independence, independence itself and the Civil War was not so pronounced in Dublin. The DMP had continued to operate in the city, albeit in a much-reduced, low-profile capacity, during the troubled 1919–23 period. It resumed more normal duties after the Civil War and was then rather painlessly amalgamated with the new Garda Síochána in 1925.

In 1926, after amalgamation, the government fixed the maximum established strength of the combined forces at 7,206. It remained set at this figure until 1933 when it was increased to 7,506, which remained unaltered until the late 1950s.[28] The actual strength of the force, as opposed to the maximum strength permitted, depended on whether recruitment was in progress or not. After 1948 when recruitment was closed, a marked divergence began to appear, and by 1951 the actual strength of the force was almost 700 below the figure approved by the government.[29] Between 1926 and 1952 the Garda Síochána policed the twenty-six counties of the Irish Free State, excluding the Dublin area, with 25–30 per cent fewer men than the RIC had done for a similar area in 1914. The new force carried out this work with 30 per cent fewer stations than its predecessor.[30] Between 1925 and 1948, fifty-six of the smaller garda stations outside Dublin had been closed.

The number of stations in the Dublin area had remained fairly static at about twenty-five. By 1950 almost half of the stations outside Dublin were manned by one sergeant and three guards. In 1930 the ratio of policemen to the general public in the Irish Free State (excluding Dublin) was 2.3 per 1,000.[31] While this was well below the RIC figure for 1911 (3.1) it was well above the corresponding average for English counties (1.2) or boroughs (1.5). Britain managed with fewer police because most English villages had just one constable who could call upon the assistance of an unpaid auxiliary special constable if the need arose. In contrast, every station in Ireland had at least one sergeant and three guards. Furthermore, the Irish guards were forced to devote approximately 30 per cent of their time to non-police duty on behalf of various departments of state. Dublin, however, had fewer policemen in proportion to its population than most of Europe's main cities.

By 1952 very little had changed in the administration and organisation of the Garda Síochána.[32] The moulds made in the formative 1923–5 period were still shaping the entry requirements, training, distribution, organisation and strength of the force twenty-five years later. Irish society may not have changed a great deal in the second quarter of the twentieth century. However, the procedures and organisation of the guards were modelled on the RIC, many of whose structures predated the mid-twentieth century by almost 100 years. As the winds of change began to blow gradually across Ireland in the late 1950s, the anachronistic element of the force's structure began to become apparent.

5

PROMOTION

THE EARLY DAYS, 1922–24

The overwhelming majority of promotions for the period 1922–52 took place during the years 1922–4. The 1922 organising committee had recommended that promotions be made from the ranks by competitive examination. However, the awarding of promotion was haphazard and governed by expediency. A new police force had to be set up very quickly, in which one in four men would from the beginning occupy a position of promotion. In the pre-mutiny period, February–May 1922, promotion to the rank of sergeant usually involved the recommendation of a superior officer without any examination. The new sergeants were mostly IRA officers or RIC men. By December 1922 a more structured approach to future promotions was put in place. Promotion was confined to men recommended by their officers on grounds of intelligence and efficiency. A literary examination in Irish, English, arithmetic, history and geography was followed by a professional examination in law, police and detective duties, as well as general orders and regulations. The commissioner then conducted an oral examination of the successful candidates. In June 1924 over 600 sergeants who had been appointed in 1922 had to sit the sergeant efficiency test. While a good many were reduced in rank as a result, very few were discharged from the force.[1] By June 1924, all sergeants had passed a qualifying examination, although this did not necessarily mean that they were fully prepared for their position.[2] During 1923 and early 1924 examinations for promotion from sergeant to inspector were introduced. In the summer of 1924, sixty-three inspectors who had not previously completed an adequate written examination had to sit the efficiency test. They included nine RIC, one RUC, one British army, one DMP, two Irish Republican Police, one civil servant, forty-four IRA and four others. The vast majority of these were in their late twenties or early thirties. Forty-eight of them passed the test.[3]

A great number of the superintendents in the pre-mutiny days of the Civic Guard had been promoted to that rank on their first day of appointment or very shortly afterwards. Many of them were either RIC men or IRA officers. An examination for promotion to officer rank was held in the RDS training depot in April, and was open to all ranks. As well as suggesting that officers should be appointed temporarily and sit an examination before being made permanent, the Kildare enquiry also recommended that an officer training corps be established. When O'Duffy took over control of the force in September 1922, he found the superintendents to be a motley group. Some were dismissed or resigned, while others were reduced in rank. The first six months of 1923 witnessed a small number of young inspectors doing the job of superintendents over very large areas. If O'Duffy was satisfied with their work, they could then sit the promotion examination for superintendent. From February 1924 former RIC members were excluded from competing in the promotion examination for sergeant to inspector or inspector to superintendent.[4] In the very early days many of the officers above the rank of superintendent had been asked by Michael Collins, Commissioner Staines or the government to join the force. As with superintendents, the majority of these had received commissioned rank on their first day of appointment or very shortly afterwards, and many were RIC or IRA men. The Kildare enquiry recommended that officers appointed to chief posts should be IRA men who were not formerly connected with the RIC or the DMP. This did not deter O'Duffy, however. By early 1924 he had appointed twenty chief superintendents from among existing superintendents, at least six of whom were disbanded RIC men.[5]

CADETS, 1923

In February 1923, O'Duffy got government approval to recruit a cadet class in order to fill vacancies in the rank of superintendent. Notices were placed in the press, advertising a competitive examination for thirty cadetships, which was open to the general public and to members of the civic guards. All candidates had to have the approval of the commissioner before sitting the examination, which was held in May. The subjects examined were Irish, English, arithmetic, geography, Irish history, dictation, précis writing, reading aloud, elementary principles of law and laws of evidence. The commissioner had the right to grant bonus marks to any candidate for good police service in the guards, good IRA/volunteer service or general fitness for command. The garda authorities were very disappointed with the response. Some candidates withdrew on their own initiative, others were found to be unsuitable for any position in the force, while others were found to be suitable as guards but not as cadets. Others were rejected on medical grounds, while most of the remainder failed the examination. Only four of the original 301 candidates were successful.[6] The commissioner decided to accept the first eighteen placed candidates, which included twelve guards. These eighteen began a six-month course of training at the depot in July. Another examination for fifteen cadetships was held at the beginning of August, entry being confined exclusively to officers of the National army. The pass mark was reduced from 60 per cent to 40 per cent, and fifteen new cadets were accepted for training. Included in this group was Captain Turlough Mac Neill, son of Eoin Mac Neill, Minister for Education. By early 1924 both cadet classes had finished their training. Thirty of the thirty-three passed the final examination and were very soon given superintendent rank and sent out to various districts.

Most of these men were very well educated by the standards of the time. The entry examination was approximately equivalent to the standard required at the completion of second year in a secondary school, a far cry from third-class primary-school standard required for entry to the force as a guard.[7] Most cadets had previously been in the Volunteers or the IRA. The thirty cadets included farmers, bank, post office and railway clerks, chemist and solicitor assistants, students and a teacher. The cadets constituted almost one-quarter of the total authorised strength of superintendents. These men were in their early to mid-twenties when promoted to superintendent.

A large proportion of the officer class of the RIC had been cadets who came from the higher social classes. The Royal Ulster Constabulary (RUC), which replaced the RIC when Northern Ireland was set up, continued using a cadet system to provide some members for the officer class. O'Duffy's request for permission to recruit a cadet class in 1923 appears to have stemmed from very practical considerations. A large number of officers were urgently required for the newly emerging force, which did not have available to it men with years of police experience and who were suitable for promotion. The 1923 cadets were unique, the garda authorities never repeating the exercise. Some of its members provided headquarters with its finest officers, while a higher than normal proportion of cadets (28 per cent) had been dismissed from the force by 1943.[8] There is no doubt that the rank and file of the Garda Síochána disliked the idea of a cadet system, which would blight their prospects of promotion, just as their predecessors in the RIC had resented such a system. Of greater importance, perhaps, in ensuring that the cadet system was not reintroduced was the fact that the overwhelming majority of officers were appointed at the same time, while they were all young, and so there was no need for a great number of suitable officers in the period 1924–52.

NCOs, 1924–52

From April 1924 until May 1925, the Garda Síochána relied on the old RIC 'p' or promotion examination in literary subjects to select candidates for advancement. This was followed by an examination in professional subjects. In 1925 new promotion regulations came into effect. There were now three sets of examinations. Class III examination was for promotion from garda to sergeant, class II for promotion from sergeant to station sergeant, and class I for promotion from sergeant to inspector. Each class had two separate examinations, literary and professional. Any guard wishing to do so could sit the literary examination, class III, which was about fourth or fifth-class standard in primary school, and was conducted by the civil service commissioners. It was qualifying in nature and those who passed might be selected to sit the professional examination. The latter was conducted by a promotion board consisting of senior garda officers. The chief superintendent of each division, relying on the various superintendents, decided who was suitable to be called for the professional examination. The latter covered police and detective duties, regulations and circulars issued to the force. A proportion of vacancies to be filled was reserved for the candidates who got the highest aggregate mark in this examination. Their names were arranged in order of merit. The names of the other successful candidates were arranged underneath these in order of seniority. Vacancies were filled beginning at the top of the list.

In 1926 the representative bodies of the Garda Síochána complained about superintendents having total control over who could sit the professional examination.[9] They suggested an appeals procedure for those prevented from sitting the examination. The request was not granted. In 1927 they protested in vain against the selection of men with less than two years' service to sit the professional examination for sergeant. They claimed that the promotion regulations allowed 'men of short service and mediocre education with a book knowledge of professional subjects to be promoted'.[10] Many of those attempting the literary examination put a lot of effort into their preparation, some even paying for and attending classes three or four nights a week throughout the winter. Advertisements were appearing in the *Garda Review* towards the end of 1926 with claims from private colleges in Dublin: 'We get all men on our books through the class III exam'.[11] In 1928 the representative bodies wanted the professional examination to be qualifying in nature, with all positions then filled on the basis of seniority. O'Duffy disagreed. He did state, however, that no guard would be eligible for promotion until he had served at least three years in his present rank. Both the commissioner and the representative bodies agreed that 25 per cent of vacancies for sergeant should be reserved for efficient, capable men who were not required to pass the literary promotion examinations. The 1929 promotion regulations granted this request.

By 1930, O'Duffy was very happy with the promotion procedure generally and especially with that for sergeant.[12] The standard of the professional examination had been raised each year from 1925. For O'Duffy the most important element in the whole procedure was the selection by their superior officers of the proper candidates for promotion. From the early 1930s onwards, recommendations by divisional officers as to which gardaí should be allowed sit for the professional examination for promotion were influenced to a great degree by seniority. Actual appointments to vacancies continued to be based on a mixture of merit and seniority. In the early 1930s the members of the force were reasonably happy with the promotion procedure.[13]

By 1936, however, the force was beginning to get a little restless with the scarcity of promotional opportunities. In the 1922–6 period a massive number of young men had been promoted. Many guards were now in their late thirties, married, with young families to support. With no natural retirements, there was very little opportunity for promotion. In 1938 the garda authorities stipulated that one-third of the total number selected to sit the professional examination would be members who had a proficiency certificate in Irish. This had no dramatic effect on promotion opportunities, as most senior guards seeking promotion had acquired the certificate. The standard of the literary examination for promotion to sergeant had increased during the late 1940s. By 1950 it was roughly equivalent to that of first or maybe second-year level in secondary school. In April 1949 the editorial of the *Garda Review* stated: 'The present system . . . for promotion to the lower ranks is good as regards efficiency and seems to satisfy the men themselves.'[14]

From 1926 until 1952 the number of sergeants in the force remained constant at about 1,200. The overwhelming majority of these had been promoted to sergeant in the 1922–5 period, with less than three years' service in the force.[15] Throughout the 1930s and 1940s promotion prospects for guards were very poor, as very few sergeants were retiring. Not all men sought promotion as this entailed added responsibility and being transferred. In general, senior garda officers appear to have carried out their selection of men to sit the professional examination in a fairly impartial manner, though the system was open to abuse.[16] Some members attempted to use the influence of public representatives in order to gain promotion. While it is impossible to gauge accurately the extent of this, it appears as if it was not successful on any widespread scale.[17] Merit rather than seniority decided who was promoted in the 1920s. As the force became more established in the 1930s, seniority began to play a more important role. The vast majority of sergeants in the thirty years from 1922 to 1952 were appointed in the mid-1920s when they were in their early twenties and had very little police experience. Those guards who became sergeants in the 1930s and 1940s were much older when promoted, although many of them had also joined in the early years. As the 1950s approached, a great proportion of all sergeants were nearing retirement.

The Dublin metropolitan division (DMD) continued to operate as an autonomous unit for promotion purposes. In general, there were few transfers between the country divisions and the DMD. To be eligible for promotion, Guards had to have served for three years in the Dublin area. Sergeants in the Dublin metropolitan division with at least five years' service and who passed the class II literary examination were eligible for selection to sit the professional examination for station sergeant. Promotion to the rank of inspector in the DMD was confined to station sergeants who had passed the class I literary examination. Outside the Dublin metropolitan area, sergeants with five years' experience in the rank were eligible for selection to sit the professional examination for inspector.[18] There were fifty-three inspectors in December 1925, and this had increased to seventy-seven by 1950. The rank of inspector was really one of superintendent-in-waiting. Inspectors substituted for absent or ill superintendents, and the majority of inspectors were eventually promoted to superintendents.

OFFICERS, 1924–52

The 1924 promotion regulations envisaged the phasing out of the inspector rank and the promotion of sergeants directly to superintendents. These regulations also divided the rank of superintendent into three grades with different levels of pay. A third-grade superintendent was not eligible for promotion to second grade until he had completed at least three years' service in the former grade. A second-grade superintendent had to have five years' service in that grade before he was eligible for promotion to first grade. The 1925 promotion regulations reintroduced the inspector rank. Henceforth, all new superintendents were to be drawn from this rank. Once a member had attained the rank of inspector, he no longer had to sit any literary examination to be eligible for further promotion. Suitable inspectors were selected by their chief superintendent and called for a special oral and written examination in professional duties, held by the commissioner. By 1930, inspectors had to have a minimum of three years' service in that rank to be eligible for promotion to superintendent. By 1950, this had not changed, although the position of third-grade superintendent had been abolished in 1947. Throughout the period 1930–52 promotion from one grade to a higher one was automatic after the required number of years, upon a favourable report being furnished to headquarters by the chief superintendent of the division. In 1925 there were 133 superintendents, by 1950 there were 129.

Approximately 330 men served as superintendents at some time or other in the 1922–52 period. Almost 60 per cent of these were appointed in the first four years of the force's existence.[19] This had profound implications for those wishing to become superintendents, as well as affecting the age at which men were appointed to that rank. In the thirty-year period under review (1922–52) the mean age at which men were appointed superintendent increased considerably, as Table 5.1 illustrates.

Table 5.1: Mean Age of Superintendent upon Appointment, 1922–52

Years Appointed	Mean Age
1922–25	31
1926–35	39
1936–52	49

Source: Officers' register; Appointment of officers 1923–52 (NAI).

In the early 1920s the majority of such officers were under thirty-five years of age, had very little policing experience and had not come through the ranks as was normal in an established police force.[20] The opportunities for promotion were extremely good. As the late 1920s and early 1930s progressed, opportunities for promotion were very few. Superintendents tended to be somewhat older upon appointment, although still quite young men. They had more police experience and usually came up through the ranks. This trend continued right up to 1952, with older men, frequently in their late forties, appointed to such officer rank. This resembled most established police forces. The superintendents appointed throughout the entire period 1922–52 were drawn almost exclusively (with the exception of the Dublin metropolitan area) from the 1922–3 recruits, many of them having been in the IRA. Consequently, by 1952 the vast majority of all serving superintendents were in their fifties, and had joined the force thirty years earlier.

The appointment in the early 1920s of so many young men to such responsible positions of authority was fraught with dangers. The vast majority of these superintendents had very little police experience themselves, yet they were expected to instruct and organise their subordinates. They became superintendents almost overnight, without the experience of the job that usually preceded promotion, and without the maturity that usually accompanies age. Consequently, a sizeable minority were found to be unsuitable or decided themselves that this was not the life for them. From 1925 until the early 1930s a total of thirty-two were dismissed from the force, four were reduced in rank, and two resigned. Dismissals were usually the result of debts incurred or excessive drinking, others were because of insubordination, while a very small minority were caused by 'immorality' or misappropriation of public funds.[21] O'Duffy had made a concerted effort to get his band of superintendents into line, and by the time that he was sacked as commissioner in 1933 he had largely succeeded. In 1941, five superintendents who were in serious debt, had a serious drink problem or were inefficient were compulsorily retired. With very few promotional opportunities in the ranks of chief superintendent, the vast majority of superintendents had reached the pinnacle of their career when they were not yet thirty-five years of age. While the majority of superintendents were able to deal with this lack of promotional opportunities, the good salary while very young and the demands of the job, a number were clearly unable to do so, hence the high percentage of men who did not remain as superintendents for one reason or another. Those who did remain were kept under tight discipline. One superintendent was fined £5 for selling turf for profit in 1935. Lesser transgressions frequently warranted a reprimand and an unfavourable record entry beside the superintendent's name in the officers' register. In 1949 a superintendent received one such entry because he owed a debt to a local publican. In fact, 50 per cent of the total officers in the 1922–52 period had at least one unfavourable record entry of some sort during the thirty years. These ranged from not completing important paperwork to 'tippling', to being in debt — especially to publicans — and to being absent without leave. Of course, a great many superintendents, including the above group, also had favourable records for very good and efficient police work.

With over half of the total force coming from the farming/labourer class, it was inevitable that a very high percentage of superintendents should come from this background. However, former teachers, students and clerks, benefiting no doubt from either extra education or valuable experience, secured a disproportionate percentage of the positions of superintendent.[22] In general, the men promoted to superintendent rank in the 1922–52 period were fairly well educated by the prevailing standards of the time. A small number had received an education well in excess of the required minimum for the rank.[23]

Merit was usually more important than seniority in deciding who became superintendents. Chief superintendents recommended, on merit, suitable inspectors for promotion to superintendent. An interview was then conducted by the commissioner, his two assistant commissioners and a police duty instructor. Following this, a list of inspectors in order of merit for promotion to superintendent was drawn up. As vacancies arose, these men were promoted, beginning at the top of the list. Seniority tended to have a greater role, although not a monopoly in who was promoted to superintendent in the Dublin metropolitan division. Many of the inspectors in this division had twenty-five or more years' service in the force, having joined as DMP men. A junior inspector had to be of outstanding quality to merit prior consideration.[24]

Chief superintendents occupied a crucial position in deciding which inspector went forward for interview for promotion. In general, they exercised this authority in an impartial and fair manner, though of course the system was open to abuse by the prejudice of an individual chief superintendent. Such abuse appears to have been the exception, however.[25] The selection system to decide which inspector went forward for interview was also vulnerable to influence from another quarter. Politicians or other people in positions of power could ensure that favoured inspectors were called for interview and were promoted. This did happen, although it was a minority who advanced in this manner.[26] The vast majority of inspectors were promoted to superintendent rank as a result of the selection procedure and interview without any outside interference. While the government had the statutory authority to appoint superintendents, in reality, the vast majority of promotions from 1922–52 were decided by the garda authorities and merely approved by the government.[27]

The promotion regulations of 1924 divided the rank of chief superintendent into first and second grade. All new appointees automatically became second-grade chief superintendents and were eligible for promotion to first grade when they had completed three years' satisfactory service in the former. The 1925 promotion regulations did not alter the situation. The Dublin metropolitan division was not treated as a separate unit for the purpose of promotion to chief superintendent rank. After amalgamation, chief superintendents were selected from all existing superintendents. There were twenty-four chief superintendents in December 1925 and this had increased only to twenty-six by 1950.

In the 1922–5 period twenty-nine chief superintendents were appointed.[28] By 1951 there were only three of these original pre-1925 men still occupying that position. The remainder had departed because of retirement, death, reduction in rank, compulsory retirement, dismissal or resignation. While there was an almost complete change in the personnel of chief superintendents between 1925 and 1952, this did not mean that there were great promotional opportunities for superintendents. On average, only one superintendent out of 130 was promoted each year between 1926 and 1952.

In the early years of the Garda Síochána most chief superintendents were appointed when very young, with very little police experience and without coming through the ranks. This gradually changed as the force became more established in the 1930s and 1940s. Almost all chief superintendents appointed in the 1922–52 period were drawn from the recruits of 1922–3. The majority of them had been in the IRA, many as officers. Six chief superintendents had been in the RIC. A small number had been in the DMP. By 1952, nine of the thirty cadets were chief superintendents. The background of men who became chief superintendents in the 1930s and 1940s varied.[29] Quite a number of them were farmers, while others were teachers, clerks, army officers, carpenters, blacksmiths, boot merchants, post office workers, civil servants, chemist assistants and surgical-appliance makers. While not all chief superintendents had been very well educated, a significant number of the 1930s and 1940s men had received a university education or at least senior intermediate level. All of the chief superintendents except two were Catholic. One was a Methodist who joined the DMP and was made a chief superintendent in 1924. The other was a Church of Ireland member who was promoted in 1925.

All first and second-grade superintendents were eligible for promotion to the rank of chief superintendent. Suitable candidates were selected on the basis of merit by their chief superintendent and sent to the depot. There the aspiring superintendents did a fairly rigorous interview before a team of senior headquarters staff, usually comprising the commissioner, deputy commissioner and one or two assistant commissioners. In 1940 Commissioner Kinnane decided to appoint a selection board to make recommendations to him as to who should be promoted to chief superintendent. This did not fundamentally change the process, merely giving it a more structured format. Seniority did not play any significant role in deciding such promotions. The chief superintendent informed the selection board of the various merits or demerits of his superintendents. It selected a number to be interviewed at headquarters and then compiled a list based on merit from which vacancies were filled.

Up until 1936 the appointment to the position of chief superintendent appears to have rested totally in the hands of the commissioner, without any reference to the government. In that year the government directed that no person should in future be appointed as chief superintendent without prior reference to it.[30] After this the commissioner decided whom he wished to be promoted, and submitted the name and a short résumé of his career to the government, which invariably ratified his decision and appointed the man. In the wake of the compulsory retirement of six chief superintendents in 1941 the government, for a while at least, became more involved in the process of promotion to chief superintendent. A committee comprising the Tánaiste and the Ministers for Justice and Defence scrutinised those recommended by the garda commissioner. It did not reject any of the names submitted to it. There was no significant change thereafter, with the commissioner submitting his list of recommended names for promotion to the government, which invariably endorsed it. There was little opportunity for political interference in the appointment of chief superintendents prior to 1936 when it remained exclusively the preserve of the garda authorities. Even after this, all appointments proposed by the commissioner were invariably accepted by the government. However, the procedure whereby superintendents were promoted according to merit did leave itself open to influence or 'pull' being exerted on behalf of favoured individuals. A friendly senior officer or an influential outsider in politics might manage to have someone promoted under the guise of merit. The majority of chief superintendents were appointed on merit, but a small minority of men appear to have been helped along in their careers by influential friends.[31]

HEADQUARTERS OFFICERS, 1922–52

The highest-ranking officers of the entire Garda Síochána force worked in headquarters. There were usually six such officers: the commissioner, two deputy and two assistant commissioners and a surgeon. Dr Vincent C. Ellis was surgeon to the force from 1922 until his retirement in 1958. The commissioners in the period 1922–52 were as listed in Table 5.2.

Table 5.2: Commissioners of Garda Síochána, 1922–52

Michael Staines	March–August 1922	resigned
Eoin O'Duffy	1922–133	dismissed
Eamon Broy	1933–138	retired
Michael Kinnane	1938–152	died

Source: *Garda Review*, April 1933, June 1938, August 1952.

These men had diverse backgrounds and experience prior to becoming garda commissioner, and each of them had a different reason for leaving the position. Staines had been in the Volunteers. He was a member of Dáil Éireann and voted in favour of the Treaty. He was 37 years old when appointed commissioner by the Provisional Government. He resigned in the wake of the Kildare mutiny. O'Duffy, the son of a Monaghan farmer, was 30 years of age when he took over. A civil engineer by profession, he had been assistant county surveyor for Monaghan for a number of years. He joined the IRA in 1917. He was appointed director of organisation of the Volunteers and became chief of staff of the National army on the death of Collins. He was elected TD for Monaghan in the 1918 general election and voted in favour of the Treaty. He did not seek re-election because of the rule debarring army personnel from being elected.[32] He was dismissed by De Valera in 1933. Broy, a Kildare man, was 46 when he became commissioner. Unlike his predecessors he had been a policeman for almost twenty years, coming up through the various ranks, having been a DMP constable. Like them, however, he had been actively involved in the military struggle for independence. In 1933 he was promoted directly from chief superintendent to commissioner. Michael Kinnane, a native of County Galway, was a 50-year-old civil servant when appointed garda commissioner. Unlike his three predecessors, he had no military experience, nor had he taken part in the struggle for independence. He had worked for many years in the British civil service before returning to Ireland in 1922 and becoming assistant secretary at the Department of Justice in 1928.

The appointment of the garda commissioner rested solely with the government of the day. Each government wanted an efficient commissioner in whom it had confidence. Staines had been appointed commissioner as he was one of the pro-Treaty TDs. He was replaced by O'Duffy, a former pro-Treaty TD and member of the National army. In the eyes of the Cumann na nGaedheal Government the political credentials of both men were correct. De Valera replaced O'Duffy not because he was inefficient, but because the government had lost confidence in him as commissioner. Although Broy had been closely associated with Collins, had favoured the Treaty, and had been in the Free State military and police forces in the 1920s, De Valera felt that he could have confidence in him as commissioner. He bypassed assistant and deputy commissioners in choosing Broy who was a chief superintendent. In 1938 De Valera bypassed the entire force when he selected a civilian, Kinnane, as the new commissioner. In fact, in the entire period 1922–52 no commissioner came from the ranks of assistant or deputy commissioner, as would have been normal in an established force. The appointment of a commissioner was a political one, not in the sense that a party hack got the job, but rather that the government had to have a man whom it could trust implicitly.

There were usually two deputy commissioners in the Garda Síochána in the period 1922–52. Those occupying these positions were as shown in Table 5.3.

Table 5.3: Deputy Commissioners, 1922–52

Patrick Walsh	1922	resigned
Eamonn Coogan	1923–36	resigned
William R. E. Murphy	1925	still serving in 1952
Edward Cullen	1936–39	died
Garrett Brennan	1939	still serving in 1952

Source: Appointment of assistant and deputy commissioners (NAI).

The first deputy commissioner of the Garda Síochána was Patrick Walsh, an RIC district inspector. He resigned in the wake of the Kildare mutiny but was appointed assistant commissioner in 1923. A Kilkenny man and TCD graduate, Eamonn Coogan, who was working in the Department of Local Government, was asked by W. T. Cosgrave in 1922 to join the force.[33] He was appointed assistant commissioner almost immediately, and deputy commissioner the following year while still only 24 years of age. William R. E. Murphy had

had a very distinguished career in the British army in World War I. He had joined the National army in 1922 and was appointed commissioner of the DMP in 1923. At the age of 35 he became a deputy commissioner of the Garda Síochána after the 1925 amalgamation. Edward Cullen was a native of County Meath. He was appointed superintendent in 1922, chief superintendent a few months later and assistant commissioner in 1924. He was 43 when appointed deputy commissioner in 1936. Garret Brennan was a Kilkenny man who joined the force as a superintendent in 1922. He was promoted to chief superintendent within a year. He became assistant commissioner in 1936. Three years later, at the age of 45, he was promoted to deputy commissioner, on the death of Edward Cullen.

There were usually two assistant commissioners in the Garda Síochána in the period 1922–52. Those occupying these positions were as shown in Table 5.4.

Table 5.4: Assistant Commissioners, 1922–52

Patrick Brennan	1922	resigned
Patrick Walsh	1923–36	retired
Eamonn Coogan	1922–3	promoted
Edward Cullen	1924–36	promoted
Thomas Woods	1936	still serving in 1952
Garrett Brennan	1936–39	promoted
Patrick J. Carroll	1939	still serving in 1952

Source: Appointment of assistant and deputy commissioners (NAI).

Patrick Brennan was an IRA officer during the War of Independence. A pro-Treaty TD and close friend of Collins, he resigned from the force in the wake of the mutiny. Thomas Woods had played an active part in the War of Independence. A Clare man, he was an Irish speaker and had a BA degree.[34] He joined the guards in 1923 and became a cadet later in that year. He was 39 years of age when appointed assistant commissioner in 1936. Chief Superintendent Patrick J. Carroll was made an assistant commissioner in 1939. The son of an RIC constable, he had grown up in County Monaghan and qualified as a primary school teacher from St Patrick's Training College, Drumcondra. He had secured first place in the May 1923 cadet examination.

By the mid-1920s O'Duffy had decided that vacancies in assistant and deputy commissioner positions should be filled from the ranks of chief superintendent. However, in the entire period 1926–52 only five vacancies arose, three in 1936 and two in 1939. In each case the commissioner recommended to the government who he thought should be promoted assistant or deputy commissioner. His recommendations were accepted.[35] There is no evidence of political interference by the government in the appointment of these men. However, it was unlikely that Commissioner Broy in 1936 and Commissioner Kinnane in 1939, both recently appointed by the government, would submit, to that same government, names of individuals who were unlikely to be approved. Furthermore, it is highly unlikely that a government that had sacked O'Duffy as commissioner in 1937, would feel obliged to accept the commissioners' recommendations of individuals to whom it objected.

CONCLUSION, 1922–52

When political 'pull' or influence was used to gain promotion in the lower ranks of sergeant or inspector, it was usually a case of a politician rewarding a friend or attempting to ingratiate himself with constituents. The use of such influence in promotion to more senior ranks, especially those of chief superintendent and higher, was not always to reward a friend. The government wanted men in the higher echelons of the Garda Síochána who had similar views to itself and who could be trusted implicitly to do its will. In the first six months of 1922, members of the Provisional Government, such as Collins, decided a number of key appointments to senior positions in the Civic Guard. Once O'Duffy took over as commissioner he assumed responsibility for this. The Cumann na nGaedheal Government appears to have been content to allow O'Duffy a relatively free hand in the area of promotion. It could trust him. He was its man, a former pro-Treaty TD and National army officer. Furthermore, practically all such promotions came from among the 1922–3 recruits who were pro-Treaty government supporters.

The scene was quite different in 1932 with the arrival to power of a Fianna Fáil government. De Valera was faced with a commissioner and most of his senior officers who had belonged to the other side of the Treaty divide in 1922. Over the next few years he gradually initiated a number of changes to ensure that the top-ranking officers of the force were more amenable to his wishes. He sacked O'Duffy in 1933. After 1936, promotions to chief superintendent had first to be submitted for government approval. In 1938 a new police commissioner was appointed from the ranks of the civil service, and in the early 1940s a sub-committee of the government scrutinised those names recommended to it for senior appointments in the gardaí. The Fianna Fáil government was still appointing senior officers from the ranks of the pro-Treaty

1922–3 recruits. However, it was keeping a closer eye on who was promoted.

All governments in the 1922–52 period realised the necessity of having senior officers in the Garda Síochána with whom they could work, and on whom they could depend. While the Cosgrave administration achieved this result largely by the 'hands-off' approach, using O'Duffy to implement its wishes, the De Valera administration took a somewhat more active role in vetting promotions. The end result was the same. The principle underlying these actions was enshrined in the 1923 and 1924 acts, which clearly stated that the Executive Council had the right to appoint or dismiss the officers of the Garda Síochána.

6

CONDITIONS OF SERVICE

PAY

In March 1919, the British government appointed a committee under Lord Desborough to recommend changes in the conditions of service of the police of England, Wales and Scotland. In October of the same year the government appointed a similar commission under Sir John Ross to make recommendations on reorganising the Irish police forces. This commission adopted the Desborough recommendations as far as they were applicable. In 1922 the organising committee suggested that the Desborough rates should be applied to the lower ranks of guard, sergeant and inspector in the new Civic Guard.[1] These were implemented as illustrated in Table 6.1. The pay of superintendents and chief superintendents closely paralleled that of the corresponding ranks in the RIC.

Table 6.1: Rates of Pay for Civic Guard, 1922[2]

Guard	Start at £3-10-0 (£3.50) p.w. rising to a max. of £4-15-0 (£4.75) after 22 years
Sergeant	Start at £5 p.w. rising to a max. of £5-12-6 (£5.62½) after 5 years
Inspector	Start at £310 p.a. rising to £360 p.a. after 5 years.
Superintendent	Start at £400 p.a. rising to £600 after 10 years
Chief Superintendent	Start at £650 p.a. rising to £800 after 6 years

Note: Decimal equivalents given in brackets.
Source: Conroy commission.

The rates of pay of the headquarters staff were 20–25 per cent lower than those enjoyed by the equivalent ranks of the RIC at the time of disbandment. In August 1922 the Kildare mutiny enquiry recommended a reduction in pay. It believed that the Civic Guard rates were undoubtedly influenced by RIC rates of pay, 'at a time when the latter body was practically being bribed with money in order to keep it together'.[3] Rates of pay for all ranks, however, remained unchanged until 1924.

The cost of living in 1924 was lower than it had been in 1919. To reflect this change and to save money the government introduced the Garda Síochána Pay Order, 1924. This reduced the pay of most members of the Garda Síochána. The cut was part of an all-round reduction in the pay of state employees. The starting pay and the maximum pay of a guard and sergeant were reduced by approximately 12.5 per cent. The pay of an inspector was left untouched. The starting pay of a new superintendent was reduced by over 20 per cent. However, a new lower rank of third-grade superintendent had been introduced, hence the lower starting pay. The pay of chief superintendents was largely unaffected, while the headquarters staff were not affected at all. Of course, they were already on salaries that were 25 per cent less than the Desborough rates. The real cuts came in the lower ranks. While the rank and file of the force were resentful and angry, nothing came of it. Primary teachers and civil servants also experienced severe reductions in pay in 1924. Organised opposition among guards was almost impossible as the representative bodies had not yet been fully set in place. Furthermore, the droves of new members flooding in every month did not experience an actual cut, having never been paid higher rates. Unemployment was very high in the country and the force still offered a secure pensionable job.[4] However, the cuts rankled with the guards for years afterwards. In practically every controversy between the representative bodies and the government concerning pay over the next fifteen years, the question of the 1924 cut surfaced. The basic pay of all ranks remained unchanged, except for minor modifications, for the next nineteen years.

The pay of the DMP followed the Desborough scale until 1924. In that year, DMP pay for constables and sergeants was also reduced and brought into line with the new rates of garda pay. The 1924 change in pay did not really affect officers of the DMP whose pay varied slightly from that of Garda Síochána officers.

In addition to their pensionable basic pay, members of the Garda Síochána, like their predecessors in the RIC, got non-pensionable allowances. All members, up to and including inspectors, were entitled to a boot allowance of approximately 1/5 (equivalent to 7p) per week. All such members outside the Dublin area, and those within it who needed to use a bicycle, received a cycling allowance of £6 per annum. The Garda Síochána continued the RIC principle of having its members live in stations. Where official accommodation was provided, a member was obliged to live in it unless permission to do otherwise was given. If no accommodation was provided, a rent allowance was paid in lieu. This varied from £120 per annum for the commissioner, to £13–£18 per annum for guards and sergeants in rural areas and small towns, and £26–£30 for those in large towns or cities. All uniformed members of the force were provided with uniform or an allowance for the purchase of one. Plain-clothes members received a clothes allowance. There were other allowances such as transport and subsistence but these were received only occasionally.[5] None of these allowances was affected by the 1924 pay order.

In 1926 the cycling allowance was cut from £6 to £5. In April 1928 the representative bodies met the newly appointed Minister for Justice, James Fitzgerald-Kenney. They argued that pay should be restored to the 1924 level and claimed that the rent allowance was inadequate to pay for accommodation. The minister was unmoved.[6] In 1929 the government wished to cut expenditure, and one of the main areas on which the axe fell was the Garda Síochána. It was proposed to abolish the boot allowance totally, cut the rent allowance by 10 per cent and the cycling allowance by half. The representative bodies vigorously opposed these proposals, but apart from the rent allowance reduction, the rest were implemented. The Labour party had strongly supported the case of the gardaí in the Dáil and Seanad. De Valera had denounced the reduction as an attack on the poor man's pay. During the debate, Ernest Blythe, Minister for Finance, had assured the Dáil that, 'the pay of the Garda Síochána is down to bedrock . . . they need fear nothing for the future'.[7] By 1931 the country was beginning to feel the severe effects of the Great Depression. In October, the government recommended a 5 per cent cut for guards and national school teachers among others. In early February 1932 the government, under pressure from the representative bodies and the press, relented slightly. It proposed to reduce the take-home pay by 5 per cent but without having any effect on the pension.

In March 1932, De Valera formed a Fianna Fáil government with James Geoghegan as Minister for Justice. In 1933 the government introduced a bill, which included a proposal to leave the pay of the married guard untouched, while reducing that of the unmarried guard. De Valera's bill favoured the lower ranks, especially the married lower ranks, with NCOs and officers bearing a much greater reduction in pay. The bill, which applied to the public service in general, passed the Dáil. However, the Seanad amended it to exclude the Garda Síochána from its scope. The Minister for Justice in De Valera's 1933 administration, P.

J. Ruttledge, was not an enthusiastic supporter of the bill.[8] Furthermore, there was vigorous opposition within the force. These factors may have influenced the government's decision to accept the amendment.

From early 1934 the lower-ranking members of the force began to request that the 1924 cut in pay and the 1929 reduction in allowances be repealed. They also asked that the rent allowance be increased to match the increased cost in rented accommodation.[9] No concessions were gained, however. In 1937 the campaign began to gain momentum with more frequent and less temperate utterances appearing in the *Garda Review*, as well as increased demands by the representative bodies.[10] Matters came to a head in early December 1937. Having been repeatedly rebuffed, the representative bodies, which were meeting in the depot, became even more strident. The government had obviously had enough and it told the commissioner to order the session at the depot to disband immediately.[11] While this caused consternation among delegates, there was nothing they could do about it.[12] In 1938 the government refused to move on the pay issue but did re-introduce a boot allowance for the lower ranks at a reduced £2 per annum. An improved rent allowance was granted in November 1939 but the representative bodies were disappointed by it.

The members of Taca Síochána received a non-incremental salary of £3 per week. In February 1940 a new pay order, which related only to future new entrants to the force, was issued. It reduced the pay of a new guard and lengthened the incremental scale by two years. The cost of living increased rapidly from the outbreak of the war in Europe. Civil servants received a substantial increase by way of a war bonus, and national school teachers had been given some concessions in 1938. However, in July 1940 the government refused a request from the representative bodies of the force for an increase in pay. In December 1942 the government announced that the Garda Síochána, teachers and civil servants were to receive a 7 shillings (35p) per week additional allowance as an emergency measure. Each rank from guard to third-grade superintendent inclusive received a 7 shillings (35p) per week increase regardless of number of years of service. The higher ranks got no increase. The members were not at all placated and were still hankering for the restoration of pay to at least the 1924 level. During the remainder of the 1940s the gardaí were given the benefit of the same bonuses as the civil servants, to keep pace with inflation.

From 1944 to 1951 all ranks from guard to inspector received an increase of approximately 60 per cent in basic pay. The rate at which members moved up the incremental scale had improved as well. There were also some increases in allowances in these years. By 1946, pay was no longer the contentious issue that it had been for a number of years.[13] Thereafter, attention in the *Garda Review* was turned to questions of an increase in the rent allowance, and inadequate accommodation. By late 1948, however, the lower ranks were calling for arbitration machinery to be set in place for the Garda Síochána. By 1951 this demand had grown, with less temperate language being adopted.

Table 6.2 relates the income of a guard on completion of training to the cost of living for various years between 1922 and 1952. Income is calculated to include basic pay, as well as the boot, cycling and rent allowance where applicable. The 1914 cost-of-living index figure was fixed at 100. When calculating the cost-of-living figure for subsequent years this base figure of 100 was used. The final column, by showing pay plus allowance as a ratio to the cost of living, displays the fluctuations of the income of a new guard in real terms over this period.

Table 6.2: Income of New Guards related to Cost of Living, 1922–52[14]

Year	Income p.w. £	% Increase or Decrease on 1922 Pay	Cost-of-Living Index	Income in Ratio to Cost of Living
1922	3.97		200	1.00
1924	3.47	-12.5	190	0.92
1929	3.33	-16.0	180	0.93
1935	3.33	-16.0	155	1.08
1939	3.37	-15.0	173	0.98
1945	3.93	- 1.0	290	0.69
1948	5.06	+27.0	320	0.80
1951	5.78	+45.0	330	0.88

Note: Amounts have been converted to decimal equivalents.
Sources: Civil service arbitration board (NAI); Conroy commission.

Newly trained guards were financially worse off in real terms in 1951 than their counterparts had been in 1922. This was true of guards on all points of the incremental scale. Real income suffered a 7.5 per cent cut in 1924. The 1929 reduction in allowances did not have a great effect on the standard of living of members, as the cost of living had decreased. In fact, until the outbreak of the war, the level of real income actually improved. However, most of the force got married in the late 1920s or 1930s, which gave members considerable added financial responsibility despite considerable advances on the incremental scale. Furthermore, members continually complained that the rental cost of accommodation for a married man and his family increased substantially during this period, despite a drop in the cost of living in other respects.[15] The rent allowance was found to be increasingly inadequate, and hence the frustration of many members over the question of pay and allowances from the mid-1930s onwards. The rampant inflation of the war years seriously eroded the income of the guards, and it was not until 1946 that an improvement began to be felt. By 1951 the men were moving towards, but had not yet reached, the comfortable situation they had enjoyed in 1922. The pay of sergeants and inspectors followed the same undulations as did the guards' pay through the period 1922–52. The officers' pay was almost totally unaltered from the inception of the force until 1945. The continual fall in the cost of living from 1922 until the late 1930s meant that real pay was continually increasing. Officers too were hit severely by the war inflation and had to wait until 1945 for their first increase. By 1951 their pay had improved substantially but they were still not quite as comfortable as they had been when the force started.

In 1922 the starting pay of guards, national teachers and civil servants was almost identical.[16] Of course, gardaí also enjoyed various allowances that the other groups did not. In the period 1924–40 gardaí did better than civil servants, as the latters' pay was reduced when the cost-of-living index fell, whereas garda pay was left untouched. However, when the cost of living rose steeply after 1939, civil servants were compensated to a greater degree and more quickly than were the gardaí. In general, national teachers were treated more or less the same as the guards. By Autumn 1946 the pay of a young guard had fallen considerably behind that of a skilled tradesman and civil servant. By 1951 the gap had narrowed.[17] The Garda Síochána continually referred to the remuneration enjoyed by the RUC and the British police forces. There is no doubt but that the members of the Garda Síochána were considerably less well paid than their counterparts in neighbouring jurisdictions.

From 1924 to 1952 the guards were not particularly well paid considering their unsociable hours of duty, the dislocation involved in being transferred and the consequent difficulty in securing good accommodation at a reasonable price. However, the secure pensionable job, in a country that never enjoyed full employment, ensured that there were always many wishing to join the force.

WELFARE

From the earliest days of the force a deduction of 2.5 per cent was made from the pay of each member as a contribution towards pension. The actual pension was calculated at one-sixtieth of the annual pay for every year of service up to the twentieth. Thereafter, every year counted as two-sixtieths up to a maximum of two-thirds of pay. The Garda Síochána Pensions Order of 1925 discriminated between those who joined prior to October 1925 and those who joined after that date. The former could retire after twenty-five years' service on half pay if over 50 years of age. Of course they could also continue if they wished until they had thirty years' service and receive two-thirds of their pay in pension. The post-1925 men could not retire until after thirty years' service and would receive two-thirds of their pay. Former members of the DMP could retire after twenty-five years on half pay, regardless of age. The pension regulations remained practically unaltered right down to the early 1950s. The arrangements compared favourably with those of civil servants who had a maximum pension of only half their pay after forty years. Civil servants did receive a gratuity, but in order to reach the maximum gratuity of one and a half times annual pay, they had to work forty-five years.[18]

By 1924, guards, sergeants and inspectors were enjoying thirty days' annual leave, while the higher ranks were allowed forty-two days. Leave of any sort including annual leave was a privilege, not a right. Special leave was granted in connection with a transfer, marriage, sickness or death of a relative, and this was deducted from the thirty days' annual allowance. Throughout the period 1924–52 the stipulations governing annual leave remained substantially the same. Some opted to take the thirty days together and brought the family back to the farm on which they themselves had been reared. Others chose to break up the leave into the maximum four periods allowed and use it to help save the turf or hay. In practice, the superintendent of the district decided who got what leave and when. Normally an effort was made to accommodate the member, but of course at certain key times of the year not everybody got the leave they wanted.[19] The amount of annual leave granted to the guards compared very favourably with that of every section of society, except perhaps teachers. It seems extremely generous for the second quarter of the twentieth century. However, the principle that the whole time of the policeman was, in theory, at the disposal of the police service was embodied in the Desborough commission report and continued to permeate the Garda Síochána long after independence. In fact, until the mid-1930s guards officially had a seven-day week with just one day off per month. Their generous annual leave has to be viewed in this light.

Members of the Garda Síochána were exempt from contributing to the national health insurance because of their terms of employment, which provided for salary to be paid during sickness and disablement. Members who were sick were visited by a doctor, usually the local GP. This service was free to the gardaí. If medicine was prescribed, the individual had to pay for it. If it was a long or serious illness, frequently the member travelled to the surgeon of the force in the depot, who assessed the case and decided what course of action should be followed. If hospitalisation was necessary, the individual paid his own maintenance costs unless the illness or injury was received on duty. Falling off a bicycle in the course of patrol duty was perhaps the most common cause necessitating hospitalisation.[20] The surgeon kept all hospital cases under continual review. The sick bay in the depot was made into a twenty-bed hospital in the 1930s, and members convalescing or requiring care were frequently sent there. They had to pay their maintenance costs. Others were sent to general hospitals. Sometimes a convalescing member was returned to work but assigned to light duties for a short period.

Payment of salary and allowances was determined by the origin, nature and length of the illness. Short-term sickness usually meant full pay and allowances for its duration. Any illness received in the course of duty meant that the member received full pay for six months, as long as there was a reasonable chance of full recovery. Usually half pay was given for the next six months, with an extension of a few months being granted in individual cases. If illness or injury resulted from wilful neglect, no pay was received. Members who were permanently disabled as a result of injuries received in the course of duty got a special pension. This depended on the extent of the disablement and the length of service. Any individual with at least ten years' service who was unable to do his work because of infirmity of mind or body (not resulting from duty), was entitled to an ordinary pension for life. Members with less than ten years of service received just a gratuity.

If a guard, sergeant or station sergeant with at least five years of service died, his widow received a pension of £30 per annum, while her children each received £10 per annum (to a maximum of three children) until they reached 16 years. When a member with less than five years' service died, his widow received a gratuity. The widow of an officer received £50 per annum and £15 per child. The regulations governing sickness, injury, pensions and gratuities were firmly in place by 1925 and were to remain substantially the same for the next twenty-five years.[21] Throughout the 1930s and 1940s the representative bodies agitated to have the widow's and orphan's allowance improved. In 1951 a revised pensions order increased widow's and orphan's allowances, as well as removing the limit on the number of orphan children to whom an allowance could be paid.

From the earliest days of the force it was realised that the death of a member or one of his family could cause severe financial difficulties. As a result, a Garda Benevolent Society was started in August 1925 by the representative bodies at the instigation of Commissioner O'Duffy. Any member of the force could join the society for an annual subscription of approximately 0.3 per cent of his pay. The society helped to defray the funeral expenses of unmarried subscribers and of subscribers' wives. On the death of a subscriber, it gave a grant to his widow and children. Necessitous orphans up to the age of 16 could each receive an annual grant.[22] Most of the members of the force joined the Benevolent Society. The families of deceased members who had been discharged prior to death were practically dependent on assistance from this fund.

Tuberculosis was a major illness and killer in Irish society. The guards were not exempt. Between 1923 and 1933 eighty-three members either died or were discharged from the force because of the disease.[23] Treatment frequently involved long periods in hospital followed by convalescence. After six months' illness a member received only half pay. Out of this, he had to provide for his family and pay his hospital costs. In 1930 one guard with seven years' service was receiving half pay of £1-17-0 (£1.85) per week while in Newcastle sanatorium. He paid £1-8-0 (£1.40) to the hospital and was left with 9 shillings (45p) to feed and clothe his wife and family.[24] In 1933 the government agreed to Commissioner Broy's request that £10,000 of the reward fund be used to set up a Medical Aid Society.[25] Its aims were to alleviate hardships caused by a member's illness over a protracted period of time. Assistance depended entirely on each individual's circumstances. It was never intended to indemnify the member against the cost of every illness. Membership was open to all members of the force for a subscription of approximately 0.125 per cent of pay. The vast majority of members joined. By the early 1940s, as the force got older, there was a substantial increase in the number of claims for assistance received by the society. TB continued to be a major source of illness. In November 1947 the government introduced significantly improved arrangements regarding sick pay for members of the force who had TB. From its inception in 1934, until 1950, the Medical Aid Society gave assistance in over 9,000 cases. By that year, however, the initiatives of Minister Noel Browne were beginning to take effect and there was a substantial decrease in the number of claims coming before the society. Neither the Benevolent Society nor the Medical Aid Society was expected to provide a comprehensive welfare system for members, but they did help alleviate cases of hardship and financial distress caused by death or ill-health.

TRANSFERS

Being transferred to another area was an integral part of the life of a member of the Garda Síochána. A death, resignation or sickness necessitated the transfer of a replacement. When a member married a woman from the vicinity of his station, he was automatically moved. Suitable married quarters in stations were not always available and this influenced transfers. Promotion invariably involved a transfer. Proficiency in Irish influenced transfers to the Gaeltacht region. Transfer could also be used as a means of disciplining a member, although this was rare. The expense involved in moving was borne by the state unless the individual himself had requested the transfer. At least one week's notice had to be given to unmarried men and two weeks' notice to married men regarding a transfer. The chief superintendent of each division had a great deal of influence and power in deciding transfers. The stipulations governing transfers remained basically the same for the first thirty years of the force's existence.

In the early years of the Garda Síochána, members were frequently transferred as the authorities grappled with many organisational problems. By the early 1930s the policy of the authorities was that once a location was found suitable, it should be permanent.[26] The exigencies of a new force frequently interfered with this principle. In 1935 the representative bodies claimed that indiscriminate transfers were causing untold hardship. By 1936, 65 per cent of the members were married with young families and not enthusiastic about moving. In the 1940s the number of transfers decreased a great deal and by the late 1940s involved annually only about 7 per cent of the entire force. Throughout most of the period 1926–52 transfers were usually not arbitrary. A married guard who did not seek promotion was frequently left in the one area for years.

From the late 1930s most transfers were at the request of members themselves.[27] Many sought transfers in the 1940s so as to allow their children to avail of secondary education. In general, the garda authorities did their best to accommodate married members, although it was not always perceived in this way. Former DMP members could not be transferred outside Dublin unless they requested it. Temporary transfers for a few days or weeks were very common.

Some members of the force who failed to get a transfer through the ordinary channels had recourse to outside influence. They, or frequently their wives, enlisted the aid of public officials in high office in church and state. This practice of attempting to influence a transfer was widespread throughout the 1930s and 1940s.[28] It is impossible to ascertain the degree to which such attempts were successful, but sufficient numbers obviously were successful to prompt numerous others to attempt it. Occasionally a guard might find himself transferred if he had offended a superior officer. Members could also be transferred as a result of politics. If a guard were friendly, or indeed hostile, to a particular political party, his superiors might transfer him. Of course, this was open to abuse and a conscientious guard impartially enforcing the law might find himself and his family transferred to a very remote district at the behest of local political activists whose toes he had trodden upon. In 1937 a guard in a town in Mayo raided a pub for after-hours drinking. Those caught had been at a political party meeting, which had taken place earlier in the evening. Pressure was applied on the guard to drop the case but he refused. He was transferred to Achill Island and then to Glenamoy where there was not even a national school for miles around. The family had to split up, with the mother and children going to live in rented accommodation in Ballina, so as to allow the children to attend secondary school. The father visited them for twenty-four hours each month. [29] There is no way of knowing the extent to which this sort of thing occurred but there can be no doubt that it did occur in some instances and caused much misery to the garda and his family who were involved.

DISCIPLINE

The disciplinary code of the Garda Síochána did not differ radically from that of the RIC.[30] There were about thirty offences against discipline. Tyrannical conduct towards inferiors was high on the list. Disobedience to orders was followed by neglect of duty, which included gossiping on duty. Communicating with the public press on any matter without prior authority, and signing any unauthorised petition regarding the force were regarded as serious offences. Accepting bribes or allowing oneself to get into debt were other offences. Malingering, absence without leave and being unpunctual were all cited as ill discipline. Use of unnecessary violence towards prisoners was also mentioned. Five of the thirty disciplinary offences related to drink and intoxication, whether on or off duty. Communicating with officials in order to influence a transfer, expressing political opinions or lending money to, or borrowing money from, other members of the force were also offences. Marrying without permission, gambling or wearing an emblem on uniform without permission were not acceptable. The punishments were dismissal, being required to resign (as an alternative to dismissal), reduction in rank, reduction in pay, transfer, fine, reprimand or a caution. Each member of the force against whom any disciplinary charge was being preferred was informed as to the nature of the charge and could write an explanation of his actions, which was sent, along with the charge of misconduct, to a superior officer.

The disciplinary code of the Garda Síochána was strict and was rigorously applied, especially in the early years of the force's existence. Dismissal was frequently used in the 1922–5 period, mostly for financial impropriety, general unsuitability and occasionally for 'immorality', which usually meant fathering a child outside marriage. As the 1930s progressed there were considerably fewer dismissals and these were often the result of serious drink and debt problems. The government was forced to introduce the Garda Síochána (Retirement) Regulations, 1941, which enabled it to retire compulsorily eleven officers and twenty-three men from lower ranks who were in serious debt, had a bad drink problem or were inefficient. The government did not want to dismiss, without pension, men who had been in the War of Independence and had served loyally in the force — hence the special regulations, which allowed them be compulsorily retired on ordinary pension.[31] The Dáil debate on the issue ensured much adverse publicity for the gardaí. Two years later in 1943, the *Leader*, a journal of current affairs and politics, stated that many guards were consuming too much drink.[32] However, only a handful of dismissals occurred each year in the 1940s. From the early 1930s the most common disciplinary measure was to fine the offender. Fines usually ranged from 10 shillings (50p) to £3. By 1931 over £11,000 had been collected in fines. On the other hand, members who showed exceptional energy, ability or bravery in the course of their duty could receive a monetary award usually of 10 shillings (50p) to £3-10-0 (£3.50). By 1931 almost £18,000 had been paid out in awards.[33]

The garda code of discipline, which was officially introduced in 1926, had not altered by 1952. However, by the early 1940s it was implemented in a more relaxed and humane manner. In 1949 the *Garda Review* editorial stated:

> The administration of Garda Síochána discipline during the latter years has been characterised by an impartiality, a consistency and a degree of justice tempered with mercy, which puts to shame the erratic tyranny, nit picking and other things, which were designated as discipline in the early years.[34]

The enforcement of discipline throughout this entire period depended to a great deal on the individual sergeant or superintendent. While there was a general relaxation in the early 1940s, Tom Long, who was a young guard in 1940, remembered being called by registration number, not by name.[35] Even by the late 1940s relations between the ranks still tended to be formal and strict with little fraternising.

ARMING THE GUARDS, 1923–52

The Civil War ended in May 1923. However, in some districts, bands of armed anti-Treatyites, disbanded Free State soldiers, or just ordinary criminals, roamed the countryside, raiding almost at will. The unarmed guards were defenceless against such men. On 3 December 1923, Sergeant James Woods was killed in Scartaglen, County Kerry. On 28 January 1924, Garda Patrick O'Halloran was shot dead during a bank raid in Baltinglass, County Wicklow. On 9 February the representative bodies recommended that between three and six .38 Webley revolvers be supplied to each station and be under the control of the sergeant. It suggested that such arms be carried by members on all escort, special-protection and illicit distillation work, when serving summons and on night duty. It stressed, however, that it was opposed to the use of arms as a general principle and that these recommendations were a purely temporary measure until a more normal situation obtained.[36] The status quo remained, however, and on 6 May, Sergeant Thomas Griffin and Garda John Murrin were both shot at Cregg, Carrick-on-Suir, County Tipperary, while attempting to arrest an armed man. Griffin died immediately and Murrin died five months later. Serious attacks on gardaí, in which shots were fired, continued sporadically throughout 1924. Poteen raids also began to feature as instances when gardaí were fired upon.[37]

Much the same pattern continued in the first few months of 1925. The government did not want to redeploy the army, nor did it want to arm the general body of the Garda Síochána. Instead, the Minister for Home Affairs, Kevin O'Higgins, formed the Special Branch. About 200 men were chosen and given a six-month training course, which included the advanced use of fire arms. They were divided into groups of about ten to twelve men and sent to the twenty divisional headquarters outside Dublin.[38] They were in plain clothes and armed. On 28 December 1925, Garda Thomas Dowling was murdered at Fanore, County Clare, when he was investigating illicit distillation.

Throughout 1926 armed crime decreased. In areas where the ordinary uniformed force was finding it difficult to cope, the Special Branch was called in. However, on 14 November 1926 two uniformed members of the force were killed in separate incidences. Sergeant James Fitzsimons of St Luke's station, Cork, and Guard Hugh Ward of Hollyford station, County Tipperary, were both killed during armed raids on their stations. Another eight such attacks occurred at this time. O'Duffy believed that a young, more fanatical, splinter group of the IRA, which included ordinary criminals 'trading under the patriotic standard', was responsible for the recent spate of attacks on garda stations.[39] He strongly urged the government to give him the authorisation to arm the entire force if and when he thought necessary. Perhaps anticipating government opposition, he suggested increasing the armed detective branch to 1,000 for a year's trial as a minimum requirement. O'Higgins refused. The minister believed that the Garda Síochána, unarmed since 1923, had functioned effectively and that the threat was now much less. Furthermore, he argued that the success of the force depended on the moral support given by the community. Arming it might diminish this and remind people of the RIC and oppression. He also stated that arming would actually increase the danger for the individual member and would provide good material for anti-state propagandists.[40]

On 11 July 1929, a garda detective, Tadhg Sullivan, was killed in Kilrush, County Clare, when a box thought to contain firearms exploded, having been boobytrapped. On 20 March 1931, Superintendent Sean Curtin of Friarsfield, near Tipperary town, was shot dead by the local IRA. In June 1931 the Executive Council decided as a result of increased IRA activity to issue revolvers to all chief superintendents. It also decided to increase the detective branch by 200. O'Duffy strengthened the Special Branch units in counties Tipperary, Kerry, Donegal, Leitrim and Cork. In November 1933, Commissioner Broy decided that he wanted twenty uniformed guards available in each division for protection duty, which would entail carrying arms. Suitable uniformed members were called up in batches for an intensive course of training in musketry and small arms instruction at the depot.[41] Throughout the rest of the 1930s there were occasional incidents in which the guards were fired upon, but they suffered no fatalities.

From the outbreak of the Second World War in 1939 (officially called the 'Emergency' in Ireland) a number of guards were temporarily transferred to Dublin and put on armed protection duty. However, there was no radical departure from the idea of the uniformed force being unarmed. The Emergency was to witness an increased surveillance of the IRA and a growing number of armed confrontations between them and members of the Garda Síochána. In January 1940 a garda detective, John Roche of Union Quay, Cork, died having been shot in a scuffle while trying to arrest Thomas Mac Curtain, son of the Cork lord mayor killed during the War of Independence. Mac Curtain was charged with the murder but eventually had his sentence of execution commuted to penal servitude for life. On 16 August a garda raid on an IRA home in

Rathgar, Dublin, resulted in the deaths of two Special Branch members, Garda Richard Hyland and Sergeant Patrick McKeown. Two of the captured men, Patrick McGrath and Thomas Harte, were subsequently executed for the murders.[42] On 9 September 1942 another Special Branch member, Sergeant Denis O'Brien, was ambushed and shot dead outside his home at Ballyboden, County Dublin. Three weeks later, Garda Michael Walsh was shot dead in Ballyjamesduff, County Cavan. Less than a month later, Garda Detective George Mordant was shot dead while searching a house in Donnycarney, County Dublin. An IRA man, Charles Kerins, was arrested and executed for O'Brien's murder, while another IRA man, Maurice O'Neill, was captured and executed for Mordant's murder.[43] In January 1948, Chief Superintendent Sean Gantley of the Special Branch was accidentally shot dead by a fellow detective while trying to apprehend an armed criminal. Shortly afterwards, the Minister for Justice, Seán Mac Eoin, issued tighter regulations governing the issuing and use of firearms by the force.[44]

From 1922 to 1952 members of the Garda Síochána could possess and use firearms. The number of men who could do so was in no way limited. Generally speaking, however, the vast majority of the uniformed guards were unarmed, with the exception of a small number, while assigned to special duties. All of the detective branch was armed. Members issued with firearms usually wore plain clothes and concealed the weapons. Arms were generally issued only to members who had firearms training. From the mid-1920s the representative bodies appear to have been content to have an unarmed force, backed up by armed detectives. The fact that the guards were unarmed greatly helped to differentiate them from their predecessors in the RIC whose latter years had been associated in the public mind with a semi-military role. Kevin O'Higgins appreciated the importance of the force being unarmed in helping it to be accepted by the divided community. Successive governments believed that the gardaí could weather occasional increases in armed violence without recourse to general re-arming. This belief was reinforced by the fact that while most garda murders were the result of IRA activity, only two had been premeditated, as that organisation did not include the members of the force in its list of 'legitimate targets'.

The decision in late 1922 and early 1923 to send out unarmed policemen was both courageous and ambitious. In many respects, the new force had modelled itself very closely on its predecessor, the RIC, but this was a clear break with tradition. This decision influenced the public perception of the force and greatly facilitated its acceptance by all sides of the community. It was, perhaps, the most significant decision taken by any government concerning the Garda Síochána in the period 1922–52.

7

ACCOMMODATION

1920s

Before the outbreak of the First World War, the RIC had 1,129 barracks in the twenty-six counties that would become the Irish Free State. These barracks served as public offices, as well as providing accommodation for single men and for some married men and their families. The new Free State government intended to continue this practice. (The term 'barracks' was used by the RIC and continued to be used by the Garda Síochána; as the 1930s progressed, this was often replaced by the term 'station', although the terms were interchangeable right up to the 1960s.) There was great difficulty in securing accommodation for the new force in the 1922–4 period. Almost 75 per cent of the RIC barracks had been burned down during the War of Independence.[1] The government owned only half of the RIC barracks, the remainder being the property of private individuals who leased them annually to the RIC.[2] The long-term solution lay in rebuilding and repairing the old RIC barracks. The Department of Finance wanted to repair the government-owned barracks as cheaply as possible and to get the private landlords to repair their own and lease them to the guards. However, many owners wanted compensation before repairing damaged barracks, and others sought exorbitant rents for undamaged barracks. The immediate problem was to secure some form of accommodation for the new force. The Department of Finance provided a small grant towards repairing government-owned barracks, and put pressure on landlords to repair premises that were privately owned. The government passed the Civic Guard (Acquisition of Premises) Act, 1923, which gave it the power to acquire premises compulsorily and, if necessary, to fix the amount of rent to be paid to the owner.

By May 1924 the immediate problem of securing some form of accommodation for the force had been overcome. Guards were now occupying 756 stations out of a proposed total of 837. However, half of these were unsuitable for permanent occupation, with many being 'little better than hovels'.[3] Many members were operating from temporary rented accommodation in places where the local RIC barracks had not been repaired by the private landlords. The state had reconstructed only a small number of the burned barracks that it owned, preferring instead to acquire existing premises for rent, either by negotiation or compulsion. The situation gradually improved throughout the remainder of the 1920s. The Board of Works was responsible for providing accommodation for the Garda Síochána. The garda authorities had no control over spending on accommodation. By 1929 the number of stations deemed by the Board of Works as unsuitable for permanent occupation had dropped to eighty. The government built a number of new stations. It also reconstructed some badly burned RIC barracks, as well as carrying out essential repairs on others that were less severely damaged. A number of private individuals did repair the barrack properties that they owned, and let them to the force. The Acquisition of Premises Act, 1923, strengthened the Board of Works' hand when negotiating for barracks accommodation.[4] By 1931 a small number of lucky station parties occupied new purpose-built barracks. A larger number occupied premises that were not designed as barracks and were rented from private landlords. A great many occupied former RIC barracks, some owned by the government, the majority owned by private individuals.

In the latter part of 1922, the headquarters' staff of the Garda Síochána was stationed in Dublin Castle. In January 1923 they moved to the Phoenix Park depot as a temporary arrangement, so that senior officers could be in close touch with those officers in charge of training large numbers of recruits. By 1926 there were no longer large numbers being trained. The offices in the depot were unsuitable — mostly dormitory and squad rooms that had been temporarily adapted. O'Duffy pressed for new accommodation. He wanted eventually to move back to Dublin Castle but, as this was not yet ready, he suggested securing temporary accommodation at the Royal Hospital, Kilmainham. It was not until 1931 that Garda headquarters actually moved to Kilmainham. It remained there until July 1950 when it moved back once again to the

Phoenix Park, where it is still situated today.

One of the earliest issues of the garda magazine *Guth an Gharda* in 1924 complained about the very poor conditions of the stations.[5] In September 1926 the representative bodies requested that, where piped water was available, baths and flush toilets be provided in all stations and that married quarters have an entrance separate from that used by the public. In 1927 a photograph of a thatched dilapidated cottage, which served as a barracks in the west of Ireland, appeared in the *Garda Review*. It consisted of three small rooms, including one measuring 14 x 12 feet where four men slept. There were holes in the thatch, so the roof leaked. Clothing left against the wall became mildewed very quickly. It was 'an evil smelling hovel, reeking with damp'.[6] The writer did admit, however, that in general the situation had improved a fair deal over the previous few years. During the 1920s the *Garda Review* had numerous editorials and articles, all criticising the terrible conditions of many of the stations.

In the 1920s most members of the force were single men who lived in dormitories in the barracks. Married men had also to live in the barracks if married quarters were provided. If not, they found their own accommodation and received a rent allowance. In July 1928 the representative bodies claimed that there were still sixty-six barracks unfit for human habitation. They cited one rat-infested premises in County Cork, which had been condemned by the local medical attendant after an outbreak of typhoid in which one guard died.[7] Most of the force in the early to mid-1920s worked and lived in fairly appalling conditions. However, the majority were healthy, young, unmarried men, not overly concerned with their living conditions. Therefore, the poor accommodation and the slow progress in improving it during the 1920s, while a source of irritation, was endured fairly stoically.

1930s

The accommodation problem was greatly exacerbated in the 1930s by the fact that the vast majority of the force got married.[8] If the sergeant was married, he was expected to occupy the official married quarters. Many of these were found to be very unsuitable. By 1935 fewer than half of the married sergeants and practically none of the married guards were housed in official accommodation. Barrack accommodation was a major source of friction between government and members of the force in the early 1930s. In November 1929 the representative bodies cited a long list of bad health resulting from poor accommodation, including two deaths of members based in Burnfort station in County Donegal. By

December 1930 only half of the married quarters had an entrance separate from that used by the general public. For the remainder, the sergeant's family's front door was used by those members of the public who had official business in the barracks. Almost a quarter of the married quarters consisted of a mere three rooms, while most of the remainder had just four. Many of the married quarters had just one toilet for both the station party and the family. This was almost invariably outside and was frequently of the pail or pit type. Very few married quarters possessed an efficient range, accessible water supply, bath, yard or garden.

During the second half of the 1930s, barrack accommodation became a less contentious issue between members of the force and the government. A small number of new barracks were built each year to replace the worst of the old ones. Also, more men got married and no longer lived in the barracks. For the few hundred sergeants and the small number of single guards who continued to live in barracks, conditions were far from comfortable, however. The following description by Mrs Margaret Delaney, the sergeant's wife at the barracks in Clogherhead, County Louth, from the mid-1930s to the early 1950s is quite typical:

> It was originally a private dwelling built by a fairly prosperous family and had no separate entrance to the married quarters. The stairs faced the front door, which added to the lack of privacy. The public office or day room, which had forms or benches on which to sit, was very close to the kitchen. It included a cell, which was rarely used. There was also a very small office for Con's [her husband, the sergeant's] use. The kitchen had no presses of any sort, no water or sink, a range whose oven had a large gaping hole in it and a cement floor. The dust continually rose up from it. The sitting room had a bay window and fireplace. There were two bedrooms upstairs for the family of seven. The walls of the bedrooms were completely bare, with no furniture at all in the married quarters when we first arrived. The nearest well for water was a half mile down the village and each night after work Con fetched the next day's supply on foot. The toilet for the men was situated between the house and the entrance to the back garden. It was a dry closet of the pit type, which was emptied now and again in an open wheelbarrow by a man from the village. We [the family] had a chemical toilet outside. There was no bath.[9]

By 1950 the family was still using oil lamps, and the barracks was one of the last houses in the village to get electricity. By 1960 the barracks had still not got running water. There was a good-sized garden attached to the station.

Even the new stations being built in the mid-1930s were not meeting the full approval of the force. The rooms in these single-storey stations were considered too small for the average family and some of them were without fireplaces.[10] Furthermore, these stations made no provision for baths.

In October 1930 the editorial of the *Garda Review* devoted itself to highlighting the inadequacy of the rent allowance for those members who did not live in barracks and were forced to pay increasingly higher rents. By September 1934 over 90 per cent of the married members of the force had to find their own accommodation. They encountered difficulties in procuring such accommodation, both with regard to standard and price. Gardaí were frequently transferred from one area to another and this made landlords either reluctant to take them on as tenants, or, if they did, inclined to charge them higher rents. Landlords were also more likely to give better housing to long-term tenants than to a garda who would probably be gone in five or six years. The representative bodies' campaign to improve the rent allowance gained momentum throughout the 1930s as both the number of married men increased and the allowance became increasingly inadequate to meet the actual cost of renting accommodation. Despite repeated calls, however, nothing happened until the end of 1939 when the government produced a somewhat improved allowance.

1940s

By 1942, over 50 per cent of the total garda stations in the country, were in need of replacement or major renovation.[11] Over half of these were former RIC barracks. Most of the stations in need of repair belonged to private landlords. While almost half of the force worked in substandard barracks, only a small number of single men and some sergeants and their families were forced to live in such conditions. During the early 1940s the government continued to build a small number of new stations each year. In July 1944 the Department of Justice proposed that 285 new stations be built and 133 existing ones undergo major renovations. However, the government provided only £50,000 per annum for the purpose. This amount was sufficient to erect only about fifteen sub-district stations. The late 1940s witnessed increasing impatience on the part of the garda authorities with the slow progress being made in providing new barracks.[12]

Barrack accommodation became a contentious issue between members of the force and the government in the second half of the 1940s. Over 1,000 young men who had been recruited in the 1943–8 period were now living in the antiquated dormitories of many barracks throughout the country. In the *Garda Review* of February 1949 a young garda described living conditions in his barracks. What he described was fairly typical. The sanitation consisted of the bucket system. The bedding was old and of very poor quality. The walls were dripping with damp. In many barracks the large cold dormitory was unfurnished and lacking a wardrobe or even a bedside chair. When rural electrification came to a village the garda station was frequently the only house not to apply for connection. Similarly, when the county council provided water to an area, the station often did not apply for connection. The Board of Works may have been reluctant to incur extra expenditure on very old buildings that might be abandoned in the near future. The 1950 commission of enquiry into the Garda Síochána found that there had been little improvement in barrack living accommodation from that provided for the RIC over 100 years earlier.[13]

By 1942, most of the members of the force were married and the vast majority of them were living in rented accommodation. Married men still had difficulty in procuring suitable accommodation at a reasonable price. The lack of available housing meant that some married men were separated from their families.[14] The situation was exacerbated by the general housing shortage of the post-war period. By 1950 no effort appeared to have been made to provide houses for the guards, and members were angry as they were ineligible for state-subsidised housing being built by local authorities.[15] By 1943 the force was pressing the government for an improvement in the rent allowance, because of inflation. In 1945 married guards throughout the country were usually paying rent ranging from 25 to 60 per cent above their rent allowance.[16] In 1950 the rent allowance was increased by 10 per cent.

Barrack accommodation within the Dublin metropolitan area was never quite the serious problem that it was for the rest of the country. The DMP stations had not suffered as much as RIC barracks during the War of Independence. Married members working in the Dublin area were also more fortunate in securing accommodation for their families where no official quarters were provided. They would not be transferred outside the Dublin area and so could secure better terms for renting, or could even make a long-term commitment regarding the purchase of a house. By 1948 over 50 per cent of Dublin gardaí were tenant purchasers of their own houses.[17]

CONCLUSION

In the period 1922–52 the garda authorities tried to provide accommodation in each station for single men, and one set of married quarters to be occupied by the sergeant if he was married. The general principles covering Garda Síochána accommodation were almost identical to those of its predecessor, the RIC. As late as 1952 the garda authorities still maintained the housing tradition of the RIC, which postulated a life in barracks for every man not specifically authorised to live out.[18] In practice, this was modified somewhat because of the large number of married gardaí who were forced to secure rented accommodation. By 1952 most guards worked in barracks that were uncomfortable and unsuitable. Many sergeants lived with their families in this inadequate accommodation. Most of the force lived in rented accommodation, which was difficult and expensive to procure. Of course, many members of the general public were living in poor housing conditions at this time. Furthermore, the gardaí received a rent allowance, which eased the burden. Notwithstanding this, however, most guards lived and worked in unsatisfactory accommodation thirty years after the force had been founded.

8

Daily Routine

HOURS OF DUTY

A guard was never 'off duty', in the sense that he was expected to be alert in detecting and preventing crime even if not officially on duty. His recreation was not a right, but a privilege to be granted when circumstances allowed.[1] Guards worked an eight-hour day (called outdoor duty) seven days a week, with just one day off per month. In addition, each guard had to do barrack orderly duty (called indoor duty) in his turn. This meant that one member had to remain in the barrack dayroom for a twenty-four-hour period. Whether single or married, he had to sleep in this dayroom, usually on a camp bed. The duty roster was made out daily by the sergeant. Under normal circumstances, most villages and rural areas did not have a guard on patrol from approximately midnight until about 10 the following morning. A fairly typical roster involved a member being on duty from 10 a.m. until 2 p.m. and again from 6 to 10 p.m. The next day he might not start until 2 p.m., have a few hours off in the evening, and not finish duty until midnight.[2]

During the 1920s most of the men were single and lived in barracks. In theory, when off duty they were not allowed to leave the barracks, except for two hours of recreation daily. In practice, many sergeants allowed the single off-duty men to leave the barracks as long as they remained in close proximity to it, and married men were in barracks only when on duty. In addition to an eight-hour stint of duty, guards had to attend police duty classes for one hour each morning, six days per week. Furthermore, they had to attend a daily parade at 9 a.m., six mornings per week. All single men not on duty had to be in barracks for roll-call at 11 p.m. throughout the year. In 1927, O'Duffy reduced the number of outdoor duty hours from eight to seven and extended the recreation period to three hours.

During the 1930s the situation became somewhat more relaxed. As most of the men got married and moved out of barracks, their off-duty time became their own to use as they pleased. Police duty classes were held much less frequently and Sunday duty was reduced to four hours.[3] The barrack orderly system became a source of grievance, however. It was monotonous and, with many of the force now married, it caused inconvenience and disruption to family life. Sergeants were not obliged to do barrack orderly duty. By 1930, in almost half of the stations, each guard had to sleep in the dayroom one night out of three. In effect, a guard was either on ordinary outdoor duty or on barrack orderly duty for almost 100 hours each week. This was increased if another guard was sick, on leave or collecting agricultural statistics. In 1939 the barrack orderly system was altered to allow a sharing of the duty during the day, although night barrack orderly duty remained as it was. The representative bodies were not satisfied with this change. Throughout the 1930s the members of the force had campaigned in vain for one rest day per week, like that enjoyed by English forces.

With the outbreak of the Second World War, hundreds of guards were temporarily transferred to Dublin, leaving many stations with depleted manpower. Barrack orderly duty had to be undertaken more frequently, as well as a plethora of new Emergency duties.[4] Many of the extra duties were removed in 1945, with the ending of the War. However, the members of the force were not pleased with their working hours. In 1947 they complained that there was no provision for overtime payment and that night work was not recognised by a special rate. In effect, the guards were being paid for their outdoor duty hours, not for their station orderly hours.

By 1950, guards had to do seven hours of outdoor duty daily, except on Sundays and the day after station orderly duty when they did four hours. In almost half of the stations the men had to do orderly duty two or three nights every week.[5] The station orderly system had its origins in the RIC practice of keeping one member continually in barracks to guard the arms stored there. By mid-century it had become rather obsolete, particularly with the availability of phones and modern transport. By 1950, guards worked fewer total hours than in 1925. They also did considerably less outdoor work, but had usually to do more station orderly duty. They now enjoyed two days' leave per month. Their working hours, however, were long and unsociable. Station orderly duty continued to cause disruption to family life, and leave and recreation continued to be viewed as a privilege.

The duty hours of the Dublin area differed from the rest of the country. Dublin guards, like their DMP predecessors, did not have to do barrack orderly duty, which was done by the station sergeant. The day was divided into three eight-hour shifts, usually beginning at 6 a.m. The city was patrolled for the full twenty-four hours each day. A guard in the metropolitan area did two months' day duty, followed by one month's night duty. He got three-quarters of an hour off for a meal during each turn of duty. He worked eight hours each day, seven days a week. Unlike his rural counterpart, he did his daily duty in one tour, not two. He got one day off per month. From the early 1930s, guards in the Dublin area on 6 a.m. to 2 p.m. duty on a Sunday were allowed four hours off to attend divine service. The night duty imposed considerable hardship on the members, and this theme was continually heard in the *Garda Review* during the war years. During the 1939–45 period, guards were frequently called upon to do extra hours of duty. By 1950, guards in the Dublin area were doing an eight-hour day, with three-quarters of an hour off for a meal, six days per week. They also worked for four hours on a Sunday. They had two days off each month of day duty, and three days off each month of night duty. While they had to do night duty, their actual hours of duty were considerably fewer than those of their rural counterparts who had to do station orderly duty. Just as the guards countrywide inherited and only slightly modified the RIC regulations regarding hours of duty, so too the Dublin guard's duty rota was based heavily on the DMP system that it replaced.

POLICE DUTIES

The official work of the gardaí fell into two categories — police and non-police duties. The former were basically the prevention and detection of crime — what is normally associated with the work of any police force. The latter involved the gardaí carrying out a plethora of administrative duties in their own locality on behalf of the state. Agrarian crime, illicit distillation and licensing laws, and ordinary crime against persons and property were the main areas of police duty. Larceny of all sorts, frequently petty in nature, occupied a considerable amount of garda time. Goods such as timber and grain were frequently stolen, and in 1926 at Broadford, County Clare, a local farmer stole a full garda clothesline.[6] Theft of bicycles was quite common. Smuggling, poaching of salmon, illegal betting, illegal possession of fire arms and the speeding of an occasional motor car were typical of the occurrences that kept gardaí busy. Traffic was not a problem in rural Ireland but was fast becoming one in the city.

The manufacture of poteen, or illicit distillation as it was officially called, was a major problem facing the force in the 1920s. It was carried on extensively along the western seaboard, although there were pockets of it in other parts of the country. Those involved in the manufacture of poteen saw it as a sort of sport in which they tried to dodge the guards.[7] It was a not insubstantial source of income in the poorer areas of the Gaeltacht. The general breakdown of law and order in the period 1919–23 greatly facilitated the poteen trade. By 1923 it had reached alarming proportions. By the mid-1920s the efforts of the guards to suppress this trade had won praise from the national press on numerous occasions, as well as from the Presbyterian Temperance Committee.[8] While the problem was by no means eliminated, by the late 1920s it had been confined to a smaller area and poteen manufacturers were increasingly harassed.

There was also a very serious and major problem relating to the licensing laws. The absence of an effective police force in many parts of rural Ireland from 1919 to 1923 meant that the existing licensing laws, which were quite lax to begin with, were frequently flouted. This caused immense hardship to a great many families in the 1922–3 period.[9] The return to more settled conditions and the work of the Garda Síochána in enforcing the licensing laws very soon brought a marked improvement in the situation. The success of the gardaí won them much acclaim among the establishment. Perhaps more important, however, was the gratitude felt by many Irish people, especially wives and mothers, to the gardaí for their work in combating the drink problem.

From the late 1920s up to the mid-1930s there was an average of about 7,000 crimes reported each year. About 50 per cent of these resulted in the gardaí securing convictions in court. The overwhelming majority of detected offences related to cars, lights on vehicles, wandering animals, school attendance, drink, dogs and larceny.[10] Much of the actual police work undertaken by the force was of a preventative nature — for example, the daily patrols and barrack orderly duty. Guards were also on special duty on occasions such as markets, fairs and meetings. Frequently they had to attend court, as well as occasionally escorting prisoners or the mentally insane.

During the Second World War, there was a fairly dramatic increase in the responsibilities placed on the Garda Síochána. In 1939 a Local Defence Force was set up throughout the country. In 1940 it was divided in two: a Local Defence Force under army control and a Local Security Force under garda control. The latter group was voluntary, usually unarmed, and was an auxiliary police force as well as a fire-fighting service in the case of attack.[11] The local sergeant was responsible for the Local Security Force in his sub-district. He and the local guards gave lectures to these men at least once a week. In the Dublin metropolitan area too, the War brought a great deal of extra work. Ports had to be kept under observation. There was much extra protection duty of ambassadors' residences and of key buildings in the city. Hundreds of men were drafted up to Dublin for a few months or longer to assist with these duties. Some, such as Garda Michael Hegarty who was temporarily transferred from Stradone in County Cavan to help protect the German embassy, found it a very welcome change and felt that the eight-hour tour of city duty passed more quickly than the four-hour stint in their home area.[12] Others were anxious to return to their normal routine.[13]

During the early part of the War a number of proposals had been drawn up outlining the duties of the Garda Síochána in the event of the country being invaded.[14] The gardaí were to hand over all weapons to the Irish army. The members of the force were to remain non-combatant as they were not part of the defence forces, and consequently, if caught committing hostile acts against the enemy, would be treated as civilians and shot. They were to co-operate with the Irish defence forces in making preparations for resistance if their area had not yet been attacked. They were to destroy all information on membership of unlawful associations or 'aliens'. They were to stay in their own locality and continue to act as policemen for as long as possible. If asked by an occupying power to perform duties of an oppressive nature against their own civilian population, they could resume civilian life. None of these proposals were implemented as Ireland was not invaded.

After 1945, the duties of the Garda Síochána, by and large, returned to the pre-war situation. While there was a substantial increase in the number of offences detected, most of this related to motoring offences, the result of a rise in the number of vehicles using Irish roads.[15] Dublin was beginning to account for a growing proportion of the country's indictable crime.[16] By 1950 the police-duties aspect of the gardaí's work had altered very little from the mid-1920s. Crime prevention and minor infringements of the law constituted most of it. Station orderly duty and bicycle patrols in rural Ireland and twenty-four-hour beat patrols in Dublin were still the essential ingredients. Only thirty district headquarters outside the Dublin area enjoyed the luxury of a car by the year 1951. In 1948 the *Garda Review* complained that the police patrol in rural

Ireland, which had no definite purpose other than to 'show the flag', was an anachronism and a sheer waste of police time. It wanted motor cycles and cars to be made available to the force.

NON-POLICE DUTIES

During the 1920s various government departments imposed new administrative duties on the gardaí. By 1930 the force was carrying out an extensive range of such duties for the state.[17] For the Department of Finance, it furnished reports regarding income-tax defaulters and land drainage schemes, executed income-tax warrants and issued firearms and betting certificates. For the Department of Industry and Commerce, it certified unemployment claims and collected a multiplicity of agricultural and commercial statistics. About seventy sergeants underwent special training and examinations and were appointed weights and measures inspectors for this department, engaged full time in the inspection, verification and stamping of the weighing equipment used by traders. For the Department of Local Government and Public Health the gardaí annually revised voters' and jurors' lists, as well as ensuring that food and drugs acts were implemented. The enforcement of the Department of Education's School Attendance Act used up a lot of garda manpower. For the Department of Agriculture, the guards enforced the various orders relating to livestock breeding, sheep dipping and diseases of animals. The Garda Síochána also had responsibility for traffic control, especially in the Dublin area. The force carried out a plethora of other functions for every government department.

In 1930, O'Duffy had calculated that non-police work performed by the gardaí amounted to one-sixth of the total work of the force. The volume of non-police duties continued to increase in the 1930s and 1940s. The 1950 enquiry into the reorganisation of the Garda Síochána stated that 40 per cent of the time of rural policemen was devoted to non-police duties, although this was lower in the Dublin area.[18] The committee pointed out that for six to eight weeks of the summer most of the time of members in small stations was devoted to collecting agricultural statistics. The guards delivered pension books from 1934, and by 1950 this amounted to 161,000 deliveries annually.

The range of non-police duties carried out by the Garda Síochána in the 1922–52 period meant that the force soon became an indispensable cog in the wheel of government administration. This also greatly helped in the community's perception of it as a civilian police force. The force was the medium through which the individual came into contact with the departments of the state. Every form and every query had to be filtered through the local gardaí. This had a two-fold effect: it ensured close contact on a regular basis between the police and the public; it also ensured that the guards had an intimate knowledge of just about everything in the local area. The guards were thus facilitated in their prevention and detection of crime.

INSPECTIONS

Inspections of guards and sergeants by superior officers were an integral part of Garda Síochána organisation from the force's inception in 1922. Guards in every station had a short daily inspection carried out by their sergeant each morning. A more formal inspection was conducted by the superintendent on a regular basis, by the chief superintendent on a less regular basis, and by headquarters staff on very rare occasions. The men's appearance and their knowledge of the law and police duties were examined. A detailed inspection of the entire barracks took place, including the married quarters. The station records were carefully examined to ensure that they were up to date. Station parties were sometimes forewarned of impending inspections either officially or by neighbouring stations. Frequently, however, as 1922 recruit Tom Boland remembers, such inspections came as a total surprise.[19]

During the early years of the force's existence O'Duffy personally inspected quite a number of stations, frequently in a blitz-like fashion. At 6.45 p.m. on 26 June 1923 he inspected Garretstown station in Dublin and by 11 p.m. he was arriving in Trim station, having inspected five other station parties of County Meath.[20] In Navan he remarked that the bedrooms were very tidy and in Trim he noted that all the guards were members of the Pioneer Total Abstinence Association. On another inspection O'Duffy visited the gardaí in Enniskerry, County Wicklow, who were occupying the parochial hall, which also served as a local library. The commissioner was not impressed when he found articles of soiled linen belonging to the guards stuck here and there among the books! In the Roscommon area O'Duffy observed a sergeant and guard enter a pub in the middle of the day, but these men informed him that they were on dog-licence duty.

By 1925 the force was more fully organised and a pattern of inspections was established which was not substantially altered for the next thirty years. The superintendent conducted a daytime inspection of each station once a month, which lasted about an hour. He also did a night-time inspection at least four times a year, which lasted only a few minutes and was normally conducted before the early hours. The superintendent frequently went out and checked on the men on patrol.

Inspections by the chief superintendent were less frequent. These inspections could occur at any time.[21]

Every station had a great number of record books in which every occurrence, both major and minor, had to be meticulously recorded. These included station diary patrol book, demand for stationery book, receipt book, a record of offences book and a mess book. Each station also had a number of reference books supplied by headquarters. The Garda Síochána 'code' issued in 1928 covered every possible regulation, including a thirteen-line account of the correct way to dress one's bed in barracks. A drill book was produced in 1929, and a garda manual of police duty shortly afterwards. 'Routine orders' were printed and circulated quarterly in booklet form. Practically all the books of instruction or reference that the Garda Síochána used were very heavily reliant on those used by its predecessor, the RIC.

In 1928, O'Duffy, under pressure from the force, abolished the inspection of married quarters. During the 1920s inspections were fairly frequent and often feared. As the 1930s progressed, the men had grown more accustomed to them and were much better versed in their duties. Most officers were reasonable in their expectations during inspection, but occasionally an ambitious officer, wishing to impress his superiors, found plenty to criticise.[22] One irate guard who had to do station orderly duty every second day during 1943 reached breaking point:

> We will not put up with an officer coming into the station like a hysterical female, and subjecting the unfortunate members to a Chinese inquisition, with the addition of gross offensiveness and personal abuse.[23]

While such instances did occur, they appear to have been the exception. The system of inspections meant that officers kept a close watch on the workings of all station parties, and that guards carried out their work knowing that an inspection could take place at any time.

DAILY LIFE

The daily patrol was an integral part of a guard's life. In Dublin it was usually a foot patrol, especially in the centre-city area. In the rest of the country, foot patrols were carried out only in towns and small villages. The rural countryside was patrolled on bicycle. The distance varied, but most guards cycled a total of 12–18 miles per day on patrol.[24] This was continually interrupted by visits of a social or professional nature to houses along the route. John Hartigan, a young guard stationed in County Tipperary in 1928, wrote in his personal diary:

> On duty . . . called to friends house, had game of cards, called to another house, conversed at length . . . on return patrolled the village.[25]

In the 1920s, the rough country roads took their toll on bicycles, and frequently this young guard ended up walking miles back to his station. He had to do night duty for a number of weeks in an attempt to catch a suspected arsonist, and wrote: 'Was completely wet as a result of heavy rain all night'.[26] One day, while patrolling the village, he noticed that the chief superintendent was on an inspection, so he delayed his return until it was almost over. He frequented his friend's house during duty and even managed to meet his girlfriend occasionally for a very short time. He regularly met a tout in order to procure information. The following is representative of the majority of entries in his diary:

> On duty in the village . . . entered several houses . . . met and conversed with some people, made discreet enquiries, nothing of any importance occurred.[27]

When a fairly serious larceny occurred, it dominated his work for a number of weeks. While guards frequently socialised when officially on duty, they were also engaged in detective work when officially off duty. In January 1928, Garda John Hartigan was off duty and returning from his own family home at 2.30 a.m. when he saw a suspicious car. He made extensive enquiries and eventually found an innocent explanation. He got to bed at 6.30 a.m.

Patrols of the imagination took place on occasion.[28] Graphic accounts of the journey were described in the patrol book without the member actually going anywhere.

Guards on barrack orderly duty were not engaged in clerical work all of the time. They frequently played cards, read the newspaper, talked to the sergeant's family or listened to the radio from the kitchen of the married quarters.[29] In the 1922–52 period the actual amount of work to be done was frequently insufficient to occupy a guard's time totally during his long daily hours of duty. Thus, the line between leisure and duty frequently became blurred. This was accentuated by the nature of police work, which demanded that a guard meet, converse with and discretely elicit information from the general public. Young Garda John Hartigan used almost verbatim accounts in his diary to describe both his hours of duty and an evening spent with 'the lads' while on a few days' leave: 'Had a conversation regarding things in general, nothing of any importance occurred'.[30] John Hartigan 'the lad' and John Hartigan the guard were indistinguishable.

9

LIFE OUTSIDE BARRACKS

In the period 1922–52 the life of a guard when off duty was closely connected with his professional life as a member of the Garda Síochána. With the encouragement of Commissioner O'Duffy a great many of the force actively participated in sports in the 1920s. The vast majority of guards got married during the 1930s. Marriage impinged on a guard's professional life as it usually involved an immediate transfer. The social life or entertainment enjoyed by a garda was influenced by the fact that he had to maintain certain standards as an upholder of the law. It was a guard's job that in large part defined his status in the local community. This chapter looks at aspects of garda life under the headings of sport, marriage, entertainment and status.

SPORT

In the early years of the state's existence there were almost 7,000 young men in the Garda Síochána, most of them in their early twenties. A high proportion of them were actively involved in sports. Eoin O'Duffy was very enthusiastic about participation by the guards in Gaelic sports. He stated that the new force would not play either rugby or soccer.[1] From the earliest days at the RDS in 1922, internal sporting events were arranged, as well as events in which the guards competed with the general public. The first annual garda sports were held in Kildare in September 1922. In February 1923, O'Duffy issued a general circular to all stations urging the civic guards to join local hurling, football and athletic clubs. In 1923 the annual Civic Guard sports day was held on 15 August in Croke Park. Special train services from each divisional area were laid on for the occasion. In 1923 a number of members of the force set up Conradh Gaelach an Gharda. Its aim was to promote the Irish language and national pastimes in the Garda Síochána.[2] The depot in Dublin came to dominate sport as hundreds of recruits were being trained there. In 1923–4 hurling, football, boxing, athletics, cycling and handball clubs were formed at the depot. In 1924 the Garda Síochána football team reached the Dublin county final. On 6 July 1924 the annual garda sports were held in Croke Park, the proceeds helping to establish a benevolent fund. Many of the divisions throughout the country organised their own annual sports day, as well as sending participants to Croke Park in July. Croke Park was again the venue for the 1925 annual sports.

In 1925 O'Duffy set up *Coiste Siamsa* (the entertainment committee) to organise sport and recreation in the force, as well as promoting the Irish language. It organised football, hurling, handball, boxing, cycling, gymnastics, athletics including cross-country running, swimming, rowing, tug-o-war, tennis, golf, billiards, chess and card tournaments. The riding hall at the depot was converted into a recreation hall and was used for boxing tournaments. Playing pitches in the Phoenix Park were improved and an existing pavilion was rebuilt. A cinder running track of 130 yards was constructed and a gymnasium was fitted with boxing equipment. Two tennis courts were provided at the depot also, and viewing galleries were added to the ball alleys. Almost 75 per cent of the cost of these facilities was provided by the members themselves through a sports fund.[3] In the divisions some recreation facilities such as ball alleys were provided by the men. In the ten-year period 1922–32 members of the force won an amazing number of sporting titles.[4] In athletics, gardaí won forty-four Irish, six British and fifty-four Irish provincial titles. In Gaelic football they captured two Dublin senior championships and two senior leagues. In hurling they won five Dublin senior championships, two provincial championships, and gardaí representing Dublin won the All-Ireland title in 1927. A number of gardaí were also on All-Ireland winning football and hurling teams representing their native or adopted counties. In handball, members of the Garda Síochána won eleven national senior, six provincial, and fourteen county titles. The garda tug-o-war team won the world championship at Wembley in May 1924. Members of the force also had an extraordinary list of successes in boxing.

In July 1926 Coiste Siamsa organised Aonach an Gharda in Dublin. This was an annual garda sports, which lasted five days. Members from all over the country participated in sporting, Irish language and dancing competitions. By the end of 1927 almost every garda division in the country had a sports organisation promoting sporting activity among the force. By 1929, major garda athletic meetings were held annually at seventeen different venues in various parts of the country. The garda band frequently travelled from the depot to play at these meetings, which were a very important local social event. Many members of the Garda Síochána were involved in sport in the locality in which they worked, either participating in or promoting it. The following extracts from the history of a hurling club in Clonmel, County Tipperary, illustrate this point:

> The influence of Clonmel gardaí on St Mary's hurling club and on all GAA clubs in the town in the 1930s was immense. . . . In Clonmel, the garda sports, which was held in the showgrounds in August 1929, attracted 12,000 spectators. . . . The garda gymnasium . . . was always at the disposal of St Mary's.[5]

In terms of success in provincial, national and international competitions, pride of place among garda sport went to boxing. Major William R. E. Murphy, a keen sportsman, helped to establish the garda boxing club in 1924, when he was commissioner of the DMP. From the late 1920s he was president of the Irish Amateur Boxing Association. In 1924 Tommy Maloney, a former British army boxer of only 5 feet 2", was employed as boxing instructor at the depot. His pay was borne by the garda sports fund. Interest and success in boxing among the members of the force grew rapidly. Gardaí competing as individuals began to dominate local, provincial and national competitions. Garda boxers formed the backbone of many Irish international boxing teams. A garda boxing team was formed at the depot and garda boxers began to travel quite frequently to Britain and mainland Europe for competitions. The annual Aonach assumed an international flavour, with police boxing teams from England, Scotland and France attending.

While O'Duffy defended the amateur status of his boxers, in reality they were at least semi-professional. Dick Hearns had qualified as a physical training instructor with the National army, which he left in 1925. He became interested in boxing and entered a number of contests near his native Ballina. In 1929 he applied for the guards but got no reply. O'Duffy heard of his boxing prowess and he was called, although recruitment had practically closed. He was not particularly keen on boxing, but the garda authorities felt very strongly that he should continue with it.[6] Any boxer showing promise was left in the depot and usually did sentry duty. In reality, boxers did considerably less garda duty than ordinary members of the force. This small group of approximately ten garda boxers usually trained six days a week for a number of hours per day. To circumvent the ban on cash prizes for amateur sportsmen, victorious garda boxers sometimes received vouchers that could be cashed in a city store.[7]

Garda boxers fought in Northern Ireland, sometimes against the RUC, all over England and in Scotland, Italy, Poland, Germany, Norway, France and Chicago. By 1932, garda boxers had won thirteen international team contests, two European police titles, fifteen national contests and two Amateur Boxing Association championships. They also dominated local and provincial contests. The more prominent garda boxers at this time included Jack Chase, Matt Flanagan, Jack Driscol, Willie Blackwell, Frank Cooper, Jack Forde, Jim Murphy, Paddy Hanly, Jim Branigan and Gerry Mulligan.[8] Dick Hearns' boxing career spanned eleven years (1928–39). In that time he was Irish national champion five times, British Open ABA champion, and European police champion for six consecutive years. In 1939 he became boxing and drill instructor at the depot, a post he held until his retirement from the force in 1964.

Garda footballers and boxers continued to notch up impressive achievements up to the mid-1930s. In fact, the depot football team was the victim of its own success. Having totally dominated the Dublin championship in the 1927–35 period, it was felt that the team was too strong for the opposition, and so it disbanded.[9] However, from about 1935 onwards there was a gradual but inexorable decline in active participation by gardaí in sports. O'Duffy, who viewed sport as 'the pulse of the nation', was sacked as commissioner in 1933.[10] The new commissioner, Broy, was not as enthusiastic about sport as his predecessor had been. The new Fianna Fáil government began to give priority to reviving the Irish language among the force, which somewhat eclipsed sporting activities.[11] In 1939 Aonach an Gharda was abandoned through lack of entries. However, the fundamental cause for a decline in sporting activity was the age structure of the force. By the mid to late 1930s, most of the men were approaching middle age and were married. Consequently, they were less capable of indulging in active sports and were less free to do so. During the late 1930s and for most of the early 1940s, sport of the type that had been central to many a young guard's life in the 1920s was almost moribund. Golf did grow in popularity, however, at this time.

In May 1945, *Brugh an Gharda*, a new social and sports club, was opened at the recently established garda boat club premises in Islandbridge. The influx of new recruits in the mid-1940s witnessed a partial renaissance of sport in the force. The garda football team won the 1948 County Dublin senior championship and was beaten in the replayed final in 1949. In the late 1940s the *Garda Review* recalled the golden era of sport of the late 1920s and early 1930s for its younger members. However, it was impossible to repeat such outstanding achievements. The existence of almost 7,000 single, healthy young men in the force at one time, coupled with an extremely energetic commissioner who was very committed to the idea of sport, ensured a very fruitful but unique union.

MARRIAGE

In the 1920s most guards were single, young men. In 1923 O'Duffy had complained while inspecting a station party in Greystones, Co. Wicklow that guards in uniform were gossiping with ladies in the main street.[12] The Garda Síochána had very strict regulations governing marriage.[13] All members had to get permission from the commissioner to marry. No member could marry a woman if there was any doubt as to her 'moral' character. The sergeant of the district where the woman resided had to send a detailed confidential report to the commissioner concerning her suitability. Guards had to have at least five years' service before being granted permission to marry, unless over thirty years of age, when three years sufficed. If required, a member seeking permission to get married had to prove that he had at least £60 at his disposal. By 1928 almost 25 per cent of the force was married. In practice, most guards who had not the required five years of service but sought permission to marry were allowed to do so. However, they had to sign an undertaking to forego the married rent allowance until they had completed the minimum service requirement. This situation persisted until the late 1940s.[14] The compulsory furnishing of a confidential report on the character of a woman whom a member wished to marry was abandoned in the early 1930s. By 1950 all members of the force were still required to obtain the commissioner's permission before marrying.

A married member of the force could not serve within 50 miles of his wife's native place. In practice, this usually meant that the new bride of a guard found herself living in rented accommodation miles away from friends, relatives and family. By 1930 the situation had improved, in that a married guard was now only prohibited from serving in his wife's native county. By 1950 a member was not allowed to be stationed in any area that lay within 30 miles of any place where he or his wife had relatives permanently residing.[15] In the 1920s if a member's wife worked outside the home, her husband was stationed a minimum of 50 miles from her place of work, which rule would necessitate the separation of guards from their families. By 1928 there were only fifty-five 'working wives' among the 1,800 married members of the force. Many of these were primary-school teachers. There was little ambiguity in O'Duffy's mind as to where the guard's wife should spend her time. He stated that there was

> no necessity among the non-commissioned ranks for the salaried wife . . . the member can terminate the unnatural separation from his wife by the simple expedient of foregoing her salary and bringing her to his home, where she belongs.[16]

The number of guards' wives who worked outside the home remained small throughout the 1930s and 1940s. For the minority of families who did decide to continue with the two incomes, family life was severely disrupted. The guard usually lived in the barracks or in rented accommodation. He travelled 30 or more miles, usually by bicycle, to visit his family on his one or two days off per month. He occasionally travelled to see them on a Sunday as he had a half day. Much of his free time was spent in travelling.[17] During the summer he would spend his month's holidays with his family. If a guard's wife owned a shop or, more importantly, a public house, the guard was inevitably stationed well away from that locality. By 1950 the situation had not changed substantially.

During the 1920s most of the force lived in barracks, sleeping in the dormitory and eating their meals in the kitchen. The position of messman rotated among the station party. He was responsible for purchasing the food. Most stations employed a barrack servant, usually a woman of mature years. Her pay and the cost of the food were borne by the men themselves. Some of these barrack servants treated the young guards like their own family, fussing and worrying about them. Others were continually scolding the men, giving rise to humorous stories about them in the *Garda Review*. All this changed when the members of the force got married and moved out. The barrack servant frequently found herself redundant.

By 1930, one-third of the force was married. By 1933 this had reached half. By 1944 over 80 per cent of the men were married.[18] Marriage added considerably to the financial responsibility of members of the force. Many married members found it difficult to provide adequately for their families in the 1930s, and especially during the rampant inflation period of the Emergency.[19] A great number of sergeants and guards eased their financial situation by growing their own vegetables. Most sergeants who lived in married quarters that had a garden grew sufficient vegetables to provide for their own families.[20]

Guards living in rented accommodation frequently grew vegetables if there was a garden attached; if not, they usually leased a plot. Many Dublin-based guards cultivated their own gardens or rented plots. The Board of Works actually leased plots in the grounds of the Royal Hospital, Kilmainham.[21]

Many guards and sergeants saved their own turf. This fairly common practice became much more widespread during the 1939–45 period, because of the difficulty in getting imported fuels. Saving turf was not confined to rural guards, with many Dublin members taking turf banks each year on Glencree Bog outside the city. Some even brought a wheelbarrow, in pieces, on their bicycles, to the mountain.[22] It was taken for granted that the guard spent much of his free time in the garden or on the bog. Occasionally, the lure of the bog or garden, especially during a break in inclement weather, was too great for some guards who were supposed to be on duty. John McGahern captures the atmosphere very well in his novel, *The Barracks:*

> He [the sergeant] was too tired at his turf banks as well as doing the police work . . . he didn't return, he must have risked staying the day on the bog . . . loose clay on the policeman's boots . . . night and morning he had the radio on long before news time to get the weather forecast and he watched the skies always.[23]

The life of a guard's family was greatly influenced by his occupation. Transfer, an integral part of a member's life, meant moving house, uprooting children from school and friends, and moving to a new locality. The daily routine of the family was also affected by the unsociable working hours, including Sunday and station orderly duty. In addition, the behaviour of a guard's wife and family was expected to be above reproach, an expectation shared by the garda authorities and the local community in which the family lived.

ENTERTAINMENT

In the 1920s Eoin O'Duffy revelled in pomp and ceremony and greatly enjoyed a gala occasion. In his capacity as commissioner, he attended the 1923 international police conference in New York. There he met Colonel Walter Scott, the honorary commissioner of the New York city police. A very wealthy, public-spirited gentleman, Scott was impressed with the newly established Irish police. He presented O'Duffy with a 1,000-dollar gold bond. The interest on this was to finance an annual gold medal for a member of the Garda Síochána. O'Duffy decided that the award should be for outstanding valour.[24] In 1925, Scott gave $500 for an annual silver and bronze medal. As a result of the 1929 Wall Street crash, however, Scott's gift was not sufficient even to meet the cost of the medals. After some hesitation, the representative bodies agreed to pay for them. In 1947 the awarding of these medals for bravery was discontinued. Instead, certificates for bravery were awarded to deserving members of the force. From 1923 to 1947, sixty-one members of the Garda Síochána, mostly of garda rank, received Scott medals. The majority of these awards were for members showing outstanding courage when facing armed men.[25]

In 1924, Colonel Scott travelled to Ireland to present the first medal to Garda James Mulroy in the depot on 18 August. O'Duffy ensured that the occasion was a memorable one. Over 4,000 people attended, including the President of the Executive Council, W. T. Cosgrave, and hundreds of recruits who were being trained in the depot at the time. From 1926 until 1932 the awarding of the Scott medals formed the centrepiece of the annual Aonach. The week's sporting, cultural and social events began with the commissioner's garden party at the depot, during which the Scott medal ceremony took place. About 200–300 attended this party, including the Governor General, the President of the Executive Council, most of the cabinet, and many of the judiciary, members of the Oireachtas, most of the diplomatic corps, army chiefs, senior civil servants, eminent physicians, consultants, educationalists, journalists, lawyers, famous athletes — in fact, it was a Who's Who of Irish society.[26] The party was a very glamorous occasion, with dress suits being worn by the men, and their spouses arrayed in the height of fashion.[27] Numerous bands attended, including the garda band, all adding colour and atmosphere to the occasion.

The garden party was O'Duffy's annual showpiece of the force. The accession of De Valera to power in 1932 totally changed this. The highlight of Aonach an Gharda was no longer the elaborate garden party, which all but disappeared. Instead, the Gaelic aspect of the week's activities was emphasised. The Scott medal presentation now took place in the recreation hall rather than on the main square. The garden party became a thing of the past. Garda headquarters ceased to be the scene for one of society's great annual social events.

In the early months of the Civic Guard in 1922, Commissioner Staines had appointed a civilian, Daniel J. Delaney, as director of music. He began a programme of intensive training for members of a garda band, which was based at the depot. In 1923 the band played at forty-three engagements. It charged a fee per engagement, refundable if it was for charity. It also gave a dozen free recitals in the Phoenix Park. A great deal of both duty and recreation time of the members of the band

Top Left: Michael Staines in full volunteer dress. Staines was the first Garda Commissioner. He resigned from office in August 1922 following the Kildare Mutiny.

Top Right: Michael Staines in Civvies.

Bottom Left: Kevin O'Shiel in later life. O'Shiel was chairman of the Kildare Mutiny Enquiry

Commissioner Eoin O'Duffy addressing recruits in the Garda Depot, Phoenix Park.
O'Duffy replaced Michael Staines and served as Garda Commissioner until 1933
when he was dismissed by De Valera.

Commissioner Eamon Broy (left) and Justice Minister P. J. Ruttledge at a ceremony at the
Garda Depot c. 1935. Unlike his predecessors, Broy had been a policeman for almost twenty
years before becoming Commissioner, a post he held from 1935 to 1938.

W. T. Cosgrave who was president of the executive council of the Irish Free State from 1922 to 1932.

Eamon de Valera and detective garda, Sandymount, Co. Dublin. On the arrival to power of Fianna Fáil in 1932, De Valera was faced with a Commissioner and most of his senior officers who had belonged to the other side of the Treaty divide in 1922.

Michael Kinnane who served as Garda Commissioner from 1938 until his death in 1952.

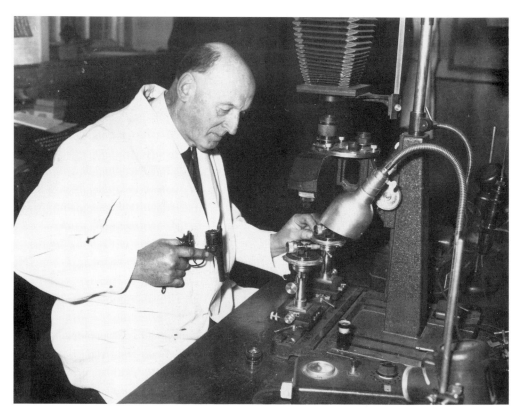

Detective Superintendent Don Stapleton, Ballistics, Technical Bureau, 1950s.

Group at Headquarters, 1954.

Front: Ch sup F. Burke; Surgeon V.C. Ellis; Ass comm P.J. Carroll; Dep comm W.R. E. Murphy; Mr Gerald Boland, Minister for Justice; Comm D. Costigan; Mr Justice Thomas Teevan; Dep comm G. Brennan; Ass comm T. Woods; Ch sup H. Duffy. **Middle:** Ch sups R. Downey; J.N. Gilroy; W. Mooney; J. Dowd; G. Butler; J. Neill; R. F. Creagh; J.J. Kelleher; A. O'Neill; H. O'Meara; P. Cronin. **Back:** D. Connolly; T. Collins; F. O'Driscoll; P. Doyle; T.J. McCarthy; T. Direen; E.A. Reynolds; J.A. O'Shea; W.P. Quinn; G.A. Flynn; P. Carroll; M.A.J. O'Reilly.

Garda Andrew Smith, Dublin Metropolitan District, on point duty at College Green in 1950.

Top: Harry Phelan, the first guard to be murdered, had gone into a shop in Mullinahone, County Tipperary, when he was set upon and shot dead.
Right: Gardaí continue to risk their lives in the course of their duties. In June 1996 Det. Garda Jerry McCabe was shot dead in Adare, County Limerick, during an IRA attempted robbery.

Garda Joy Treacey (**left**) and Garda Alice Kennedy. In 1959 women (banghardaí) were recruited for the first time. By 1996, seven per cent of the force were women. The term Bangharda was officially dropped in 1991.

was devoted to band duties. Delaney continued as musical director and in 1926 was given the rank of superintendent. In the same year, the garda band broadcast a recital on the new radio station, 2RN. Following the success of this, a broadcasting studio was set up in the depot, which facilitated band recitals being broadcast on radio. The band also moved around the country attending engagements. The DMP had a band of its own, which had been established in 1873. In 1926 the committees of the DMP and garda band were amalgamated. They pooled their funds but remained as distinct bands. Individual band members were given a small annual sum from the receipts received for engagements.[28]

During the 1920s, members of the Dublin metropolitan division organised garda dances to raise funds for various charities around the city. From the early 1930s, Garda Síochána annual dances were held in each division and the proceeds donated to charity. These were expensive formal-dress affairs, usually with supper served, and numerous photographs of such gatherings appeared in the *Garda Review*. As the 1930s progressed, a growing number of divisional and district forces co-operated with the representative bodies to raise funds for garda charities such as the benevolent fund. This involved organising dances, whist drives and sporting events. This social aspect of Garda Síochána life showed a marked decline in the late 1930s because recruitment ceased and the vast majority of members of the force were approaching middle age.[29] Organised social events received a bit of a fillip in the 1940s, with the establishment of a 'Garda Boys' Club' and a committee to co-ordinate garda social functions in the Dublin area.

Garda-organised social events were only occasional occurrences and did not constitute a full social life. In the 1920s most of the guards were single, energetic young men who took part in the same leisure activities as their peers who were not in the force. While having a few drinks with friends in the local pub was not encouraged by the authorities, it was not prohibited.[30] Guards, in common with other young men, also went to the local pictures, attended dances, visited friends, met girlfriends and went for walks. During the 1920s and early 1930s when many of the guards lived in barracks, young men from the local area frequently spent evenings there playing cards, draughts and rings. In some instances the garda barracks served almost as a local club or meeting place at night time.[31]

Marriage and its consequent financial responsibilities meant that there was less money and less time for socialising in the 1930s. In some Dublin stations a wet canteen continued to exist right up to the late 1930s. However, the majority of the men in the force socialised with members of their local community. They went to the local pub and mixed with the clientèle — as long as it included no lawbreakers.[32] The garda authorities were always particularly vigilant in trying to ensure that a member's drinking habits did not compromise his position as a law enforcement officer. A guard who drank while on duty, was known to drink after closing hours, drank to excess, or was in debt to a publican was regarded as a serious liability to the force.

STATUS IN COMMUNITY

In the Ireland of the first half of the twentieth century, knowledge of people's family background helped to ascertain their status. A guard, however, was stationed well away from his native place and consequently could not be categorised so easily. It was his occupation that gave him his status in the community. Set apart by his uniform, his formal training and his pensionable, secure job, he occupied a position of considerable importance in the local community at a time when an individual's dealings with the state apparatus usually necessitated a visit to the local barracks. Above all, he had authority — he was the law, and as such was generally respected and looked up to by members of the community.[33] In small towns and rural areas the local doctor and solicitor, the priest and the better-off businessmen constituted the social élite. While the guard was not accorded the same social standing as these, he was viewed as belonging to the lower echelons of this group.[34] Very many of the force secured a secondary education for their children at a time when only a minority of the population, mostly the middle class, got the opportunity. Most were unable to afford boarding school but obtained a transfer either to a town with a secondary school, or near enough to one so that the children could cycle or take the bus.[35]

Society's expectations of the standard of living of a garda were frequently greater than his means permitted. Consequently, there was sometimes tension between social expectations and financial reality. As one TD, the son of a garda, remarked:

> The local guard suffered the contradiction of having a high standing in the local community but . . . poor remuneration.[36]

By 1952 the vast majority of the members of the Garda Síochána were approaching retirement age. However, from the mid to late 1940s over 1,000 new recruits had joined the guards. These young men lived together in the stations, were active in sports and willing to travel long distances to a good dance. As the 1920s men neared retirement, the 1940s recruits were only setting out on their careers. The Garda Síochána was coming of age, and a new generation was about to take over.

10

GAELIC AND CATHOLIC

GAELIC

When the Irish Free State was set up in 1922 approximately 10 per cent of the population used Irish as their everyday language.[1] Most of these people lived in Gaeltacht regions on or near the western seaboard. A large majority of the people in the country had little or no knowledge of Irish. Fewer than half of the state's primary teachers were competent to teach the language.[2] It was the schools, however, which were to become the focal point of the language revival campaign. Both the legislators and the revival pressure groups believed that compulsion rather than voluntary effort was the only way to ensure that the schools produced Irish-speaking pupils. From 1922, Irish was to be taught in primary schools for at least one hour each day where there were teachers competent to teach it. In 1924 the programme for secondary schools stressed the Gaelic element of the curriculum. From the school year 1927–8, Irish became a necessary subject for the Intermediate Certificate.[3] It is against this background that the efforts of government and various garda commissioners to revive the language among the force, must be viewed.

Commissioner O'Duffy, 1922–33

The 5,500 recruits attested to the Garda Síochána in the years 1922–4 did not sit an examination in Irish as part of their entry procedure. In 1923,

O'Duffy decided to reserve 500 places for Irish-speaking recruits. A fairly extensive recruiting campaign in the Gaeltacht area met with little success, however. Some applicants were physically unsuitable and others, while fluent Irish speakers, were unable to read or write the language. Irish was included as a compulsory examination subject for admission to the cadets in 1923. Elementary Irish accounted for 10 per cent of the total marks of the efficiency tests conducted by O'Duffy in 1924 for guards who had originally been admitted without an adequate written examination. From 1924, Irish was included as an optional examination subject for anyone wishing to join the guards. By the late 1920s, Irish was still not compulsory for admission to the force. However, marks received in the Irish examination, which involved simple conversation and translation, were added to a candidate's overall marks, thus enhancing his performance.

In the five-year period 1923–8 (after which recruitment was virtually suspended) there was positive discrimination towards Irish speakers wishing to join the Garda Síochána. Irish was introduced as part of the entrance examination, mainly to facilitate the recruitment of native speakers. The vast majority of those recruited from Gaeltacht areas, while physically of good health, were educationally very weak.[4] The civil service commissioners rarely failed an Irish-speaking candidate in the entrance examination, leaving it to the discretion of the commissioner whether to accept or reject such an applicant. In 1928, O'Duffy stated: 'There are hundreds of men in the guards today who would not have the remotest chance of admission were it not for their knowledge of Irish.'[5] Preferential treatment continued to be given to native Irish speakers throughout the early and mid-1930s.

During 1922 most recruits received no instruction in the Irish language during training. In 1923 instruction in Irish for at least one hour per day became a regular feature in a recruit's training. By 1924, five native Irish-speaking members of the force, with previous teaching experience, were employed full time in teaching Irish in the depot. For the remainder of the 1920s Irish remained central in a recruit's training, with two hours of class each day and an examination at the completion of training.

From 1923 to 1932 over 4,000 men turned up at the depot in Dublin to join the guards. Table 10.1 shows their knowledge of Irish at the time of recruitment.

The overwhelming majority of men who joined the Garda Síochána in the 1920s had received only a primary education, many not even completing it. The majority of recruits had no knowledge of Irish. Even those who did receive instruction in the language while in training could hardly hope to be proficient after three or four months. However, there was general goodwill towards Irish among the gardaí in the 1920s.[6] Many who had had no previous opportunity to learn the language were now keen to rectify this deficiency.

Table 10.1: Knowledge of Irish (self-assessed) of Recruits at Admission, 1923–32[7]

	%
No knowledge of Irish	68
Possessed 'a little' Irish	12
Possessed 'better than a little' Irish, fair or good at the language, small number of fáinne holders[8]	15
Native speakers	5
Total	100

Source: Temporary register.

An Irish-language enthusiast, Commissioner Eoin O'Duffy made a very concerted effort to ensure that the Garda Síochána became competent in Irish. The immediate aim was to ensure an adequate number of Irish-speaking gardaí for the Gaeltacht areas. The longer-term plan was to make the entire force competent in the language. O'Duffy saw the gardaí as being in the vanguard of the movement for restoration. In 1923 the force produced its first periodical. Although it was written mainly in English, its Irish language title, *Iris an Gharda* (Garda Magazine) and articles in Irish reflected the enthusiasm of the time for the language. In November 1923, representatives from eleven garda divisions met in the depot and formed Conradh Gaelach an Gharda, with the aim of promoting the Irish language, dancing and debating. *Iris an Gharda* was replaced in 1924 by *Guth an Gharda* (Garda Voice), which continued to encourage the men to study the language. In 1925 it, in turn, was replaced with the *Garda Review*, which actively encouraged and promoted the language with at least two or three articles each month in Irish. It also had a section helping the student to learn the language, complete with exercises and questions on grammar.

By 1924, 4 per cent of the members of the force were either native speakers or holders of the fáinne, 44 per cent stated that they had a fair knowledge of the language and 45 per cent said that they were learning it. Only 7 per cent stated that they were neither competent nor making any effort to become so.[9] Officers accounted for a disproportionately large number of fluent speakers. By 1925, Irish was spoken 'wholly, chiefly or to an appreciable extent' by the general public in almost 10 per cent of the country's total garda sub-districts.[10] These lay mainly along the Atlantic seaboard from Donegal to Kerry, as well as in West Cork and in Waterford. Most of these areas had guards who were either fluent Irish speakers or had a good knowledge of the language. Even in these Irish-speaking districts where daily garda work was conducted through the medium of Irish, official correspondence continued to be carried out through English. O'Duffy had, and was still having, administrative problems, however, in ensuring that the Gaeltacht areas were adequately supplied with fluent Irish-speaking gardaí. In 1924 a major controversy erupted when hospital workers on a picket line at Letterkenny mental hospital insisted on giving their names in Irish to the gardaí. They were brought for a short time to the local station. Letters to the press expressed outrage. The matter was raised in the Dáil.[11] Some of the best officers and men were fluent Irish speakers but O'Duffy needed them in areas other than 'backward Irish-speaking districts'.[12] The lack of amenities and the remoteness of many Gaeltacht stations were a positive disincentive. In 1926 a government-established commission on the Gaeltacht (Coimisiún na Gaeltachta) recommended that members who could perform their duties entirely through Irish should receive extra pay.[13] The government did not agree.

In the 1920s, station parties usually made their own arrangements to study Irish. Some employed Irish teachers whom they paid for themselves. Others studied on their own or attended Gaelic League classes. In some stations the sergeant conducted classes for the men. While the attempts to master the language varied, there is no doubt but that many members of the force made a very considerable effort to acquire competency in Irish. The Garda headquarters and training depot in the Phoenix Park was to the fore in the Irish language revival. From early 1922 it had established a very active branch of the Gaelic League. Coiste Siamsa organised the five-day Aonach an Gharda from 1926 onwards. One day of this annual event was devoted to Aeridheacht, a festival of Irish culture with debating and drama in Irish, as well as céilí dancing, singing and music. Although most of the officers at headquarters were competent Irish speakers, the majority of civil servants who worked there had little or no Irish. The language was rarely used for official purposes.

From 1923, Irish became a prerequisite for all promotion. In June of that year, all sergeants and inspectors who had been appointed in 1922 were compelled to sit an efficiency test in which Irish was an essential component. For the remainder of the 1920s many members wishing to be promoted went to considerable trouble to improve their level of Irish. Sergeant William J. McConville travelled from Navan to Dundalk to attend an Irish course, one night per week, over a period of two winters, in preparation for the examination for inspector.[14] In general, those seeking promotion attained a competency in Irish, which ensured that the language did not impede their progress.

For the first six years or so of the force's existence, O'Duffy appears to have believed that the members would become bilingual, mainly through their own efforts. By 1928, however, progress had been slower than expected. While the force was still generally well disposed towards Irish, the demands of duty, irregular hours, a shortage of proficient Irish teachers and long, bright summer evenings made it somewhat difficult to master the language. Of much greater significance, however, was the fact that individuals soon realised that fluency in the language frequently meant being posted to a remote Gaeltacht area with little chance of serving outside that region in the future. One member, writing to the editor of the *Garda Review*, described his station in Connemara as being very remote:

> The áras [station] is four miles from the nearest church, eight miles from the nearest railway station, twenty miles from the nearest doctor, nineteen miles from the nearest District Court, thirty three miles from the nearest District H.Q. . . . thirty six miles from the nearest Divisional H.Q. 99% of the people speak no English at all. There is no field for hurling or football.[15]

By 1928, O'Duffy assumed that with all primary-school children learning Irish, every member of the force would of necessity have to be bilingual in five to ten years. In 1929 he proposed to the government the introduction of two schemes by which the force would become bilingual within seven years.[16] The first, called the Gaeltacht scheme, was designed for those who had some knowledge of Irish. O'Duffy believed that Gaeltacht areas, which tended to be remote, were unlikely to lose the language quickly. He proposed to move out a number of Irish-speaking members from those areas to stations throughout the country where they could help others to acquire competency. Non-fluent members serving in the Gaeltacht area would have a great incentive to become fluent, as this would almost automatically mean a transfer out of the Gaeltacht. All unmarried non-fluent members of the force would have to go to the Gaeltacht for a few months. Married members were to have this option. O'Duffy also proposed that examinations would be held at regular intervals to see whether members had practical fluent Irish. Officers were expected to furnish periodic reports on the progress of the men.

O'Duffy also proposed the Linguaphone gramophone course for those members who had little or no Irish. Each barracks was to have a Linguaphone instrument and Irish language records. Each guard was to have his own Linguaphone textbook and the station members were to spend one hour per day together studying Irish. They were also individually to devote one full day per week (a barrack orderly day) to Irish. The Linguaphone scheme, which concentrated on everyday conversation, was a two-year course. O'Duffy hoped that this scheme, coupled with the arrival of fluent Irish speakers from the Gaeltacht to stations throughout the country, would enable those members with little or no Irish to become fairly competent after two or three years. At this stage they would go to a Gaeltacht station for a few months to become fluent. To supplement both the Gaeltacht and the Linguaphone schemes, O'Duffy proposed running special courses in Irish for 600 men at the depot. These men were then to be allocated to stations throughout the country.

In 1930 the Executive Council agreed to the scheme, which came into operation shortly afterwards. There does not appear to have been any major opposition to it. Almost every member of the force contributed the equivalent of one day's pay towards funding the scheme, and the remainder was funded by the government. On numerous occasions O'Duffy praised the men for their voluntary contribution. In reality, they felt pressurised into contributing. Failure to do so was looked upon very unfavourably by the authorities — some members felt that they could even face an unwanted transfer if they did not pay up.[17] O'Duffy's attitude towards his men learning the language in the early 1920s was one of exhortation and praise. By 1930 this had generally changed to one of compulsion and threat. In that year he warned that any member who was not fluent in the language by December 1938 would be dismissed.[18] Competency in the language was to be ascertained by performance in a written and oral examination called the Irish proficiency test.

As the plan for Irish was implemented, some individuals were certainly annoyed with being compelled to pay for it, forced to study it, and threatened with dismissal if they failed to master it. The enthusiasm and idealism of early youth began to wane somewhat as the early 1930s progressed. The addition of extra non-police duties almost every year left many of the men with less time and in a less receptive mood for learning the language. Furthermore, most of the men were getting married at this time and this new added responsibility, coupled with living out of barracks, did not help attempts to master Irish. Notwithstanding all of this, the early 1930s witnessed the most active and concerted effort by the force to learn the language. O'Duffy's seven-year plan for making the entire force bilingual had reached its halfway mark by 1933 when he was dismissed by De Valera.

Commissioner Broy, 1933–8

De Valera, his Fianna Fáil government and the new garda commissioner, Eamon Broy, appear to have been even more committed to reviving the Irish language than the Cumann na nGaedheal government and O'Duffy had been. Under the new government, the Aeridheacht element of the annual Aonach week took prominence, with De Valera himself on occasion officially opening the event. Approximately 7 per cent of the 400 men recruited in the 1933–4 period were native speakers, with a further 23 per cent possessing a fair knowledge of the language. The remainder had little or no Irish. In 1934 the Galway-west division was designated an all-Irish division. Only officers and men capable of performing all of their duties entirely through Irish were stationed there. Other Gaeltacht areas also demanded similar treatment. De Valera, on a visit to Letterkenny, was handed a letter from a deputation of Fianna Fáil cumainn. It stated (in translation):

> The guards without Irish and the people without English . . . we know that the Gaeltacht is only a dumping ground for the most inefficient grade of the guards.[19]

In 1935, three all-Irish districts were established in the Donegal division and another two were established in the Kerry division. Broy insisted that Irish become the sole medium of communication in these Irish-speaking districts. All correspondence, including official correspondence with Dublin headquarters, was now to be through Irish. To meet the demands of policing the new all-Irish division and districts, 105 of the 170 recruits attested in 1935 were native Irish speakers. The entry requirements were relaxed to allow some of these men to join the force. Their training was conducted entirely through the medium of Irish, which posed practical problems as not all of the depot's instructors were competent Irish speakers and most of the textbooks were available only in English. Consequently, these recruits received a less than comprehensive training. In 1937, Irish was made a compulsory subject for entry to the Garda Síochána.

In 1935, gardaí stationed in the Galway-west Irish division had great difficulty persuading insurance companies to accept correspondence in the Irish language. In December 1935, Broy ordered every member in all-Irish-speaking garda districts to give evidence exclusively in Irish to the courts.[20] There was much controversy, however, when the presiding judge in a Kerry larceny case was unable to read the garda depositions which were in Irish, and so had to adjourn the case.[21] A sergeant from an all-Irish-speaking Kerry district was called as a witness for the prosecution in a case in Limerick. He insisted on giving his evidence in Irish, and as there was no interpreter available, the proceedings were delayed. The attorney general's office instructed that the sergeant in the circumstances should have given his evidence in English. It cited the Supreme Court decision of 22 March 1934, which in effect stated that while accepting the primacy of the Irish language in general, it must never be allowed to impair the operation of justice.[22] In the wake of the controversial court cases in Limerick and Kerry, the secretary to the Minister for Justice wrote to Commissioner Broy in 1936, outlining the minister's views on Irish in the force:

> It is desirable to recognise that the gardaí are considerably in advance of the general public regarding the Irish language, and the minister is reluctant to assent to the expenditure of public money towards widening the gap between gardaí and the general public.[23]

Irish speakers were inevitably sent to the Gaeltacht and left there for a long time in remote areas with few social amenities. The language was seen as a hindrance, and gardaí frequently refrained from using it or acknowledging that they were fluent.[24] In order to transform this attitude towards the language Broy persuaded the government in 1934 to pay an additional 7.5 per cent non-pensionable allowance to gardaí while serving in all-Irish districts. In the same year the commissioner announced an incentive to encourage members to pass the Irish proficiency test, whereby they would receive £5 if successful before 1936. From the early to mid-1930s the Linguaphone course of instruction continued to be the main element in the attempt to make the force bilingual. In 1936 a new shorter *Irish Press* Linguaphone course replaced the old Linguaphone course. Small-scale schemes were also organised to promote Irish in the force. In 1937 the authorities organised a one-month summer course in Irish for gardaí in a County Kerry Gaeltacht. In 1936 a voluntary movement known as Biorán na Gaedhilge was established at the depot. Its aim was to get fluent speakers to help members with a knowledge of Irish to improve sufficiently to acquire the fáinne. These schemes offered incentives to the men in the form of extra holidays if they successfully completed the course.

O'Duffy's plan for the Gaeltacht and Linguaphone schemes to work in tandem to ensure a bilingual force had run into problems even before he was dismissed in 1933. The Linguaphone course was not suited to the general linguistic competence of many of the men. Progress was very slow and the numbers moving into the Gaeltacht were very small. Consequently, the release of great numbers of fluent Irish speakers from the Gaeltacht to be scattered throughout the country did not materialise, and the small stations did not get the fluent speaker who would have instructed them in the language. It was a vicious circle. Broy pressed ahead vigorously with O'Duffy's idea of training selected gardaí to be sent out as Irish teachers to stations all over the country. However, less than one-third of those selected for the course passed the final examination. Practically all of the men who had been specially trained as instructors were diverted to the all-Irish-speaking districts, as were almost all of the 105 native-speaking new recruits. By 1938, after eight years of Linguaphone study, the vast majority of the men were not bilingual. Furthermore, with the exception of the Gaeltacht areas, most stations did not have a fluent Irish speaker. O'Duffy's optimistic forecast in 1929 that the garda stations' map of Ireland would soon be dotted with 800 Gaeltacht pins had not become a reality.[25]

Broy's five years as commissioner (1933–8) were characterised by great efforts to make the force bilingual. His general approach was to encourage and induce the men to learn the language rather than to threaten them. He rarely if ever alluded to the threat of dismissal for members who were not competent Irish speakers by 1938. The 'Routine orders' were issued in bilingual form from March 1936. The creation of an all-Irish-speaking Galway-west division and the Donegal and Kerry districts appears to have been successful. These areas frequently held their own garda Aeridheacht, which were great cultural festivals. The *Garda Review* for its part played a key role in promoting the language, with numerous articles in Irish appearing each month. However, none of this changed the men's perception that fluency in Irish frequently meant banishment to a 'bog station'.

Commissioner Kinnane, 1938–52

Commissioner Kinnane's approach to the promotion of the language within the force was somewhat more low key than that of his immediate predecessor. The Taca members of 1939–40 were the first recruits to undergo a compulsory entrance examination in Irish. This posed no problem as many of them had attended secondary school. They did not receive any instruction in Irish during their short 5–6 weeks of training. Irish accounted for 20 per cent of the total marks in the entrance examination for recruits in the 1940s.[26] Comhdháil Náisiúnta na Gaedhilge (National Council of Irish) was not satisfied, however. It wanted new recruits accepted only if they were proficient in the speaking and writing of Irish.[27] The commissioner disagreed. He was already experiencing difficulty in securing sufficient recruits for the force and felt that if fluency in Irish was now to become a prerequisite for entry, he would get only a fraction of the recruits required.

In 1944 Comhdháil Náisiúnta na Gaedhilge urged the Minister for Justice to use the Irish language as the medium for instructing recruits while in training. It claimed that the depot was 'now as un-Irish as it was in the time of the RIC'.[28] Practically no instructor was capable of giving police instruction through Irish. The commissioner favoured bilingual instruction, and by October each recruit received one hour per day instruction in law and police duties through Irish. This was in addition to his ordinary police duty classes through English. In effect, it was a total duplication of the earlier English class.[29] A big effort was made to get recruits to enter for the fáinne examination. The official aim was to produce bilingual gardaí capable of serving in Gaeltacht or non-Gaeltacht areas. In reality, the new gardaí were far from bilingual. Although half of them had usually a fairly good knowledge of the language upon entering, training did not do much to improve this and was of very little benefit for those who were poor at the language.[30] The rote learning of police duties in Irish did not help the recruit to carry on an ordinary conversation in the language. Furthermore, certain sections of the police duties manual on which the instructor concentrated tended to appear on examination day.[31]

From 1938, Kinnane decided to reserve a third of the places of candidates selected to sit the promotion examination for those members possessing the Irish proficiency certificate. In fact, on several occasions he had to deviate from this as there were insufficient numbers. However, those possessing the Irish proficiency test enhanced their chances of promotion. In 1939, Kinnane had the members of the force graded according to their knowledge of Irish, so as to be in a better position to judge future progress. 'Routine orders' continued to be produced bilingually until late 1939, when war rationing forced retrenchment and only the English version appeared. By 1943 programmes for study were still appearing very regularly in the *Garda Review*, to be followed in conjunction with the Linguaphone scheme. All of this was to help the individual members to pass the proficiency test. In 1947, Kinnane praised the new recruits for their competency in Irish and exhorted them to wear the fáinne on all occasions. Photographs in the press of large groups of garda recruits at fáinne presentations were somewhat deceptive, in that members who were not receiving the fáinne were frequently drafted in to swell the numbers at the ceremony.[32]

Kinnane was less enthusiastic about the language than his predecessor, Broy. He did not initiate new schemes to promote Irish, and in fact allowed many existing ones to lapse. The arrival of the Emergency and its plethora of extra duties left much less time and energy for studying Irish. At this stage, most of the men were married and had young families. All of these factors combined to ensure that the study of Irish within the force went into a fairly rapid decline towards the end of the 1930s. During the 1940s the members were still officially expected to study Irish for a few hours per week, use Linguaphone and complete the *Garda Review* exercise. In reality, little or no study was done, the gramophones collected dust, and inspecting officers who were supposed to check the men's copybooks rarely did so.[33] From the late 1930s and especially during the 1940s, the *Garda Review* was not nearly as zealous as earlier in its advocacy of the Irish language.

By the 1940s, the men, apart from a small dedicated minority, were largely indifferent to the language. While officially maintaining the policy of daily Irish classes, the garda authorities in practice appear to have accepted the reality that there was little chance now of making this force of largely middle-aged men, bilingual. The statistics for proficiency in Irish among the force in March 1946 tell their own story.

Table 10.2: Proficiency in Irish of Garda Síochána (as assessed by civil service commissioners), 31 March 1946[34]

Rank	Total Strength on 31/3/1946	Oral and Written	Oral Only	Written Only
Chief Superintendent	27	4	—	7
Superintendent	134	18	—	26
Inspector	78	9	—	22
Station Sergeant	58	9	—	4
Sergeant	1,257	158	2	164
Garda	5,800	456	20	550
Total	7,354	654	22	773

Source: 'Use of Irish' (NAI).

The examination on which the civil service commissioners based their assessment of proficiency had both a written and an oral section. The written part was very easy and success therein was of little significance.[35] Less than 9 per cent of the members of the Garda Síochána could both speak and write the language after twenty-four years of the force's existence. While Comhdháil Náisiúnta na Gaedhilge was not pleased with the position of Irish within the Garda Síochána in general, it did acknowledge in 1944 that the situation in the Gaeltacht was quite satisfactory. By 1950 there were twenty-one all-Irish-speaking stations in Galway, twenty-two in Donegal and fifteen in Kerry, in which all members were competent in Irish.

Conclusion

A number of factors accounted for the failure of the force to master the Irish language. In the early 1920s, when the men were fairly enthusiastic, the lack of an organised scheme of instruction, coupled with the necessity of becoming familiar with police duties, inhibited mastery of the language. The Linguaphone scheme of the 1930s was found in many instances to be impractical, unless followed in conjunction with the aid of an actual Irish teacher. The marriage of the majority of the force in the 1930s meant that they were no longer living in barracks with the same time and opportunity to study. Commissioner Kinnane, while certainly not opposed to the language, was not as enthusiastic about Irish as his predecessors had been. The perception, frequently substantiated by fact, that fluency in Irish would mean being stationed in a very remote area, lacking in social amenities, persisted right up to the 1950s. This had a detrimental effect on those who had the language using it, and on those who did not have it, attempting to learn it.

The major underlying reason, however, why the guards did not become bilingual was summed up by Commissioner Kinnane in 1944 when he stated: 'The real problem is that the people don't want to use Irish.'[36]

It appears as if the Minister for Justice, P. J. Ruttledge, as early as 1936, had come to the conclusion that there was no sense in making the force bilingual when the rest of the country was not. He believed that henceforth the position of the language in the Garda Síochána would be 'sufficiently maintained by the recruitment of Irish speakers whenever possible and by consolidating the present position in the three Gaeltacht counties'.[37] This is precisely what happened over the next fifteen or twenty years. The position of the language among gardaí in the Gaeltacht areas was consolidated, while attempts to make the entire force bilingual lost impetus. By and large, the objective of providing service in Irish for the Gaeltacht areas had been achieved, but the larger purpose of creating a fully bilingual force had not.

This failure by the Garda Síochána to become bilingual must be seen in the context of the failure of the wider revival effort in post-independence Ireland. Despite much goodwill towards Irish, it was English that remained the working language of government ministers in the Dáil and in Cabinet. Those hoping to join the civil service had to pass an Irish examination, but the daily business of the service was carried on almost entirely through English.[38] The success of the Garda Síochána in providing service in Irish for the Gaeltacht areas was not matched by other areas of the public service, except perhaps by primary teachers. Even their enthusiasm for the language was beginning to wane by 1941 when the Irish National Teachers Organisation issued a report that was highly critical of teaching other subjects through the medium of Irish to children whose home language was English.[39] Despite its best efforts in the 1920s and 1930s, the Garda Síochána could not on its own revive the Irish language.

CATHOLIC

In 1926 almost 93 per cent of the Free State's population was Roman Catholic.[40] The Catholic Church had considerable influence over government legislation, especially in the area of social and moral issues. The decision to deny facilities for divorce in the Irish Free State, which had existed for the wealthy under British rule, and the introduction of film and publication censorship in the 1920s, are just two examples of this influence. There was also a certain triumphalism about being an Irish Catholic at this time.[41] The elaborate celebrations in 1929 marking the centenary of Catholic Emancipation typified this triumphalism. The Eucharistic Congress, which was held in Dublin in 1932, was an even greater celebration of Catholicism, with Cosgrave, De Valera and Sean T. O'Kelly acting as canopy bearers in the main procession. It was inevitable that the Garda Síochána, with over 98.7 per cent Catholic membership, would be strongly influenced by the prevailing ethos of the state.

In January 1923, O'Duffy wanted a full-time chaplain appointed on a temporary basis to the depot while there were large numbers of recruits being trained there. He contacted Archbishop Byrne of Dublin who selected Fr Patrick McAuliffe to reside in the depot. He was to receive £365 a year from public funds. In 1923 the former RIC riding school in the depot was converted into a chapel, most of the cost being borne by the recruits themselves.[42] A weekend retreat was held in 1923, during which strict silence was observed. On Sunday, 1 April 1923, almost 1,500 guards paraded on the main square of the depot at Phoenix Park. In a religious ceremony in front of a massive picture of the 'Sacred Heart', they dedicated their work as policemen to the service of God.[43]

Similar religious services occurred in many barracks throughout the country.[44] By 1924 there was no longer any need for a depot chaplain as the number of recruits had greatly decreased.

From 1925 onwards the garda authorities had places reserved for recruits at mass in the local Aughrim Street Parish Church. A week-long retreat or mission conducted by the Passionist Fathers was held in the depot in a converted temporary church. This was an annual event, which dominated depot life, with great numbers attending all ceremonies. There had always been a close association between the Passionist Fathers of Mount Argus and the DMP, and this continued with the Garda Síochána. In 1928, gardaí presented a marble throne to Mount Argus, and in 1938 they donated a new altar.[45]

In 1928, O'Duffy led a 250-strong garda pilgrimage to Rome. The party included ten chief superintendents, eighteen superintendents, four inspectors, seventy-seven sergeants and 138 guards. They were received in special audience by Pope Pius XI. The commissioner addressed the pope in Irish. The pope in his address praised the Garda Síochána for being unarmed.[46] O'Duffy later had a meeting with the Italian leader, Mussolini. On the return journey the group stayed in Paris for a few days, where they attended a reception given in their honour at city hall. The garda boxing team was also in Paris at this time. The sense of achievement, pride and triumphalism was palpable in the numerous accounts of the pilgrimage given in the *Garda Review*.[47]

In the following year, 1929, O'Duffy was chief marshal at the main event of the Catholic Emancipation centenary celebrations attended by almost 250,000 people.[48] In 1930, he once again led a garda pilgrimage, this time to Lourdes. Over 340 gardaí of all ranks travelled.[49] On their return journey they also visited Paris where they were once again the centre of a municipal reception. The Eucharistic Congress of June 1932 was a mammoth organisational task for the Garda Síochána, which it carried out with vigour and efficiency. The July issue of the *Garda Review* featured on the cover a picture of the papal nuncio with the President of the Executive Council, Eamon De Valera, and the editorial was devoted to the congress.

The Pioneer Total Abstinence Association (PTAA) was a Catholic organisation devoted to promoting temperance in society. Its members, called Pioneers, took a pledge to abstain from all alcoholic drink for life. Some took a temporary pledge for only a short period, such as the duration of Lent. Members wore a small emblem of the 'Sacred Heart'. Towards the end of 1922 a branch of the PTAA was formed at the depot.[50] The general intemperance that prevailed in the country in the 1922–4 period was a cause of grave concern to clergy, politicians and the general public. In an extremely strongly worded statement in 1923, O'Duffy warned his members that any impropriety with regard to drink would have very serious consequences.[51] He wanted a sober, efficient police force that would gain the respect of the people. In a country ravaged by drink he wanted the guards to lead by example. He encouraged the spread of the Pioneer movement among the force.[52] The wearing of any emblem on uniforms was prohibited, but the commissioner made an exception with regard to the Pioneer pin. Many recruits joined the PTAA while in training in the depot. Of course, not all of these remained Pioneers when distributed to the various stations throughout the country. When a procession to celebrate the silver jubilee of the PTAA took place in Dublin in June 1924, over 150 gardaí, accompanied by the garda band, turned out for the occasion. At this stage there were approximately 1,000 gardaí full members of the Pioneers and another 1,000 holding a temporary pledge.[53]

From the late 1920s until the mid-1940s the depot branch of the PTAA was moribund, as relatively few recruits joined the force during this period. The influx of large numbers of recruits in the mid 1940s saw the depot branch of the PTAA reactivated. Of the 474 recruits who passed through the depot in the 1946–8 period over 60 per cent either became full Pioneers or took a temporary pledge.[54] This was in addition to a considerable number of recruits who were already Pioneers before joining the force. In 1949 the PTAA held celebrations in Dublin to mark its golden jubilee. The *Garda Review* carried a large photograph of the garda members of the Pioneers in uniform marching to the celebrations in Croke Park.[55]

St Joseph's Young Priests Society was founded in 1895. Its main aim was to provide financial support for those studying for the missionary priesthood. An RIC branch of the society proved to be its mainstay in the earlier years. The first ordained priest sponsored by the society was the son of an RIC man. This branch ceased when the RIC was disbanded in 1922. In 1926 the society was re-established by Assistant Commissioner Walsh, who had previously been involved in it when a member of the RIC. Almost 82 per cent of the Garda Síochána favoured reactivating the society within the force when circularised about it.[56] The object of the garda branch of the society was to provide for the secondary education and first few years of seminary training of boys who were the sons of members of the force. Over the next twenty years the garda membership of the society remained at about 80 per cent of the force, and the contributions totalled around £340 per annum. By 1948 a total of fifty-four sons of members had been adopted by the society for education to the priesthood.[57]

Eoin O'Duffy frequently reminded his force that they were not merely men carrying out an ordinary job, but policemen doing a Christian duty. In 1928 the editor of the *Garda Review* spoke of the pilgrimage to Rome as showing that 'the Garda Síochána are obeying a higher law than their own'.[58] A garda commissioner who was resolutely Catholic, a government that was closely associated with and influenced by the Catholic Church, and the *Garda Review* which lauded committed Catholics, were not of themselves sufficient to make the members of the force earnest Catholics. Many of the individual members, however, took their religion very seriously and appear to have been imbued with a strong sense of Catholicism. During 1923 three confessors were required for the greater part of each Saturday for the recruits in the depot.[59] In 1928 over 200 members of the force sacrificed half of their annual leave and the equivalent of nine weeks' pay to go on pilgrimage to Rome. In 1930 over 300 made similar sacrifices to go Lourdes. The private diary of Garda John Hartigan gives a good insight into the religious observance of one young man over a nine-month period in the late 1920s.[60] During that time he attended mass twice each Sunday morning if not prevented from doing so by his tour of duty. He usually went to confession two or three times per month. He attended mass on some Friday mornings and frequently attended daily mass during Lent. He also attended evening devotions. John Hartigan's religious observances in no way stifled his enjoyment of life. He attended dances until 3 or 4 a.m., returning to friends' houses for tea and a chat afterwards. He regularly attended the local cinema and frequently enjoyed a drink with his peers.

The departure of the flamboyant O'Duffy in 1933 and the financial responsibilities of many of the force meant that there were no more pilgrimages to Rome or Lourdes. Occasions for Catholic celebrations, such as the 1929 centenary or the 1932 Eucharistic Congress, did not arise in the later 1930s or 1940s. Catholicism, however, while not as overt in public celebration, was still very powerful and influential. The 1937 Constitution enshrined the Catholic ethos in the laws of the land. Within the Garda Síochána, the retreats, specifically organised for members in the Dublin area and the members of the depot, continued. The Catholic ethos was very apparent in the *Garda Review*, with frequent photographs of family members or relatives of members of the force who were ordained to the priesthood. In March 1939 the front page and an article were devoted to the death of Pope Pius XI. The 1940s editions of the magazine had numerous references to the activity of the PTAA and St Joseph's Young Priests Society.

Only 1.3 per cent of the total members who had joined the Garda Síochána in the 1922–52 period were Protestant.[61] In 1923 O'Duffy issued instructions to all stations: 'Where members of different creeds are in the same station, care will be taken to avoid religious discussions.'[62] There is no evidence of Protestant members of the force having suffered any discrimination from the authorities or from fellow members.[63] While there was no hostility towards them, they were a very small minority among an overwhelmingly Catholic majority in a force with a strongly Catholic ethos. Their position within the guards mirrored their position in the state at large during the thirty years or so after independence.

Independent Ireland from 1922 to 1952 supported Gaelic games, the Irish language and the Catholic Church. Both the Garda Síochána authorities and the men themselves tended to do likewise.

11

THE VOICE OF THE GARDAÍ

GARDAÍ AND THE VOTE

The setting up of the Civic Guards in 1922 was closely associated with the political crisis of that time. The first commissioner, Michael Staines, and a number of the high-ranking officers were pro-Treaty TDs. The overwhelming majority of the men recruited in 1922 were in favour of the Treaty. The enquiry set up in the aftermath of the Kildare mutiny concluded that the force's close association with politics and politicians had been detrimental to its development. It recommended that no elected representatives be allowed to serve in the new police.[1] The new Free State Government went a step further. It included a clause in the Electoral Act, 1923, which excluded civic guards from the franchise. The Labour party opposed this exclusion, but the government, influenced no doubt by the recent happenings at Kildare and the ongoing Civil War, was adamant. It felt that it was essential for the impartial enforcement of the law that the civic guards be above party politics. It saw the disenfranchisement of the guards as considerably strengthening this separation of police from the divisive politics of the time.

The idea of denying the vote to police was not new. The RIC regulations had forbidden its members to vote. From 1923, civic guards could not vote at Dáil or Seanad elections, although they could vote at local and municipal elections if they wished. In 1925, Commissioner O'Duffy threatened with dismissal any member of the force who joined what he termed a 'political society'.[2] The overwhelming majority of the force did not become involved in political activity. In 1928 the Garda Síochána 'code' included a very strong recommendation to members that, in the interests of maintaining impartiality, they abstain from voting in local and municipal elections. The majority of members appear to have abided by this.[3]

During the 1920s the force does not appear to have been unduly concerned about being disenfranchised. However, the 1929 reduction in garda allowances changed this attitude. The editorials of the *Garda Review* and the resolutions of the representative bodies began to demand the enfranchisement of the force.[4] O'Duffy and the Minister for Justice, James Fitzgerald-Kenney, while in agreement in principle with granting the franchise to the force, were firmly against doing so at that time.[5] The members were sorely disappointed at the minister's refusal. The government's recommendations of a 5 per cent pay cut in 1931 accelerated the demand among the force for the vote. The *Garda Review* editorial of February 1933 complained that members of the army, but not the gardaí, were allowed to vote. When the threat of a pay reduction was removed in October 1933, the demand for enfranchisement abated somewhat. The activities of the Blueshirts and the IRA may have influenced the representative bodies to adopt a more low-key approach to the question of the gardaí getting the vote at this time of heightened political tension.[6] In 1936 the representative bodies again requested that members be allowed the right to vote. Commissioner Broy favoured the request, but the Minister for Justice, P. J. Ruttledge, was opposed.

Very little further was heard about the garda franchise until 1943 when the representative bodies again raised the issue. They stated that the police forces had the vote in other democratic countries, even in Northern Ireland where political feeling ran higher than in most countries.[7] In 1944 they stepped up their campaign. Commissioner Kinnane and the Minister for Justice, Gerard Boland, had no objections. However, the Department of Local Government and Public Health (which had responsibility for electoral reform) was not convinced that there was a strong reason for changing the status quo. In 1944 the government decided that the matter would 'be borne in mind when legislation amending the electoral acts was contemplated'.[8] By the late 1940s the men themselves, their representative bodies, the garda commissioner and the Department of Justice were all in favour of the guards getting the vote. The Department of Local Government appeared to be dragging its feet.[9] By 1952 the members of the force still could not vote at parliamentary or presidential elections. Throughout the period 1922–52 the garda campaign to secure the vote was motivated by practical considerations rather than lofty ideas of exercising one's democratic right. The gardaí saw enfranchisement as a means whereby they could better defend their position and conditions of service.

REPRESENTATIVE BODIES

In 1919 the RIC and the DMP were allowed to set up representative bodies for each of their lower ranks.[10] In 1923 the Garda Síochána (Temporary Provisions) Act provided for the establishment of representative bodies for the new force. The terms of this act were almost identical to those that had governed the RIC and DMP. Gardaí could not join a trade union or go on strike. The representative bodies had no executive power whatsoever. They were a conduit through which the men's views were channelled to the garda authorities, the Department of Justice and occasionally the government. The decisions and views of these three groups were in turn channelled back to the members of the force through the representative bodies.

There were two representative bodies — one for sergeants and guards, the other for all higher ranks. Every member of the force was entitled to make proposals to his representative body. Members did not have to pay any financial subscription. The representative bodies were organised at district, divisional and provincial level. District meetings were held once or twice a year, resolutions were passed and members were elected to the divisional committee. The procedure was repeated, with some members of this committee being elected to the provincial committee. Ireland was divided into three provincial areas: Leinster, Cavan and Monaghan; Connaught and Donegal; and Munster.[11] The provincial committees and the depot then elected members to the central representative body, which met once or twice a year in headquarters. Members were elected for a two-year term.

The two representative bodies — the lower and higher ranks — frequently met in joint session and drew up a list of recommendations that members of the force had suggested. These were then forwarded to the commissioner who dealt with what came within his remit. Pay and allowances could be adjudged upon only by the Minister for Justice. The commissioner would not send to the minister any recommendations that he considered to be outside the scope of the representative bodies or to which he strongly objected. Proposals to which he was not strongly opposed were sent to the minister without any comment. Proposals of which he approved were always accompanied by a favourable comment.[12] In effect, the garda commissioner exercised total power of veto over the recommendations of the representative bodies.

In 1927 revised regulations governing the representative bodies were introduced to take account of the amalgamation of the DMP with the Garda Síochána two years previously. The Dublin Metropolitan division area became a fourth electoral area for sending representatives to the central representative body. Furthermore, the two representative bodies were now replaced by three. One chief superintendent and four superintendents now represented these ranks on the central representative body. Two inspectors, one station sergeant and four sergeants represented the NCOs on that body. Eight guards represented that rank on the central body.[13] The gardaí serving in the Dublin metropolitan area were not happy with the revised regulations as they felt that their interest could not be safeguarded by a mainly rural body. Nothing was changed, however.

The representative bodies met in January and again in February 1924. They made recommendations concerning such mundane matters as the issue of waterproof clothing for members on cycling patrol, as well as addressing more fundamental issues such as the cadet system which they wanted abolished. At this time the government was considering reducing the pay of the force. The representative bodies were incensed that they had not been consulted.[14] The pay cut was implemented a few weeks later. In 1925 they complained that the placing before them of various orders relating to pay, pension and other matters was merely a perfunctory exercise. The Department of Justice defended its record in helping the force and claimed that it had abolished the cadet system and issued winter protective clothing. Throughout the remainder of the 1920s the representative bodies put forward recommendations ranging from a request that all stations be issued with Jeyes fluid, to a demand that the pay cut of 1924 be reversed. Several minor concessions were granted by O'Duffy but the major issues with relation to pay and allowances were rejected by the government. In 1929 the representative bodies persuaded the Minister for Justice not to proceed with a 10 per cent reduction in the rent allowance. However, they were extremely disappointed with their failure to prevent a range of further reductions in allowances. They threatened to resign as they felt that they served no useful purpose. O'Duffy persuaded them to remain in existence for the present at least.[15] The latter part of 1931 was dominated by the government's proposals to reduce garda pay by 5 per cent.

In 1932 the representative bodies pointed out to the new Fianna Fáil government that the previous government had never really consulted them, and they expressed the hope that this government would treat them better.[16] In May 1933 the government agreed to the representative bodies' long-standing wish to set up a medical aid fund, and in October the proposed pay cut was withdrawn. The new commissioner, Broy, agreed to meet delegates of the representative bodies in a weekly conference for a frank discussion on any resolution or grievance of the force. P. J. Gallagher of the representative bodies stated that the interview that he had had with Commissioner Broy concerning these proposals was 'one of the happiest' he had ever had.[17]

Sergeant P. J. Gallagher played a pivotal role in relations between the garda authorities, the Department of Justice and the members of the force over a thirty-two-year period from 1925 until his death in 1957. A native of County Sligo, Gallagher had been a teacher and in the IRA before he joined the guards in 1923. He was elected secretary of the representative bodies and also secretary of the Benevolent Society in 1925, posts he held until his death. He played a very active role in the establishment of the Medical Aid Society and in the formation of the St Joseph's Young Priests Society. For over twenty years he was secretary and assistant editor of the *Garda Review*.[18] From the mid-1920s until 1942 he contributed a monthly article to the *Garda Review* entitled 'Representative Body Notes', outlining the concerns, successes and failures of the representative bodies. From the early 1940s and afterwards he continued this work under a new title 'Without Prejudice'.

During the mid-1930s the representative bodies became more militant both in their demands and in the tone in which these demands were expressed. While they continued to request improvements in duty hours, length of leave and the approach to learning Irish, it was the restoration of 1929 allowances and the reversal of the 1924 pay cut that increasingly dominated their meetings. In 1934 they managed to get the approach for making the force bilingual changed from one of threat to one of inducement. Thereafter, they began to grow somewhat disillusioned with Commissioner Broy who appeared less receptive to their proposals.[19] They grew increasingly annoyed with the Department of Justice, its minister and the government who appeared to refuse almost every request they made. In 1935 the Minister, P. J. Ruttledge, breaking with the practice of previous years, did not attend the central committee meeting of the representative bodies at the depot.

Throughout 1937, anger, resentment and frustration continued to grow among the rank and file of the force. Resolutions came pouring in from all parts of the country to the representative bodies.[20] Matters came to a dramatic climax towards the end of 1937. The representative bodies, meeting in the depot, decided to confine their discussion solely to the restoration of the 1929 allowances and the removal of the 1924 pay cut. They sent a letter to the Minister for Justice supporting their claim, as they had done already the previous June, but without eliciting a response. Having got no satisfaction this time either, the central committee asked the minister to receive a deputation from them but he replied that he was ill. In desperation, the committee asked De Valera to receive the delegation. Members of the government, in particular the Minister for Finance, Sean McEntee, were very annoyed with the tone of the representative bodies' letter, which had been published in the *Garda Review* and which had also appeared in some of the national papers.[21] De Valera refused to meet them and the government ordered the session at the depot to disperse and its members to return to their stations immediately. The government had acted within its authority and the delegates, although deeply resentful, had to comply with its wishes. The force in general also deeply resented the government's action.[22] Despite some minor concessions by the government in 1938, disillusionment continued, with the representatives of one particular division resigning as they felt that they were achieving nothing.[23]

During the Emergency, 1939–45, the representative bodies concentrated on getting an improved rent allowance and an increase in pay in the face of rampant inflation. The increases granted in both of these during the war years did not at all satisfy them, although they had a good personal relationship with the new Minister for Justice, Gerard Boland.[24] However, the 1945 and 1946 new pay orders met with a favourable response. In January 1946 the editorial of the *Garda Review* stated that 1944 and 1945 had been the best years to date for the representative bodies and that they had made a serious contribution towards a solution of the vexed pay question. During 1946, discussions took place between the representative bodies' delegates and the Department of Justice, including, at times, the minister himself. The resulting new pay and allowances order was warmly welcomed by the representative bodies. They regarded it as a considerable advance for the force, as it recognised, at least partially, that gardaí were entitled to be treated in a special category for purposes of pay. The representative bodies also felt that it was the first time that the principle of negotiation between the Minister for Justice and the elected representatives of the force had been conceded.

By 1948, pay was again to the forefront, with a complete revision of Garda Síochána pay being requested. The departure of Gerard Boland as Minister for Justice, when Fianna Fáil lost the 1948 election, removed the sympathetic ear that the representative bodies had enjoyed. In December 1948 the representative bodies met the new minister, Seán Mac Eoin, but were not satisfied with his proposals. In early 1949 the force displayed an increased militancy. Some groups of gardaí proposed to hold a protest march at midnight through the streets of Dublin, but

Commissioner Kinnane refused permission. The representative bodies felt that they were being treated by the Department of Justice as an instrument for relaying orders that worsened garda conditions of service. They demanded that the force have access to arbitration machinery for settling disputes. This claim dominated the early 1950s.

While there was general approval in the 1920s for the setting up of the representative bodies, there was no great avalanche of men rushing to attend meetings or to be elected as delegates. The 1929 cut in allowances, the 1931–3 proposed pay cut, the cost of accommodation and the struggle to support a family on a garda's pay, all combined in the 1930s to make the force more interested. Such interest reached a climax in 1937 only to be shattered by the forced dissolution of the central committee's meeting in December of that year. For the next four or five years, interest in the representative bodies waned somewhat as a result of that action by the government. The arrival of the Emergency in 1939, which imposed considerably longer hours of duty on members, may also have been a contributing factor in this decline. Some districts, however, continued to be actively involved in the representative bodies, while in others the organisation was practically moribund.[25] From about 1944, interest increased once again. Rampant inflation during the years of the Second World War had seriously eroded the men's standard of living. Questions regarding pensions were now of more than academic interest as the vast majority of the force moved closer to retiring age. The influx of over 1,000 new recruits in the 1943–8 period also helped to revitalise the representative bodies.

In the 1923–52 period the representative bodies were successful in effecting a number of changes in the daily routine of the lives of their members. However, with regard to major issues, such as a radical improvement in accommodation and a substantial increase in pay and allowances, they were almost invariably unsuccessful. The effectiveness of the representative bodies depended on the goodwill of the garda commissioner, the Minister for Justice and the government of the day. The gardaí had no strike weapon and the government ultimately held the whip hand. During the 1944–7 period the representative bodies enjoyed a status more akin to that of a full trade union, in that their views and arguments were taken seriously by Minister Boland. By 1949, however, it would appear that the status quo had returned somewhat, with the new government apparently using the representative bodies to relay unpopular decisions back to the rank and file. The 1950 demand for arbitration machinery was an acknowledgement that the severe limitations under which the representative bodies had worked for the previous twenty-six years were no longer acceptable to the force.

COMMISSIONERS, MINISTERS FOR JUSTICE, POLITICAL PARTIES AND THE GARDA SÍOCHÁNA

The garda commissioner occupied a position of great importance and influence in relation to the members of the force. He had absolute authority in the internal management of the Garda Síochána. Michael Staines was commissioner for less than six months, during which time the Kildare mutiny took place. Despite this crisis, Staines was regarded by most of the early members of the force as a decent and honourable gentleman.[26] In his ten and a half years as commissioner, Eoin O'Duffy campaigned vigorously on behalf of his men for any cause that he believed was right.[27] Between 1923 and about 1926 he supported the majority of issues raised by the representative bodies. Thereafter, he was somewhat more discriminating in what he supported although it would be very unfair to regard this as a 'U-turn' of any sort. Although a strict disciplinarian, O'Duffy was very popular among the rank and file of the force. In 1923 when he made lightning, unexpected inspections of various stations throughout the country, the men felt that 'he was someone you could talk to', he was on the side of the gardaí.[28] In 1928 the new Minister for Justice, James Fitzgerald-Kenney, referred to the fact that O'Duffy was extremely popular with his men.[29] When O'Duffy was sacked in 1933 there was genuine regret throughout the force, although the members accepted the government's prerogative to act as it did. O'Duffy demanded the highest standards from his men. Equally, he exerted great efforts in defending their legitimate concerns. He had a paternalistic attitude towards the force and his concern for, and pride in, his men shone through his ten years as commissioner.

Although the members of the force may have been upset at O'Duffy's departure, the appointment of Eamon Broy as commissioner was well received by them. The new commissioner gave a very favourable response to the majority of resolutions forwarded to him in the first year of his new job. In early 1935, however, the honeymoon between Broy and the force came to an end when the commissioner gave a quite negative response to resolutions of the representative bodies. By 1936 the representative bodies felt that the commissioner fully supported their resolutions where the decision lay with the government, but where the decision lay with him, he refused their requests.[30] In 1936 he did relinquish responsibility for the *Garda Review*, handing control of it over to the representative bodies. Broy's style as commissioner was less paternalistic and more democratic than O'Duffy's had been. He was also less of a disciplinarian than O'Duffy, especially in the 1933–5 period. The relationship between Broy and the members of the force was somewhat less personal than that which had existed between the members and O'Duffy.

There was widespread regret among the men when the government appointed an outsider, civil servant Michael J. Kinnane, to the top job in the force in 1938. Nevertheless, the members welcomed him as their new commissioner once the appointment had been made.[31] Kinnane adopted a very low profile and dealt with the day-to-day problems of administering the Garda Síochána. He responded to the representative bodies' proposals, granting some, refusing others and forwarding the remainder to the Minister for Justice. In the mid-1940s he did put a good deal of pressure on the government to improve garda pay.[32] Kinnane's style reflected that of the civil servant in many ways. He was an efficient and capable administrator with a low public profile and did not adopt a very personal approach when dealing with the members of the force. His style as commissioner was the antithesis of what O'Duffy's had been. When he died in office in 1952 the editorial of the *Garda Review* referred to the 'respect and esteem' that he had earned 'so unostentatiously'.[33]

The Minister for Home Affairs (later Justice) occupied a key role in relation to the conditions of service enjoyed by the members of the force. Demands for increased pay and allowances had absolutely no chance of success unless approved by the Minister for Justice, who would then attempt to persuade the Department of Finance to grant the necessary extra funds. The representative bodies were largely impotent unless they managed to enlist his support. Eamonn Duggan's term as Minister for Home Affairs in 1922 was too short to allow any distinctive style of approach to the force to emerge. He was replaced by Kevin O'Higgins who held the portfolio from September 1922 until his assassination in July 1927. O'Higgins was very firm in his dealings with the gardaí and presided over the 1924 pay cuts, which affected all ranks of the force. O'Duffy felt that the Department of Justice under O'Higgins was intransigent in its dealings with the gardaí.[34] However, in 1926 O'Higgins had resisted a proposal to reduce the boot allowance, as he believed that the gardaí had endured enough with the 1924 pay cut.

James Fitzgerald-Kenney was Minister for Justice from 1927 to 1932. He was cordial when he met the representative bodies, which he did on a number of occasions. He presided over the 1929 reduction in allowances and was minister when the idea of a 5 per cent pay reduction was mooted in 1931. The representative bodies were not pleased with his response to their demands although he had dropped the idea of reducing the rent allowance in 1929 and was prepared to modify the proposed pay cut of 1931.

The new Fianna Fáil Minister for Justice was James Geoghegan who was appointed in 1932 and held the post for less than twelve months. He was replaced by P. J. Ruttledge who held the position until 1939. The new minister and the representative bodies got off to a good start with the latter stating in 1934: 'We feel we have the good will of the Minister for Justice, who has already shown, more than any other previous minister an appreciation for the welfare of the force.'[35] This did not last for long, however. The failure of Ruttledge to improve the situation with regard to pay and allowances helped to sour relations between him and the representative bodies. The government's forced disbandment of the central committee in 1937 marked the nadir in relations between the government and Minister for Justice on the one side, and the gardaí on the other.

Following the outbreak of the Second World War, the cabinet was re-organised in September 1939. Gerard Boland became Minister for Justice, a post he retained until 1948. Boland was very sympathetic to the gardaí's case regarding housing problems, and pay and allowances. However, the government's financial position meant that little was done to improve the situation. Despite this, the representative bodies held Boland in high regard. They tended to blame the Department of Finance for its inflexibility and to praise Boland's interest in the welfare of the force.[36] They were particularly gratified that the minister negotiated with them, taking at least some of their proposals on board. When Boland resigned as Minister for Justice after his party's defeat in the 1948 general election, the editorial of the *Garda Review* was glowing in its praise of him.[37] General Sean Mac Eoin was Minister for Justice from 1948 until 1951. While relations between the representative bodies and the minister were good, they tended to be businesslike rather than very friendly. There existed none of the rapport that had been the hallmark of relations with the previous minister, Gerard Boland.

The majority of the men who joined the gardaí in the 1922–8 period were pro-Treaty supporters. The pro-Treaty Cumann na nGaedheal Government of the 1920s was at pains, however, to point out to the new force that it was the servant of all the people and whatever government was elected by the people. In 1928 the Minister for Justice, James Fitzgerald-Kenney, told the guards that they must be impartial and that 'persons who were regarded as enemies of the state, must now be regarded as enemies no longer.'[38] Cumann na nGaedheal could have been forgiven for believing that the gardaí learned their lesson too well. In March 1933 the *Garda Review* carried a photograph of the former Finance Minister, Ernest Blythe (1923–32), who had recently lost his Dáil seat. It commented on his defeat, saying, 'it will not plunge the rank and file of the garda into the deepest gloom.'[39] Blythe had been one of the strongest advocates of stringent fiscal policies. The 1924 pay cut and the 1929 reduction in allowances, coupled with O'Duffy's success in instilling in his men their role as impartial enforcers of the law, meant that by 1932, the men saw themselves first and foremost as policemen.[40]

While the Garda Síochána was disillusioned with Cumann na nGaedheal by the early 1930s, it could not hope to find much solace in De Valera and Fianna Fáil who had been stern critics of the force on a number of previous occasions. De Valera believed that the state had too many police. In 1929, Deputy Little of Fianna Fáil stated during a Dáil debate that the police were 'sitting on walls, kicking their heels . . . in a great many parts of the country.'[41] In 1930 Seán Lemass expressed the opinion that 'under present circumstances a position in the Civic Guard is a soft job.'[42] There was a fairly widespread perception among the gardaí at this time that Fianna Fáil was hostile to the force.[43] By 1930 the gardaí felt that neither Cumann na nGaedheal nor Fianna Fáil could be relied upon to support their cause. However, the conditions of service for members of the force were just as good or as bad under Fianna Fáil governments (1932–48) as they had been under Cumann na nGaedheal governments (1923–32).

The Labour party vigorously espoused the cause of the Garda Síochána in the Dáil and Seanad during the 1920s, 1930s and 1940s. The individual who most consistently advocated their case was Richard Corish, TD. Corish in particular, and the Labour party in general, had strongly opposed the 1924 and 1929 reductions in garda pay and allowances. The *Garda Review* and the representative bodies were frequently profuse in their thanks to the Labour party.[44] In June 1929 the *Garda Review* carried a cover page photograph of Deputy Corish. In November 1932 the representative bodies acknowledged the support of the party, in an article in the same journal entitled 'Champion of our Cause — The Labour Party'.[45] In 1935, Corish submitted a proposal to the government for the state to build houses throughout the country to be let exclusively to the gardaí at economical rent. During the latter part of the 1930s Labour pressed the government for an increased rent allowance for the force. Individual politicians of all parties had supported the Garda Síochána's case at various times throughout the 1920s, 1930s and 1940s. In fact, in the mid-1940s there was general agreement in the Dáil that gardaí deserved an increase in pay and an improvement in housing conditions.[46] However, Labour party deputies and senators were the most active, energetic and consistent supporters of the cause of the Garda Síochána in the first twenty-five or thirty years of the force's existence.

THE *GARDA REVIEW*

In February 1923, O'Duffy launched a weekly magazine for the force, called *Iris an Gharda*. Its editor was a civilian, Donnchadh J. Kelly. It ceased publication in June 1924 when he retired as editor. The representative bodies then decided to take control and publish a new weekly journal called *Guth an Gharda*, which first appeared in July 1924, at a cost of 3d (1p). Its editorials were outspoken with regard to the recent pay cut and various issues such as housing and allowances.[47] It was found increasingly difficult to produce the magazine on a weekly basis, and so it ceased production after six months.

In December 1925, a new monthly journal, the *Garda Review*, was launched. It was started without funds and managed by a committee appointed by the commissioner. Its policy was directed by the representative bodies, subject to the approval of the commissioner.[48] The editorial of the first edition outlined the function of the journal: 'An organ for expression and for the dissemination of news and information, a domestic journal, interesting, educative, entertaining'.[49] It emphasised that the *Garda Review* aimed to bond all members together and was not an organ of agitation. Members could pay an annual subscription of 7/6 (37½p) for the magazine, which included post and packaging. The contents of that first edition comprised the following: editorial; traffic in Dublin; photography hints; first aid; detective story by Arthur Conan Doyle; national and international sport; Humbert in Killala/an historical story; list of marriages of gardaí; short story in Irish by Pádraic Ó Conaire; recent legal decisions; good police duty; Irish grammar; divisional notes from around the country; list of transfers of gardaí; student page; and weights and measures information. Many of the articles and letters in the *Garda Review* came from members of the force themselves. A mailbag or letters to the editor soon became a regular and popular feature of each edition. There was an average of 3,000 copies sold each month in the first year. Its editor, a civilian, William Harding, had previously been the editor of the RIC magazine.

Until the mid-1930s the format of the *Garda Review* remained virtually unchanged. A new section, a 'Women's Realm,' became a regular feature each month. This dealt with recipes for cooking; body and hair care; fashion and household management; as well as a plethora of other issues of interest to women at that time. About one-third of each edition was usually devoted to advertisements. Some of these included alluring females in what must have been seen as fairly seductive poses for the second quarter of the twentieth century. Cartoons, quips and jokes were sprinkled throughout each issue. O'Duffy used the magazine to advise, instruct and generally to keep in contact with the gardaí distributed throughout the country. He continually exhorted his men to reach very high standards of professional and moral conduct. He constantly praised and encouraged them. By 1929 the *Garda Review* had an average of 6,000 subscribers. The editor, William Harding, died in June of that year. There followed a succession of editors over the next four years. Pádraig Sheehan SC took over editorship in 1932 and continued in the post for over twenty-five years. By 1936 over £3,000 of the journal's profits had been spent on the promotion of professional and recreational interests within the force.[50]

The *Garda Review* always followed its own independent line of opinion. Its editorials, representative body notes and various articles were trenchant and frequently very critical of government policy as it related to conditions of service of the force. The journal criticised the Cumann na nGaedheal government in the 1920s and the Fianna Fáil government of the 1930s. It expressed its most militant comments in the 1935–8 period. This increased militancy was the result of growing resentment among the force at the government's failure to improve pay and allowances. The views and opinions of the *Garda Review* did not change after 1936 although the representative bodies now had total responsibility for the journal. Both the pre-1936 and the post-1936 issues frequently criticised the government. Both occasionally criticised the incumbent commissioner for failure to grant some concession that the force had requested. From the end of the 1930s onwards, the overall tone and opinions of the *Garda Review* are indistinguishable from those of the 1920s and early 1930s.

By December 1952 the *Garda Review* had produced 325 separate editions, never having missed one month. It was highly professional with regard to literary standard, layout, typing, illustrations and photographs. It allowed the representative bodies to keep the rank and file informed of developments, as well as providing a medium through which the views of the government and the commissioner could be relayed to the members of the force. The journal remained interesting and entertaining reading for the vast majority of the Garda Síochána. Perhaps its greatest achievement was the nourishment of the *esprit de corps* among the 7,000-strong force, scattered in small isolated units of three or four men, throughout the length and breadth of the new state.

CONCLUSION

By 1952 the gardaí still had no vote, were forbidden to join a trade union and were not allowed to strike. They had representative bodies, which were fairly successful in addressing minor grievances but which had very limited success when faced with major issues. The force had a vibrant and successful journal. The gardaí could make their voice heard through the representative bodies and the *Garda Review*. Ultimately, however, it was up to the garda commissioner, the Minister for Justice and the government to decide whether or not to act upon what they heard.

12

PREMATURE DEPARTURE AND AGEING

PREMATURE DEPARTURE

Between 1922 and 1952, 10,135 men were attested to the Garda Síochána. Departure records are extant for all the men who joined in the 1922–31 period and for Taca members (1939–40).[1] Information about departure is available for over 90 per cent of members who either departed early or retired from the force in the first thirty years of its existence. By 1952 over 4,000 men had left the force.[2] Only about one-third of these had retired, the rest had resigned, been dismissed, absconded, been discharged or had died.[3] Table 12.1 illustrates what had happened by 1 January 1952 to the 7,937 men who had joined the Garda Síochána in the 1922–31 period.

Fifteen of the sixteen members who absconded did so in 1922. Most of the 396 deaths were the result of illnesses that are curable today, such as appendicitis, pneumonia, ulcers and diabetes. Pulmonary tuberculosis accounted for 25 per cent of Garda Síochána deaths. Deaths resulting from falling off bicycles were quite common right up to the late 1940s. While most discharges were on grounds of physical ill-health, a minority were the result of mental illness such as melancholia. Tuberculosis accounted for 25 per cent of discharges.

Between 1922 and 1952, 100 serving members died from TB and another 81 sufferers were discharged on grounds of ill-health. Many of

Table 12.1: Situation as on 1 January 1952 with regard to Members Recruited in the 1922–31 Period

Reason for Departure	Number	% of 1922–31 total
Absconded	16	0.2
Died	396	5.0
Discharged	324	4.1
Dismissed	968	12.2
Resigned	1,092	13.7
Retired	1,281	16.1
Still serving	3,860	48.7
Total	7,937	100.0

Source: General register.

the latter would subsequently have died from the disease. The highest incidence of TB in the force occurred in the 1925–30 period. Commissioner O'Duffy was perplexed by this as each candidate had undergone a rigorous medical examination before entering the force, and any history of tuberculosis in the family precluded a man from joining.[4] The very poor, crowded and frequently damp accommodation occupied by many of the men in the early years of the force, as well as the irregular hours and frequent wettings while on patrol, may have facilitated the spread of the disease. Although the incidence of TB among members of the Garda Síochána in the 1922–52 period was actually lower than the national average, there is no doubt but that the nature of the job was a contributing factor in members contracting the disease.[5]

Over 12 per cent of the 1922–31 recruits had been dismissed by 1952.[6] Debt and drink were easily the two most common causes of dismissal. A small minority of members were dismissed for financial fraud, general indiscipline or 'immoral behaviour'. Less than a handful were dismissed for serious criminal offences. Over 45 per cent of all dismissals took place in the first four years of the force's existence. This was inevitable considering the hasty manner in which thousands of young men were recruited, the vast majority of whom were unused to any sort of institutional discipline. By the 1940s the number of dismissals had dwindled to a handful — usually three to four per annum.

Almost 28 per cent of all members who resigned from the force did so to emigrate. A large number of other resignations were the result of members wishing to take over the family farm upon the death of a father or the emigration of a brother. Others resigned to take over the family business. Over 85 per cent of total resignations occurred in the first ten years of the force's existence. Some of the members found that the discipline of the policeman's job was not to their liking, while many single young men were attracted by the hope of a better standard of living in Britain or America.[7] Most of the guards who emigrated came from the western counties, which had a long tradition of emigration. The great depression, which hit America in 1929, and the marriage of many members in the 1930s meant that emigration was no longer a viable option for most gardaí. Almost one-quarter of Taca members recruited in the 1939–40 period were no longer in the Garda Síochána by 1952. The majority of those who left had resigned, many of them to avail of attractive opportunities for work in post-war Britain.

A total of 336 men served as officers in the Garda Síochána at some time in the thirty years 1922–52.[8] Table 12.2 illustrates what had happened to these men by 1952.

Table 12.2: Situation as on 1 January 1952 with regard to Officers Appointed in the Years, 1922–52[9]

Situation	Number	%
Departed from the force prematurely	115	34.2
Retired	55	16.3
Still serving	166	49.5
Total	336	100.0

Source: Officers' register.

Of the 115 officers who left the force prematurely, 35 per cent were dismissed, 24 per cent died, 17 per cent were discharged, 10 per cent were forced to retire under the 1941 Garda Síochána (Retirement) Regulations, 7 per cent resigned and 7 per cent were reduced in rank. Over 90 per cent of officer dismissals occurred before 1930, mainly as a result of recruitment in a very hasty manner in the 1922–5 period. Thereafter, only a handful were dismissed over the next twenty years (not including the eleven officers who in effect were dismissed under the 1941 regulations). Only a very small number of officers had resigned from the force by 1952. The security of the job and the reasonable salary that accompanied it may account for this low number.

Over 70 per cent of total premature departures in the 1922–52 period had taken place by 1930. By that date, O'Duffy had got rid of any man he found to be unsuited to the force. At that stage also, many men who detested the job had already resigned. Those who remained were in for the long haul. By 1930 the lack of job opportunities abroad, together with marriage and its attendant responsibilities, ensured that fewer men left the force prematurely. The proportion of early departures from the Garda Síochána in the late 1920s was lower than that of the RUC for the same period.[10]

AN AGEING FORCE

The vast majority of the men who joined the guards in the 1920s were in their early or middle twenties. A minority were in their late twenties, a small number in their thirties and even fewer in their forties. As a result there were very few retirements in the 1920s and relatively few in the 1930s. According to the Garda Síochána (Retirement) Regulations, 1934, guards, sergeants and inspectors had to retire at 57 years of age, and superintendents and chief superintendents at 60 years. Assistant and deputy commissioners and the commissioner had to retire at the age of 65. The commissioner could grant individual members, up to and including the rank of chief superintendent, an extension of service of up to five years. In 1939 an embargo was imposed on allowing an extension of service to any rank higher than sergeant, so as not to interfere with members' promotional prospects. During the 1940s extensions were freely granted to those of garda rank. This was to facilitate married men with young families who were older than most when they joined the force.[11]

The numbers retiring increased steadily as the 1940s progressed. The trend was accelerated in the 1948–52 period when approximately 9 per cent of the pre-1932 recruits retired. New retirement regulations in 1951 which meant that the men who had joined the force when over 27 years of age were given added years for pension purposes, helped to increase the number of retirements. In the late 1940s the representative bodies had campaigned to have the retirement age raised. They argued that trade union restrictions meant that retired gardaí were unable to secure work at a time when family commitments for many members were at their greatest.[12] In 1951 the government raised the retirement age by three years for all ranks below and including chief superintendent. Extensions of service could be granted up to a maximum of two years. From 1949 onwards the garda authorities had granted extensions of service to all members who were fit, irrespective of rank. The retirement pattern of the officers appointed in the 1922–52 period more or less reflected that of the general body of the force.

By 1950 the age profile of the Garda Síochána was dramatically different from what it had been in the early 1920s. Figures 12.1 and 12.2 illustrate the changing age pattern of the force over the period.

Figure 12.1: Garda Síochána Age Profile of Force, 1926[13]

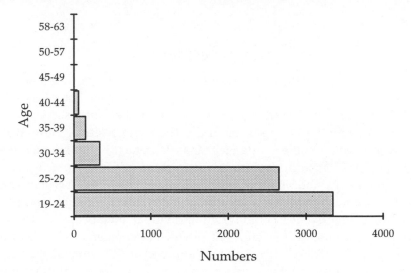

Sources: General register; Extension of Service (NAI); Shaw papers.

Figure 12.2: Garda Síochána Age Profile of Force, 1950[14]

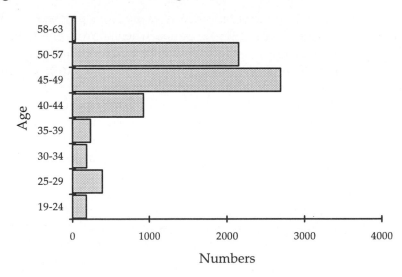

Source: Extension of Service (NAI).

Less than 19 per cent of the members of the force were under 40 years of age by 1950. These included some of the men who joined in the 1933–5 period, all of the Taca members who joined in 1939–40 and all of the recent recruits of the 1943–8 period.

By January 1952 the Garda Síochána was composed of the following groups:

Table 12.3: Composition of Garda Síochána on 1 January 1952 according to Recruitment Period[15]

Recruitment Period	%
Pre-1932 men	60.0
1933–5 men	7.5
Taca 1939–40	3.5
1940s men	15.5
DMP	11.5 [16]
Others	2.0
Total	100.0

Sources: General register; Taca; 1950 enquiry.

Despite resignations, discharges, dismissals, deaths and retirements, the men who joined the Garda Síochána in the 1922–6 period still constituted nearly two-thirds of the force in 1952. All of this was soon to change. The men who had joined in this period had reached thirty years' service and were entitled to their full pension. Each year, hundreds availed of this. The 1950s marked the end of an era. The first generation of gardaí was retiring and a new band of men recruited under very different conditions was to become the police force of the future.

13

Overview, 1952–97

This chapter is an attempt to sketch in merest outline the evolution of the force over the past forty-five years. As much of the archival material relating to the post-1952 period has not yet been released, it was not possible to use the methodology followed for the 1922–52 period. The chapter therefore relies mainly on a perusal of the *Garda Review* for the period, the Conroy commission, newspaper articles and interviews with members of the force.

The men who joined the Garda Síochána in the 1922–52 period were not paid very well and their conditions of service left a lot to be desired. However, the level of crime was very low and members of the force had a clear-cut view of their role. The administrative structures of the Garda Síochána, which it had inherited from the RIC, served the force reasonably well at this time. The advent of the second half of the century brought with it major changes in society and in the Garda Síochána.

1950s

Ireland experienced a severe economic depression in the 1950s, with poor economic growth, high unemployment and a low standard of living. Almost half a million Irish people emigrated during the decade, mostly to England. There was a general air of despondency over the country. Successive governments seemed unable to cope with the problems, with each of the three general elections in the 1950s bringing a new government into power. Britain was enjoying a post-war economic boom with the introduction of the welfare state, a substantial rise in living standards and improved job opportunities.

Over 3,500 members of the Garda Síochána retired in the 1950s. Most of these had joined the force in the 1920s. Many who had young families to support found the pension inadequate and had to seek other employment. Quite a number went to work in England. Approximately 2,800 new members were recruited to the force in this period. By 1958 the total strength of the Garda Síochána was less than 6,500, a drop of almost 1,000 on the 1948 figure. The closure of several small rural stations and the introduction of the patrol car (or squad car as it was frequently called) in many areas, to replace the foot or bicycle patrol, eased the reduction in manpower. This new generation of recruits was not prepared to put up with the harsh conditions that the earlier men had endured. Demands were frequently made for an increase in pay and allowances, improvements in barrack accommodation, shorter working hours and the removal of some aspects of the disciplinary code. This decade was dominated by the demand that conciliation and arbitration machinery be provided for the Garda Síochána, as it had been for civil servants. Members also campaigned for the right to vote. Most requests by gardaí for improvements in conditions of service cited the much better conditions enjoyed by the RUC and by the British police.

When Commissioner Kinnane died in 1952 he was replaced from outside the force by Daniel Costigan, a civil servant. In the mid-1950s some aspects of the disciplinary code were relaxed and much-improved guidelines regarding leave and recreation were introduced. A new open-necked uniform replaced the high-necked one. Improvements were also made in relation to the number of hours worked by gardaí. However, by 1957 the force was unsettled and restless. Its demands for arbitration machinery, increased pay and the franchise had not been met.

The year 1959 brought a number of changes. Gardaí were given the vote and they were granted arbitration facilities. Women (banghardaí) were recruited for the first time. They did not normally do night duty but instead had long hours of stand-by duty at night-time. Like all women working in the public service, banghardaí received less pay than their male counterparts. Their role was initially perceived as dealing with children and young girls who got into trouble with the law.

By the end of the 1950s many gardaí were working, and some actually living, in stations that were in a very bad condition. Members of the force had less time off than their counterparts in other jobs. There was no overtime payment. During the decade the force had received several pay increases but its members were far from satisfied. Although there had been an increase in crime in the latter part of the decade, Ireland remained relatively free from the type of crime that was beginning to appear elsewhere.

1960s

Ireland underwent a fairly radical transformation in the 1960s. Séan Lemass was Taoiseach, T. K. Whitaker's 'Programme for Economic Development' was in operation and there was an improvement in the world economy. The country experienced a period of unprecedented economic progress. Emigration and unemployment decreased, with a number of emigrants actually returning to take advantage of the increased job opportunities in Ireland. Free second-level education was introduced in 1967. The Second Vatican Council encouraged discussion of religious and social matters. The advent of television greatly accelerated this trend and gave Irish people a window on the wider world. Changes in the economic, social, cultural and religious spheres resulted in the emergence of a more open and affluent society. The Garda Síochána was to be faced with new, more complex problems.

Approximately 3,000 recruits joined the guards in the 1960s. By the end of that decade the vast majority of the members of the force were young men. In 1961 a pay award excluded members who had less than five years' service. There was much unrest among younger members and they organised meetings to discuss their grievances. They were unhappy with the negotiating machinery and also with the representative bodies whom they did not think were truly representative. The commissioner warned against these meetings, which were contrary to disciplinary regulations. One such meeting was held in the Macushla Ballroom in central Dublin. Senior garda officers were delegated to take the names of those attending meetings, and eleven guards were dismissed from the force. A number of young guards adopted a 'go-slow', or work-to-rule tactic in Dublin. The intervention of Archbishop McQuaid was followed by a return to full discipline within the force, the reinstatement of the eleven men, and a promise by the government to review the workings of the negotiating machinery with a view to improvements. In 1962 new representative body regulations were drafted, which allowed each group — guards, NCOs and officers — to advance its own claim, rather than being advanced jointly as was previously the case. The Garda Representative Body, under Jack Marrinan, adopted a very professional approach — for example, employing an economic consultant to prepare future pay claims. Despite a significant improvement with regard to the incremental scale in 1960 and a number of pay awards throughout the decade, there still was unrest by 1968.

The 1960s introduced some new aspects to garda work especially in the cities and larger towns. The increased volume of traffic on Irish roads occupied a great deal of the force's time. Juvenile delinquency and vandalism were on the increase and street fights between rival gangs, armed with knives, were becoming more common in Dublin in the middle of the decade. There was a marked increase in indictable offences, with the Dublin metropolitan area accounting for over 60 per cent of the country's crime. Hundreds of gardaí were posted along the border with Northern Ireland in early 1968 to prevent the spread of the 'foot and mouth' cattle disease. Influenced by events in the US, Europe and Northern Ireland, some Irish citizens later in that year took to the streets of Dublin to register their disapproval of events at home and abroad, including the Vietnam War. Such protests sometimes resulted in baton charges by the gardaí.

A number of administrative changes were implemented during the decade. In 1964 the Dublin metropolitan area was reorganised and extended to include the newly built-up suburban areas. While improvements in communications, scientific investigation and mobility were introduced, many members felt that these were beginning to supplant, instead of supplement, the man on the beat. The force disliked the economising on manpower that had occurred in most areas. A juvenile liaison scheme was set up in 1963. In 1964 the training depot was moved from the Phoenix Park headquarters to Templemore, County Tipperary. In the mid-1960s, aware of the growing importance of public relations, the force secured a five-minute slot on RTE television, called 'Garda Patrol'. There were frequent changes of garda commissioner. Daniel Costigan retired in 1965 to be replaced by William P. Quinn, who retired in 1967 and was replaced by Patrick J. Carroll. In 1968 Michael J. Wymes took over when Carroll retired. The principle of the commissioner coming from within the force was now firmly established, as all these appointees had come up through the ranks.

There was a renaissance in sport among the force, with the revival of Aonach an Gharda and some striking successes by the rowing club. The boat club premises were reconstructed with much-improved recreational facilities, and a Garda Club was established at Harrington Street, Dublin. In 1965 the full-time Garda Band was disbanded on grounds of economy, much to the annoyance of many members of the force. The Scott medal presentation ceremony was reintroduced in 1960. In 1966 a memorial was unveiled at Garda headquarters, to the members of the force who had given their lives in the service of their country. A Garda Pensioners' Association was set up. St Raphael's Garda Credit Union was founded in Dublin in 1964 and St Paul's Garda Credit Union was established in Cork in 1967.

By 1969 the actual strength of the Garda Síochána was 6,500, about the same as it had been ten years earlier. There were just five women sergeants and twenty-three women of garda rank. Throughout the 1950s and 1960s a total of sixty-four stations had been closed and a further forty-eight reduced to the status of sub-station. Garda recruits were trained for four months in Templemore, allocated to a station for a year, and then brought back to Templemore for about a month's training before being put on probation for one year. Some progress had been made in providing new stations and better living accommodation for members of the force. By 1969 one-quarter of the married men and their families, and half of the single men, lived in officially provided accommodation. The quality of such accommodation varied from recently built new stations to pre-1922 barracks. A special drive had been made in the early 1960s to provide more houses for married gardaí. The Medical Aid Society and the Garda Benevolent Fund continued to provide reasonable cover for members of the force, but there was a growing realisation that an amalgamation of the societies and a more comprehensive welfare scheme was needed. Many members of the Garda Síochána normally worked more than the required minimum of forty-eight hours per week. There was no overtime pay and while members of the force were entitled to time off in lieu of extra duty, they did not always get it. Most workers in other walks of life had more time off.

By 1968 there was serious discontent in the Garda Síochána, caused primarily by dissatisfaction over pay and conditions. As a result, the Minister for Justice appointed a commission, under Judge John Conroy, to make recommendations on remuneration and conditions of service within the force. It submitted its report in January 1970. The Conroy commission was the first full-scale assessment of pay and conditions of gardaí since the force had been set up in 1922. As well as making fairly radical recommendations regarding pay and conditions, it also drew the government's attention to a number of important areas outside the remit of the commission, which needed urgent attention. It strongly urged that an examination be carried out into the role, organisation and personnel policy of the Garda Síochána, and in particular its relationship with the Department of Justice, which appeared to exercise too much control. By 1969 the Garda Síochána was made up of relatively young members who were working in a rapidly changing society. However, in terms of organisation and administration the force had not changed a great deal since it was first set up in the 1920s, when it closely mirrored its predecessor, the RIC.

1970s

The early years of the 1970s saw prices rise with an average inflation rate of approximately 8 per cent. Ireland joined the European Economic Community in 1973. The quadrupling of oil prices as a result of the Middle East crises in that year greatly accentuated inflation, which was running at 21 per cent by 1975. This was gradually reduced in the next few years, only to increase once again at the end of the decade under the pressure of new oil price increases. Unemployment increased throughout the decade and, despite an improvement in the 1977–9 period, it was over 90,000 by 1979. The changes that had begun in the 1960s were accelerated in the 1970s. Society became more consumerist, affluent and permissive. A better-educated generation questioned all forms of authority, whether parental, school, church or state. The media began to play an increasingly important role in shaping people's views.

The 1970s was a decade of immense change for the Garda Síochána. In many ways the recommendations of the Conroy commission heralded a new era. The commission introduced reasonable improvements in basic pay and radical improvements in conditions of service. It increased the rent element of pay, gave an allowance on top of normal pay for regular night duty, reduced the working week to forty-two hours and, perhaps most significant of all, introduced the concept of overtime payment. Throughout the 1970s gardaí received pay increases under the national wage agreements. In the first half of the decade members were generally satisfied with their pay, supplemented in many instances by overtime payments, partly the result of the crisis in Northern Ireland. However, in 1975 the government introduced substantial reductions in garda overtime in order to economise. By the end of the decade pay was once again to the fore, with members claiming that they had lost much of the ground gained under the Conroy commission in 1970. They also claimed that their job had become much more difficult and dangerous.

Although the Northern 'Troubles' had begun in the late 1960s, it was not until the next decade that they began to impinge on the Republic. Bombs in Dublin and Belturbet, County Cavan, in 1972, and in Dublin and Monaghan town in 1974 killed twenty-nine people. In 1975 the Herrema kidnapping took place and in 1976 the British Ambassador to Ireland, Christopher Ewart-Biggs, was assassinated. Many gardaí were transferred to the border areas and there was increased surveillance of subversive activity in the rest of the country. Four members lost their lives during the decade. Garda Richard Fallon was shot dead by Republican bank raiders in 1970. Inspector Samuel Donegan was killed by an IRA booby-trap bomb on the Cavan-Fermanagh border in 1972.

Garda Michael Reynolds was shot dead in Dublin by Republicans in 1975, and Garda Michael Clerkin was killed by an IRA booby-trap bomb at Garryhinch, County Offaly, in 1976. As well as an upsurge in subversive activity, the 1970s also witnessed a dramatic increase in ordinary crime. The 1977 figure for indictable crime was two and a half times the 1967 figure. Armed robberies became commonplace and crime in general was more organised and more vicious. Those accused of crimes were now more aware of their rights and there were few places to detain young offenders. The media became much more critical of the force. There was much controversy concerning a so-called 'heavy gang' of gardaí and their treatment of Republican suspects.

The number of gardaí was increased by almost 50 per cent in the 1970s, so that by 1979 the total strength of the force was nearly 9,500. Advances in technology, new methods of communication, and the civilianisation of certain clerical jobs, as well as the introduction of a nationwide network of traffic units, were some of the changes that took place. In 1971 the Garda Press Office was set up. In 1972 the force celebrated its golden jubilee, and the Garda Band was re-established on a full-time basis. The following year, Commissioner Wymes retired, to be replaced by Patrick Malone, who retired in 1975 to be replaced by Edmund P. Garvey. In 1978 the government replaced Commissioner Garvey with Patrick McLoughlin.

As the 1970s progressed, it became increasingly obvious that the negotiating machinery available to gardaí for sorting out difficulties and grievances with their senior officers was ineffective and outdated. By 1978 the old representative bodies had been replaced by four representative associations, of which the Garda Representative Association (GRA) and the Association for Garda Sergeants and Inspectors (AGSI) were to become the best known. Unlike their predecessors, these bodies did not depend for their existence on the goodwill of management and they could now negotiate as independent entities in their own right. Furthermore, the conciliation and arbitration scheme was improved to increase the involvement of rank-and-file members, as well as broadening the scope of its work to include guidelines governing areas such as promotions, transfers and discipline. By the late 1970s, banghardaí received equal pay and they no longer had to retire on marriage. In 1979 the marriage ban on both men and women entering the force was removed. By then, all members were covered by the Health Act, but only lower-paid gardaí could depend totally on it — the others had to supplement it with Medical Aid Society or Voluntary Health Insurance cover.

By the end of the 1970s the Garda Síochána had a much more modern complexion than ten years earlier. In terms of pay, welfare and representative associations, the force was much more in line with the conditions of service enjoyed by those in other walks of life. However, the actual job had changed significantly and it was now much more challenging, complex and indeed dangerous. No radical changes had been made in the structure and administration of the force, although the government did appoint Professor Louden Ryan to head a committee of enquiry into the force. In 1979 the committee published its report. As well as making recommendations regarding pay, it found that the intro-duction of payments for working unsociable hours and overtime had led to wide disparities in earnings between members of the same rank. It also pointed out that the existing procedures for promotion were widely regarded as being unfair — it did not investigate whether this was the reality or just a perception. It suggested far-reaching changes in recruitment and training procedures, and also stressed the need for training programmes for all ranks, an area that had been neglected in the 1970s. Although its remit did not include the roles of the Depart-ment of Justice and the Garda Commissioner, it pointed out that there appeared to be no major problems in this area. The Ryan report drew attention to the fact that there was an increased preoccupation with money among gardaí, as there was in Irish society in general at the time. It stressed that more money by itself would not resolve the problems of the force and that changes regarding recruitment, training, promotion and management were of much greater importance for the future de-velopment of the force.

1980s

The early 1980s were characterised by high inflation, which reached a peak of 21 per cent in 1982. It dropped to single figures for the next few years and by 1989 was running at below 4 per cent. However, a spiral-ling national debt forced governments to follow a policy of fiscal rectitude. This resulted in attempts to control the size of the public service as well as its wages bill. Over 70,000 people emigrated from Ireland in the 1981–6 period, and by the latter part of the decade the rates had reached the heights of the 1950s. Unemployment continued to soar and by the early 1990s had reached 300,000. Marital breakdown and the number of single-parent families increased. Drug abuse, in particular heroin addiction, became a major problem among young people, especially in the cities.

Gardaí were reasonably happy with the pay increases recommended by the Ryan report in 1979, with the exception of young guards, ser-geants and those who did not earn overtime. However, high inflation and high taxation soon took the lustre off that settlement. A substantial curtailment of overtime in 1982 did not help. However, relatively low inflation rates and a national realisation that the country's finances had to be brought under control meant that pay did not surface again as a major issue until the latter part of the decade. A reduction in overtime in 1986 and a virtual embargo on recruitment and on some promotions were not well received by the force.

The Garda Síochána suffered eight fatalities in the early 1980s, equalling the high total of the 1922–6 period. In July 1980, Garda John Morley and Garda Henry Byrne were both shot dead by Irish National Liberation Army bank robbers near Ballaghaderreen, County Roscommon. In October, Detective Garda Seamus Quaid was shot dead by the IRA at Ballyconnick, County Wexford. In February 1982, Garda Patrick Reynolds was shot dead by an INLA robber in Tallaght, Dublin. In April 1983, Sergeant Patrick McLoughlin was shot dead by a man at Dunboyne, County Meath. In December 1983, Recruit-Garda Gary Sheehan was killed by the IRA during the freeing of kidnap victim Don Tidey at Ballinamore, County Leitrim. Detective Garda Francis Hand was shot dead by the IRA during a robbery at Drumree, County Meath, in August 1984. Sergeant Patrick Morrissey was shot dead by two INLA men after a robbery at Collon, County Louth, in June 1985.

In the early 1980s, rising crime figures caused widespread public concern. The establishment of divisional task forces and an increase in the number of armed gardaí helped to reduce the number of armed robberies, especially of banks. The level of crime actually decreased in the mid-1980s, only to begin to rise again at the close of the decade. The nature of crime changed somewhat, with 'joyriding', attacks on the elderly and armed drug-related crimes becoming much more common. The force had long campaigned for a strengthening of the law against the criminal. The introduction of the Criminal Justice Act, 1985, went some way towards meeting its demands. A Garda Síochána (Complaints Act), 1985, was also introduced, which set out the procedures to be followed in the investigation of complaints by the public against members of the force.

In 1981 the Garda Síochána had approximately 10,000 members. By 1984 this had risen to 11,200, at which level it remained for the next few years. By 1988 the effects of the earlier embargo on recruitment and the retirement of many of the 1950s men meant that numbers had dropped to about 10,500. In order to alleviate the situation. the retirement age was temporarily extended from fifty-seven to sixty. The number of women in the force increased from thirty-five in 1977 to 300 in 1983, which included three inspectors, and eight sergeants. In 1981 a new training college was opened in Templemore to provide training for senior officers. In 1985 a committee under Dr Thomas Walsh was set up to examine all aspects and stages of garda training. By the end of the decade, garda-recruits, now called student-gardaí, had to undergo two years' training. This consisted of five separate but integrated phases, two of which involved on-the-job training carried out under professional guidance. The 1980s saw an increase in the number of specialised units within the force, which now included the drug squad, crime units, special investigation units, task forces, traffic corps and protection corps, among others. A new communications system was established, and increased computerisation of the force got underway. New ventures in community policing were introduced in a number of urban and rural areas. Towards the end of the decade, more civil servants were employed so as to free gardaí for operational duties. In 1989, thirty-three gardaí were sent to Namibia as part of an international police force.

In the early 1980s a number of controversial incidents involving the force received much publicity. In January 1983, Garda Commissioner McLoughlin and Deputy Commissioner Ainsworth retired, having become caught up in matters relating to the tapping of the phones of two journalists. The Kerry babies tribunal, which examined events surrounding the garda investigation into the deaths of two infants in County Kerry in 1984, did not enhance the reputation of the force. The death of a man in garda custody in Shercock, County Cavan, received much publicity. Laurence Wren became the new commissioner in 1983. He retired in 1987 and was replaced by Eamonn Doherty, who retired the following year, and Eugene Crowley became the new commissioner.

A reorganisation of the medical aid scheme meant that by the end of the decade most gardaí were members of St Paul's Garda Medical Aid Society, which provided both ordinary and comprehensive health cover. In 1985 career breaks were introduced as an option for members. In 1986 the Garda Benevolent Society opened Raheny house as a retirement home for former members. In 1988 three new welfare officers were appointed, in addition to the one already provided for the force. Garda pilgrimages went to Rome in 1982 and to Lourdes in 1984. In 1987 the navy blue uniform was replaced by a lighter blue one. A Garda Museum was opened in the Phoenix Park headquarters in that year.

Throughout the decade the representative bodies campaigned for better pay, improved promotional and recruitment procedures, and a strengthening of the laws against criminals, and they also highlighted the increased stress that now accompanied the job. Much progress was made in the area of station accommodation. About seventy-five new stations were built, as well as a new police college at Templemore.

1990s

The economy performed well in the first half of the 1990s, with inflation remaining low. However unemployment figures remained very high. The gardaí had a number of important arms finds before, during and after the IRA ceasefire of August 1994. In June 1996, Detective Garda Jerry McCabe was shot dead in Adare, County Limerick during an IRA attempted robbery. Crime rose by 16 per cent in the 1990–96 period. There was a growing tendency on the part of criminals to use firearms. Drug-related crime increased with a small number of criminals being responsible for serious and organised crime. The investigative journalist Veronica Guerin was shot dead in Dublin in June 1996.

In 1991, Patrick Culligan replaced Commissioner Crowley who re-tired. A five-year corporate strategy plan regarding the administration of the force was introduced. New methods in deciding the personnel needs for each garda district were adopted. The concept of community policing in rural areas was extended. This was an attempt to achieve a balance between the traditional, familiar role of the rural garda and administrative efficiency. Management suggested introducing a staff appraisal scheme called 'Performance, Development and Review'. A new tenure policy was introduced whereby, in future, members taking up specialist jobs would return to mainstream policing after a specified time. Garda management felt that all of these changes were essential for the future efficiency of the force. A number of members felt that some of the new schemes were simply not suited to an organisation like the Garda Síochána. Others felt that there were insufficient personnel to make some of the innovations work effectively.

Internal divisions in the Garda Representative Association, which had been simmering for a number of years, came into the public arena in the 1990s. In 1994 the GRA split into three, with a breakaway group forming the Garda Federation and the representatives of four garda divisions remaining independent of either the GRA or the Garda Fed-eration. Attempts by the garda commissioner, an independent mediator and successive Ministers for Justice to resolve the dispute have been unsuccessful to date.

By 1996 the total strength of the force was 10,700 members. Of these, about 7 per cent were women — the term bangharda was officially dropped in 1991. In 1992 the Dublin Garda Recreation Club opened a fine new sports complex at Westmanstown. The 1990s saw gardaí serv-ing as part of UN police forces in such diverse places as Namibia, Cambodia, Croatia, Angola, Cyprus, Somalia and South Africa. In July 1996 Patrick Byrne replaced Commissioner Culligan who retired.

14

CONCLUSION

1922–52

There was great continuity between the RIC and its successor, the Garda Síochána. Some continuity was inevitable considering that the *raison d'être* of both forces was the prevention and detection of crime. In 1922, the almost total domination by RIC personnel of the seminal organising committee greatly increased the similarity between the two police bodies. However, the close resemblance between the old and new force cannot be attributed entirely to that fact. Successive Irish governments, Ministers for Justice, garda commissioners and senior officers continued, either consciously or unconsciously, to adopt and adapt traditions, regulations and mechanisms that had been used by the RIC.

The garda authorities recruited members who were almost identical to those recruited by their predecessors in the RIC. The Garda Síochána preferred to enlist men from the rural areas, especially farmers and labourers, as the RIC had done before it. Both forces received a disproportionately high number of recruits from counties Leitrim, Roscommon, Sligo and Longford.[1] Training of gardaí closely followed RIC precedent. It was a military-type training carried out in the former RIC depot, sometimes availing of RIC instructors and following the same manuals as the RIC had followed. The principle of distribution was the same for both forces — that is, a sergeant and three or four guards in each station rather than a village constable system. The ranking structures were almost identical, differing only in nomenclature. Both police forces were centrally controlled and centrally funded. The RIC and the Garda Síochána had the same problem regarding promotion, of how to strike a balance between the claims of men with long service and those with less service but perhaps more promise.[2] By and large, the Garda Síochána inherited the RIC system of discipline based on rewards, fines, reduction in rank and dismissal. The twin problems of drink and debt among their members occupied the minds of both police authorities.

Members of both the RIC and the Garda Síochána experienced problems of inhospitable and inadequate accommodation.[3] The sense of continuity between these two forces was strongly emphasised by the fact that many garda stations were former RIC barracks. The general principle governing accommodation for the old and the new force was the same. RIC members and gardaí worked long hours of duty including barrack orderly duty. They both operated under the principle that they were always on duty, leave being regarded as a privilege. Apart from times of political or agrarian unrest, the RIC had very little serious crime to deal with, especially in the late nineteenth and early twentieth century.[4] Similarly, only a small proportion of the gardaí's duties involved serious crime. The suppression of illicit distillation along the western seaboard occupied both the old and new police forces. In the early twentieth century the RIC established a boxing championship and it was also keenly involved in tug-o-war competitions. The newly established Garda Síochána continued this tradition. The members of both forces strove to secure a good education for their children as a prelude to their ascent of the social ladder.[5]

While there was great continuity between the RIC and the Garda Síochána, there were also very significant differences. Members of the RIC were armed when performing certain duties. A large proportion of the officer class were cadets who came from the higher social classes and included a disproportionately high number of Protestants. The RIC also owed its allegiance to the British Crown.

In contrast, the Garda Síochána was unarmed and it abandoned the cadet system very soon after its introduction. The ethos of the force was mainly Catholic and Gaelic. More important, however, was the fact that the gardaí owed their allegiance to an Irish government. However much the opponents of that government (the anti-Treaty side in the Civil War) might question its legitimacy and even take up arms against it, they generally did not set out to kill members of the force. The infusion of Fianna Fáil blood into the gardaí, in the form of the Broy Harriers and others in the 1933–5 period, helped to dispel many of the lingering doubts that Fianna Fáil supporters had about the force. During times of social or political upheaval, the RIC had tended to run foul of public opinion. After the turbulent first year of the force's existence, the most volatile political period prior to 1952 was from 1933 to 1935. While the actions of the gardaí may not have ingratiated them in the eyes of some sections of the community, their even-handed approach to law breakers ensured that they did not alienate any large section of Irish society.

The Garda Síochána was well regarded by the general public in the 1923–52 period. Members were well received and respected in their local communities and in the wider society in general.[6] Most of the references to the gardaí made in the Oireachtas were laudatory in nature, and the press coverage of the force tended to be likewise. In general, the Garda Síochána as a force was more popular than the RIC had been, even allowing for the fact that the latter group did not quite suffer the stigma that tradition would have us believe it did.

The conditions of service for gardaí in the period under review were not particularly good. While these conditions seem insufferable by today's standards, it must be borne in mind that they were not unduly harsh by Irish standards of the time. For most of the period 1922–52 employment prospects in the country were very poor, emigration was high and most of those who had jobs usually received quite low pay. The majority of the population lived in less than comfortable accommodation. With large families being the norm, the basic necessities of food, clothing and shelter loomed large in most people's lives. Against this background, the policeman's lot had a number of significant advantages. It offered security in employment, something that was much sought after in Irish society at that time. It also guaranteed quite a generous pension after thirty years when most members were still in their early fifties. It was one of the few jobs that afforded those with a modest education a fairly good social standing in society. The authority wielded by the guard increased the respect and standing afforded him by the community. Although not well paid, a job in the Garda Síochána offered the opportunity of security, pension and social status, which would not otherwise have been available to thousands of young men.

In the 1920s the overwhelming majority of the members of the force were young single men with few responsibilities, interested in sport, full of life and energy and not unduly worried about being frequently transferred. Their pay was more than adequate as they availed of the rent-free accommodation in barracks and had no family to support. By 1952 these men were middle-aged and married. They were laden with the responsibility of a fairly large family, usually in their teenage years. Access to secondary schooling for children and proper accommodation for the family were major concerns for these gardaí. Pay was at best adequate, and frequently inadequate, in providing a reasonable standard of living for the garda and his family.

The Garda Síochána had come into existence at the same time as the new Irish Free State. By 1952 both were reaching maturity or stagnation — depending on one's viewpoint. What contribution had the Garda Síochána made to that state by 1952? The force had become an increasingly important administrative arm of the government as a result of the myriad of non-police duties it carried out. Its presence throughout the country appears to have acted as an effective deterrent against crime. Perhaps its greatest achievement was the fact that it was accepted by all shades of political opinion and all sections of society in Ireland at the time. It was seen as an unarmed civilian police force, neither repressive nor oppressive in nature. The tragedy of the Civil War and the lack of significant economic improvement after independence quickly dampened the enthusiasm and idealism that initially greeted the foundation of the new state. The Garda Síochána, however, continued to be viewed as a notable achievement of the state and as a symbol of its success. The force was a tangible sign of independence.

1952–97

The 1952–70 period marked the beginning of change in Irish society and in the Garda Síochána. While there was some progress regarding pay and conditions it was obvious by the late 1960s that a radical review of such matters needed to be undertaken. The administrative structures of the force were also becoming increasingly anachronistic in a rapidly changing society.

The Conroy commission brought the conditions of service of the force into the modern era. It strongly suggested that a similar commission be set up to examine the role, organisation and personnel policy of the force. In the 1970–97 period a number of committees examined various aspects of the force. However, there was no radical reassessment of the entire organisation along the lines suggested by Judge Conroy. Changes in administration and personnel policy tended to be on an ad-hoc basis, reacting to immediate crises rather than amounting to long-term planning. Pay and conditions of service for gardaí have improved in the past twenty-five years. However, the job has become much more complex and difficult, and gardaí still operate in an organisation whose basic structures have not been changed since the foundation of the state. The failure to develop a cohesive personnel policy in the past, coupled with the 'stop-go' policies of various governments *vis-*

à-*vis* the force, have militated against change despite agreement between management and rank and file that such change is essential.

The difficulties faced by the force today should not obscure its great achievements. The Garda Síochána was one of the striking successes of the new state. It brought a return to peace and stability. It has weathered numerous crises while remaining a civilian-type police force, the vast majority of whose members are unarmed. Despite the soaring crime rate (which is not peculiar to Ireland), the Garda Síochána continues to enjoy the goodwill and respect of the population. Perhaps the greatest proof of the success of the Garda Síochána over the past seventy-five years is the fact that its achievements tend to be taken for granted.

References

1: POLICING IN IRELAND BEFORE INDEPENDENCE

1. McLysaght (1950), p. 202.
2. Breathnach (1974), p. 25.
3. Brady (1974), p. 7.
4. *Ibid.*, p. 10.
5. Griffin (1990), p. 26.
6. Palmer (1988), pp 360–61.
7. Griffin (1990), p. 314.
8. 'Strength and distribution of the Garda Síochána', 1924–7 (NAI, DJ, 4/10/1).
9. Griffin (1990), p. 689.
10. *Ibid.*, p. 326.
11. *Ibid.*, p. 809.
12. Lyons (1973), p. 409.
13. Brady (1974), p. 34.
14. Lyons (1973), p. 416.
15. Shea (1981), p. 65.
16. Brewer (1990), p. 79.
17. Neligan (1968), p. 129.
18. R. Mulcahy to M. Collins, 6 August 1922 (UCDA, Mulcahy papers 7/B/38) (henceforth referred to as Mulcahy papers).
19. Brady (1974), p. 27.
20. Shea (1981), p. 82.

2: GENESIS 1922

1. 'Report of police organisation committee', 27 February 1922 (NAI DT, S9049A) (henceforth referred to as Org. comm. report); 'Organising committee of Civic Guard', February 1922 (GM, P. Walsh papers) (henceforth referred to as Walsh papers).

2.   For an account of the DMP from the setting up of the Irish Free State (1922) until amalgamation with the Garda Síochána (1925) see Chapter 4.

3.   Reference to army means the Free State or National army from early 1922 onwards. Reference to IRA in this chapter means those involved in the War of Independence, 1919–21. Anti-Treaty forces refer to those IRA who refused to accept the Treaty and fought against the new Free State Government. From about the mid-1920s onwards the term IRA was used to describe those who opposed in arms the Free State Government.

4.   Org. comm. report.

5.   T. Boland in interview with author, 19 January 1991 (henceforth 'in interview' means with the author).

6.   Recollections of P. McGonagle, 1977–8 (Shaw papers in the possession of the Shaw family, Portarlington, County Laois (henceforth referred to as Shaw papers)).

7.   Recollections of Mrs P. McAvinia and M. Spellman, 1977–8 and of John Shaw c. 1982. (Shaw papers).

8.   Recollections of W. Mitchell, 1977–8 (Shaw papers).

9.   Staines to Department of Home Affairs, 11 April 1922 (NAI DJ, H 99/10).

10   T. Boland in interview, 19 January 1991.

11.   'Civic Guard routine orders', 12 April 1922 (GM) (henceforth referred to as 'Routine orders').

12.   T. Boland in interview, 19 January 1991.

13.   Temporary register of the Civic Guard (GM) (henceforth referred to as Temporary register).

14.   Evidence of Sergeant T. Kilroy, 14–17 July 1922 in 'Minutes of evidence of the commission of enquiry into the Civic Guard following the mutiny of 1922' (NAI, H 235/329) (henceforth referred to as Minutes of evidence to mutiny enquiry).

15.   Evidence of Sergeant P. J. Haugh, 21–22 July 1922 in Minutes of evidence to mutiny enquiry.

16.   North Roscommon IRA intelligence officer to Desmond Fitzgerald, June 1922 (UCDA, Fitzgerald papers, p 80/709).

17.   Recollections of P. Brady, 1977–8 (Shaw papers).

18.   Recollections of M. O'Connor, 1977–8 (Shaw papers).

19.   Collins' speech to Civic Guard at Kildare, 26 May 1922 (NAI, S 9524).

20.   'Report of the commission of enquiry into the Civic Guard following the mutiny of 1922', 17 August 1922 (NAI, S 9048) (henceforth referred to as Mutiny enquiry).

21.   Recollections of J. Daly, 1977–8 (Shaw papers).

22.   'Routine orders', 15 May–24 June 1922.

23.   Recollections of E. Sheedy, 1977–8 (Shaw papers).

24.   Mutiny enquiry.

25.   T. Boland in interview, 19 January 1991.

26.   Recollections of P. Lawlor, 1977–8 (Shaw papers); Recollections of B. Kelly, 1977–8 (Shaw papers).

27.   Recollections of J. Lennon, 1977–8 (Shaw papers).

28.   Recollections of D. Colohan, 1977–8 (Shaw papers).

29.   *Irish Independent*, 28 December 1922.

30.   Recollections of J. Connelly, 1977–8 (Shaw papers).

31. 'Activity of Civic Guard outposts', 28 July 1922 (Mulcahy papers).
32. Brennan to Mulcahy, 25 July 1922 (Mulcahy papers).
33. 'Civic Guard instructions', 9 September 1922 (GM, Staines' file).
34. 'Attacks on civic guards', April 1923 (NAI, H 99/109).
35. Recollections of R. O'Hara, 1977–8 (Shaw papers).
36. Recollections of P. Glynn, 1977–8 (Shaw papers).
37. Recollections of B. Kelly, 1977–8 (Shaw papers).
38. 'State of the country, monthly reports', February 1923 (NAI, H 99/125).
39. *Leitrim Advertiser*, 5 October 1922; *Irish Independent*, 21 February 1923; *Irish Times*, 21 February 1923.
40. Recollections of P. K. Campbell, 1977–8 (Shaw papers).
41. S.O.H., 'Opening of Carracastle Station, County Mayo,' in *Garda Review*, July 1963 (GM).
42. Recollections of P. McInerney, 1977–8 (Shaw papers); Fitzgerald papers, 22 November 1922 (p80/429).
43. Recollections of P. Meehan 1977–8 (Shaw papers).
44. 'Gnáth rialacha', 1 October 1922 (GM).
45. O'Duffy (March 1929).

3: WHO JOINED THE GUARDS?

1. Temporary register; the fact that 30 per cent of these recruits left shortly afterwards or were rejected does not materially affect the conclusions arrived at, as those not attested came from all backgrounds in roughly proportionate numbers.
2. General register of appointments 1922–31 (GM) (henceforth referred to as General register); Registry of candidates (in possession of the Ryan family, Dublin).
3. The 1922–52 statistics relate solely to those members who were recruited to the Garda Síochána in the 1922–52 period. They do not include members who were recruited to the DMP in the 1922–5 period before that body was amalgamated with the Garda Síochána.
4. Most of these IRP members would also have been in the IRA (exact statistics are not available).
5. These figures do not include members who joined the DMP in the 1922–5 period. Subsequent tables in this chapter are also exclusive of DMP men unless otherwise stated.
6. O'Duffy to Home Affairs, 4 October 1923 (NAI, 4/107); O'Duffy complained to Home Affairs in October 1923 that he had found it necessary to reject a higher proportion of army applicants than others — therefore this figure which is taken from the Temporary register may be a little too high.
7. Fedorowich (1996).
8. O'Duffy internal memo, 27 October 1923 (NAI, H 160).
9. O'Duffy to Home Affairs, early 1924 (NAI, 4/107/1).
10. All statistics regarding county, trade and religion of recruits in the 1922–31 period are based on the General register; the general population statistics are based on the 1926 census in Vaughan and Fitzpatrick (1978);

subsequent population statistics are also based on the 1926 census as the vast majority of the force joined in the 1922–6 period.

11.   Evidence of P. Brennan, 21–2 July 1922 in Minutes of evidence to Mutiny enquiry.
12.   O'Duffy to Home Affairs, February 1923 (NAI, H99/147).
13.   T. Boland in interview, 19 January 1991.
14.   O'Duffy (May 1929).
15.   For a fuller account of RIC recruitment see Chapter 4.
16.   Until the late 1940s the Registry of candidates merely recorded 'labourer' as an occupation, not differentiating between farm labourer and others. When it did begin to distinguish between these categories the ratio was about 3 to 1 in favour of farm labourers. This statistic, taken in conjunction with the fact that the majority of recruits came from the mainly agricultural west and south of the country, has been used to assume that two-thirds of those described as labourer were agricultural labourers.
17.   O'Duffy (May 1929).
18.   General register.
19.   'Application to join Garda Síochána', 1927–32 (NAI, H 235/14/1).
20.   Mary Shaw in interview, 16 March 1992, wife of Sergeant John Shaw, Church of Ireland member who served in the force 1922–53.
21.   'Oriel House CID', May 1923 (NAI, H169).
22.   Brady (1974), p.127.
23.   Temporary register.
24.   O'Duffy to Home Affairs, 21 December 1922 (NAI, H99/145).
25.   O'Duffy to Home Affairs, November 1922; 14 May 1923; 20 October 1923; Finance to O'Duffy, 23 November 1923 (NAI, H99/132).
26.   The Department of Home Affairs became the Department of Justice in 1927 but it continued to be referred to by its former name by many people for some time.
27.   See Chapter 6 for a fuller account of O'Duffy's proposal.
28.   'Commissioner's annual report', 1929 (NAI, S 6093A).
29.   'Garda Síochána establishment scheme' 1922–30, (GM).
30.   *Irish Times*, 24 February 1933.
31.   O'Duffy, in interview in *Garda Review*, June 1932.
32.   For a full account of this incident see Brady (1974), pp. 172–6.
33.   'Kilrush labour dispute', 19 December 1932 (NAI, S 2874).
34.   'Kilrush labour dispute', 29 December 1932 (NAI, S 2874).
35.   'Commissioner Eoin O'Duffy', 14–16 March 1933 (NAI, S 6485A).
36.   *Ibid*.
37.   See Chapter 4 for details of the 1925 amalgamation.
38.   All statistics regarding county, trade, religion, age and height of recruits in the period 1931–52 are based on the Registry of candidates.
39.   The term Broy Harriers more properly applies just to the seventy-nine men assigned to the Special Branch on the day of attestation; subsequent references to Broy Harriers refer solely to this small group of men.
40.   'Use of Irish', 6 April 1944 (NAI, 4/31/2); Temporary register, this recorded recruits' proficiency or lack of it in the Irish language.
41.   Martin (1975).
42.   'Representative body notes', *Garda Review*, June 1938 (henceforth referred

to as 'Rep. body notes').

43. See Chapter 8 for further treatment of the LDF and LSF.
44. The apparent aberration in the pattern which shows Dublin county grouped with a band of counties in the western half of the country is explained by Dublin's disproportionate population which was 17 per cent of the state's total.
45. The inclusion of Laois in a mainly western dominated cluster of counties can be partly explained by the fact that up to one-third of these men arrived *en masse* to join the force from Portlaoise in February 1922, see Chapter 2 for further details.
46. Griffin (1990), p.90.

4: ENTRY, TRAINING AND ORGANISATION

1. Org. comm. report, 27 February 1922.
2. 'Application to join Garda Síochána', 1923–7 (NAI, H 235/14/1).
3. *Ibid.*
4. 'Garda Síochána designations, appointments and discipline regulations', 19 June 1924 (NAI, S 4947A).
5. 'Recruiting and examinations', August 1936 (GM).
6. 'Taca', 1939–40 (GM).
7. *Ibid.*
8. T. Long in interview, 19 January 1991.
9 'Report of interview board', 3 November 1943 (NAI, S 7989A).
10. 'Garda Síochána appointment regulations', 18 October 1946 (NAI, S 9540B).
11. 'Application to join Garda Síochána', 1923–7 (NAI, H 235/14/1).
12. 'Public recruiting notice', 2 October 1922 (NAI, S 9049A).
13. 'Application to join Garda Síochána', 1923–33 (NAI, H 235/14/1-3); 'Application to join Garda Síochána', 1934–45 (NAI, 4/1/1-7).
14. 'Examination for recruits', 30 September 1937 (NAI, S 9540).
15. O'Duffy (June 1929).
16. T. Ryan in interview, 2 February 1991.
17. O'Duffy (June 1929).
18. Recollections of P. McGonagle, 1977–8 (Shaw papers).
19. 'Civic Guard general distribution', September 1923 (NAI, H 99/29).
20. 'Distribution of force in Cork', 6 September 1922 (NAI, H 21).
21. 'Report of commission of enquiry into Garda Síochána 1950', (NAI, S 7989) (henceforth referred to as 1950 enquiry).
22. Home Affairs to Executive Council, 11 May 1923 (NAI, S 3058).
23. 'List of Garda Síochána divisional offices', 31 July 1924 (GM, Staines' file).
24. 1950 enquiry.
25. 'Strength of DMP', 17 June 1924 (NAI, H 225/4).
26. J. Heffron in interview, 2 February 1991.
27. *Ibid.*
28. 'Report on the remuneration and conditions of service, commission on the Garda Síochána' (Dublin, 1970) (henceforth referred to as the Conroy commission after its chairman Judge J. Conroy).
29. 1950 enquiry.

30. *Ibid.*
31. 'Garda Síochána establishment scheme', 1930 (GM).
32. In 1926 Galway county was divided into two divisions, East and West Riding, thus bringing the number of divisions up to twenty-one, excluding Dublin; Kilkenny and Waterford were later amalgamated, thus reducing the total number to twenty again.

5: PROMOTION

1. O'Duffy (June 1930).
2. One sergeant who had passed the sergeant's examination in June 1923 and was sent to Thurles in charge of four guards had very little knowledge of police duties; recollections of J. Gallagher, 1977–8 (Shaw papers).
3. 'Promotion to rank of superintendent', 1924, (NAI, 4/82/1).
4. 'General circulars', 15 February 1924 (GM).
5. 'RIC pensioners in Garda Síochána', 24 February 1925 (NAI, H99/9).
6. 'Cadet appointments', May 1923 (GM).
7. 'Cadets', 1922–52 (NAI, 4/218/1).
8. Officers' register (GM); all statistics relating to officers are based on this register unless otherwise stated.
9. 'Representative body resolutions', *Garda Review*, November 1926 (hereafter referred to as 'Rep. body res.'); by 1927 there were three representative bodies, one for officers, one for NCOs and one for guards, who jointly forwarded their resolutions to the commissioner. They are hereafter referred to as 'the representative bodies' unless the need arises to distinguish between them.
10. 'Rep. body res.', *Garda Review*, September 1927.
11. *Garda Review*, November 1926.
12. 'Commissioner file', 3 September 1930 (GM).
13. 'Rep. body notes', *Garda Review*, April 1935.
14. Editorial, *Garda Review*, April 1949.
15. A small number were DMP sergeants appointed prior to 1922, but as almost two-thirds of the pre-1922 DMP had resigned by 1925 many DMP sergeants were post-1922 appointments.
16. Editorial, *Garda Review*, April 1949.
17. Broy to Justice, 26 August 1936 (NAI, 4/29/2); 'Use of influence in Garda Síochána', 23 June 1948 (NAI, 4/29/2).
18. The minimum service required in a particular rank in order to qualify for promotion varied — in the very early years it did not exist, by the late 1920s it was usually about three years in each rank; as the 1930s progressed it lengthened to five or seven years in some ranks. In practice, promotion after 1930 usually came to those who had far more years of service in their particular rank than was the required minimum.
19. Officers' register.
20. Almost all of the men, who were over 40 years of age when appointed officers in the 1920s were former DMP men who became superintendents in the Dublin metropolitan area after years of service and progress up the ranks.
21. Officers' register, this recorded favourable and unfavourable records.

22. 'Appointment of officers', 1923–52 (NAI, S 3385, S 8875/A/B/C/D. S 8876).
23. *Ibid.*
24. 'Appointment of officers', 15 August 1940 (NAI, S 8875A); T. Long in interview, 19 January 1991.
25. W. J. McConville in interview, 26 January 1991.
26. This view emerges from off-the-record comments in interviews with quite a number of members who served in the force in the 1920s, 1930s and 1940s, including those of garda rank, NCOs and officers.
27. 'Appointment of officers', 19 January 1951 (NAI, S 8875D).
28. All statistics relating to chief superintendents are taken from the officers' register.
29. 'Appointment of officers', 1936–51 (NAI, S 8875/A/B/C/D).
30. 'Appointment of officers,' 1923–40 (NAI, S3385, S8875, S8876).
31. Off-the-record comments in interview by various members who served in the force in the 1922–52 period.
32. *Irish Independent*, 1 December 1944; *Irish Press*, 1 December 1944.
33. B. Coogan in interview, 11 February 1991.
34. 'Appointment of assistant and deputy commissioners', 1935–9 (NAI, S 9201A).
35. *Ibid.*

6: CONDITIONS OF SERVICE

1. Although it was the Ross commission that officially set the new rates of pay for the RIC and DMP in 1919, the new scale was much more frequently referred to as the Desborough rates.
2. Conroy commission; all rates of pay for the Garda Síochána are taken from this source unless otherwise stated; decimal equivalents are given in brackets.
3. Mutiny enquiry.
4. M. Hegarty in interview, 4 December 1988.
5. The Garda Síochána code, 1928.
6. 'Report of representative bodies', in *Garda Review*, July 1928.
7. 'Reduction in salaries', (NAI S 6341/4).
8. Editorial, *Garda Review*, October 1933.
9. Editorial, *Garda Review*, May 1934; Editorial, *Garda Review*, February 1935; Editorial, *Garda Review*, May 1935.
10. Editorial, *Garda Review*, March 1937.
11. Finance to De Valera, 13 December 1937 (NAI, S9967A).
12. Editorial, *Garda Review*, January 1938.
13. Editorial, *Garda Review*, January 1946.
14. 'Civil service arbitration board', 24 May 1951 (quoting Central Statistics Office cost-of-living index) (NAI, S9967C); Conroy commission.
15. Editorial, *Garda Review*, May 1937; 'Rent allowance', in *Garda Review*, May 1946.
16. Ernest Blythe papers, 28 October 1931 (UCDA p24/147).
17. Commissioner Kinnane to Justice, 4 November 1946 (NAI, S9967B); 'Civil service arbitration board', 24 May 1951 (NAI, S9967C).
18. 'Without prejudice', *Garda Review*, January 1951.

19.   T. Ryan in interview, 22 October 1993.
20.   'Garda Síochána hospital expenses', 1928–33 (NAI, H314).
21.   Garda Síochána Pensions Order, 1925.
22.   'Benevolent Fund Society', 1924–62 (NAI, 4/41/1).
23.   General register.
24.   'Medical Aid Society', 1929–54 (NAI, 4/27).
25.   The reward fund was made up of fines imposed for disciplinary reasons on members of the force, as well as the fees that sergeants who were ex-officio inspectors of weights and measures were allowed to charge; members who showed exceptional zeal or ability were rewarded from this fund.
26.   Broy to Justice, 20 August 1936 (NAI, 4/29/2).
27.   'Rep body notes', *Garda Review*, November 1940; 'Without prejudice', in *Garda Review*, March 1942.
28.   Broy to Justice, 26 August 1936 (NAI 4/29/2); 'Use of influence in Garda Síochána', 23 June 1948 (NAI, 4/29/2).
29.   O'Toole (1990).
30.   'Garda Síochána discipline regulations', 1926–42 (NAI, S4947A).
31.   'Garda Síochána retirement regulations', 13 June 1941 (NAI, 4/60/1).
32.   Editorial, *Garda Review*, October 1943, quoting *The Leader*.
33.   O'Duffy (December 1931).
34.   Editorial, *Garda Review*, August 1949.
35.   T. Long in interview, 19 January 1991.
36.   Home Affairs to Finance, 24 July 1925 (NAI, 4/28/1A).
37.   'Attacks on Garda Síochána', January–December 1924 (NAI, H99/109/2).
38.   Brady (1974), p. 136.
39.   O'Duffy to Justice, 6 December 1926 (NAI, S5260).
40.   O'Higgins to Executive Council, 3 January 1927 (NAI, S5260).
41.   Broy memorandum to chief superintendents, 24 November 1933 (NAI, 4/28).
42.   Brady (1974), p. 235.
43.   Coogan (1970), pp. 247–8.
44.   'Garda Síochána arming', 1943–8 (NAI, 4/28/2C).

7: ACCOMMODATION

1.   'Civic Guard general distribution', 27 September 1923 (NAI, H 99/29).
2.   Home affairs to Executive Council, 30 May 1924 (NAI, S3837).
3.   *Ibid.*
4.   'Civic Guard Acquisition of Premises (Amendment) Bill', 1932 (NAI, H 235/287).
5.   *Guth an Gharda*, 7 August 1924.
6.   'Accommodation', *Garda Review*, October 1927.
7.   'Rep. body notes', *Garda Review*, July 1928.
8.   *Ibid.*, October 1936.
9.   Mrs Margaret Delaney in interview, 3 January 1991.
10.   'Rep. body res.', *Garda Review*, October 1936.
11.   'Garda Síochána building programme, planning for post-war problems', 28 July 1942 (NAI, S 12892).
12.   Kinnane to Justice, 28 June 1948 (NAI, 4/123/3/A).
13.   1950 enquiry.

14. Editorial, *Garda Review*, April 1941.
15. *Ibid.*, June 1950.
16. 'Pay and allowance', November 1945 (NAI, 4/38/2).
17. 'Without prejudice', *Garda Review*, May 1948.
18. 'Garda Síochána building programme', 1952 (NAI, 4/128/4/1).

8: DAILY ROUTINE

1. O'Duffy's reply to representative bodies in *Garda Review*, November 1928.
2. All statistics relating to hours of duty are compiled from the 1928 Garda Síochána code, the 1950 enquiry, the *Garda Review*, and interviews with retired members of the force.
3. M. Hegarty in interview, 4 December 1988.
4. 'Strength of stations', *Garda Review*, October 1939.
5. 1950 enquiry.
6. 'Garda Síochána work', *Garda Review*, June 1926.
7. Editorial, *Garda Review*, December 1928.
8. Editorial, *Garda Review*, July 1926.
9. Allen (March 1992).
10. 'Commissioner's annual report', 1929 (NAI, H 235/270); 'Criminal statistics', *Garda Review*, July 1936; 'Garda Síochána establishment scheme', 1930 (NAI, S7989A); offence is an all-encompassing term, which includes very serious crime and minor infringements of the law; crime, which usually means indictable crime, refers to serious law breaking such as murder and violent crime, and includes all larceny.
11. J. P. Cooke, 'Memories', *Garda Review*, July 1967.
12. M. Hegarty in interview, 4 December 1988.
13. T. Long in interview, 19 January 1991.
14. 'Duties in event of invasion', 23 January 1941 (NAI, S12273).
15. 'Report of the garda commissioner on crime', 1947–9 (NAI, S14741A).
16. 1950 enquiry.
17. 'Garda Síochána establishment scheme', 1930 (NAI, S7989A).
18. 1950 enquiry.
19. T. Boland in interview, 19 January 1991.
20. 'Inspections by commissioner', 26 June 1923 (GM).
21. Inspection books, 1933–51 (GM).
22. T. Boland in interview, 19 January 1991.
23. 'Letters to editor', *Garda Review*, October 1943.
24. W. J. McConville in interview, 26 January 1991.
25. Diary of John Hartigan, Emly station, County Tipperary, 1 February 1928 (GM) (henceforth referred to as Hartigan diary).
26. Hartigan diary, 29 February 1928.
27. Hartigan diary, January–November 1928.
28. There were many joking references to such patrols in the *Garda Review*, 1930–52.
29. John McGahern (1963) gives a very good atmospheric description of the daily life, especially barrack orderly routine in his novel *The Barracks*.
30. Hartigan diary, January–November 1928, 14–23 April 1928.

9: LIFE OUTSIDE BARRACKS

1. *Freeman's Journal*, 2 April 1923.
2. 'Irish language and national pastimes,' in *Iris an Gharda*, 12 November 1923.
3. O'Duffy (October 1929).
4. Coiste Siamsa, *Jubilee, a souvenir of 50 historic years of sport in the Garda Síochána 1922–72* (Dublin, 1972).
5. O'Donnell (1989), p. 48.
6. Dick Hearns in interview, 9 December 1990.
7. *Ibid.*
8. Neary (1985); Jim Branigan or 'lugs' as he was affectionately known was a garda boxer during the 1930s.
9. 'Sport', *Garda Review*, December 1935.
10. 'Recognition of sport in Ireland', *Garda Review*, December 1928.
11. 'President visits depot', *Garda Review*, September 1933.
12. 'Inspections by commissioner', 29 June 1923 (GM).
13. Garda Síochána code.
14. 'Without prejudice', *Garda Review*, February 1949.
15. 'Marriage regulations', 12 April 1948 (NAI, 4/29/2).
16. 'Rep. body notes', *Garda Review*, November 1928.
17. McGahern (1974) gives a very graphic account of the hardship involved in *The Leavetaking*, pp. 45–51, 56–8.
18. 'Rep. body notes', *Garda Review*, November 1928; 'Garda Síochána estimates', 1930–1 (NAI, H 235/251); 'Rep body notes', *Garda Review*, October 1936; 'Garda Síochána and married quarters', 14 July 1944 (NAI, S12892).
19. 'Letters to editor', *Garda Review*, February 1932; 'Letters to editor', *Garda Review*, June 1939; 'Rep. body notes', *Garda Review*, December 1942; 'Without prejudice', *Garda Review*, December 1942.
20. M. Delaney in interview, 3 January 1991.
21. T. Ryan in interview, 22 October 1993.
22. *Ibid.*
23. McGahern (1963): pp. 165–179.
24. O'Duffy (January 1932).
25. 'History of Scott medal', *Garda Review*, January, February 1959.
26. 'Aonach', *Garda Review*, September 1929.
27. B. Coogan in interview, 11 February 1991.
28. O'Duffy (November 1929).
29. Editorial, *Garda Review*, September 1939.
30. Garda Síochána code.
31. T. Boland in interview, 3 November 1993.
32. *Ibid.*
33. *Ibid*; N. White in interview, 13 January 1991; J. Heffron in interview, 2 February 1991.
34. W. J. McConville in interview, 26 January 1991.
35. P. Byrne in interview, 16 February 1991; N. White in interview, 13 January 1991; M. Shaw in interview, 16 March 1991; M. Delaney in interview, 3 January 1991.
36. Austin Deasy in interview in *Garda Review*, November 1982.

10: GAELIC AND CATHOLIC

1. 'Irish language', 6 May 1922 (NAI, H72); exact statistics do not exist for the year 1922. However, the figure of 10 per cent is a fair estimate.
2. Lyons (1973), p. 638.
3. Kelly (1993), p. 9.
4. O'Duffy to Home Affairs, 14 May 1925 (NAI, 4/31/1).
5. *Ibid.*, June 1928.
6. M. Hegarty in interview, 4 December 1988; T. Boland in interview, 19 January 1991; W. J. McConville in interview, 26 January 1991.
7. Temporary register (this register did not begin to record the knowledge of Irish of each recruit until 1923).
8. Some recruits from non-Irish-speaking areas had studied the language under the auspices of the Gaelic League and qualified for the ring-shaped badge of competence, the fáinne.
9. 'Garda Síochána Irish census', August 1924 (NAI, 4/31/1), this census appears to have been dependent on self evaluation.
10. 'Garda Síochána Irish language returns for Irish-speaking counties', 27 April 1925 (NAI, 4/31/1).
11. Internal Home Affairs memorandum, 31 May 1924 (NAI, H72).
12. O'Duffy to Home Affairs, 14 May 1925 (NAI, 4/31/1).
13. Coimisiún na Gaeltachta (Dublin, 1926).
14. W. J. McConville in interview, 26 January 1991.
15. 'Letters to editor', *Garda Review*, December 1927.
16. O'Duffy to Justice, 2 December 1929 (NAI, 4/31/1).
17. Allen (November 1978); T. Boland in interview with author, 19 January 1991; M. Hegarty in interview with author, 9 August 1992.
18. 'Routine orders', June 1930.
19. 'Garda Síochána formation of all-Irish units', 4 June 1934 (NAI, 4/31/1).
20. 'Irish language', 5 December 1935 (GM).
21. *Ibid.*, 12 June 1936.
22. Justice to Broy, 12 June 1936 (GM).
23. *Ibid.*
24. Broy to Justice, 7 June 1934 (NAI, S 5975A).
25. O'Duffy to Justice, 2 December 1929 (NAI, 4/31/1).
26. 'Garda Síochána appointment regulations', 1943 (NAI, 4/107/A).
27. Comhdháil Náisiúnta na Gaedhilge to Taoiseach, 29 February 1944 (NAI, 4/31/2).
28. *Ibid.*
29. 'Use of Irish', October 1944 (NAI, 4/31/2).
30. Kinnane to Justice, 12 May 1946 (NAI, 4/31/1).
31. G. Allen in interview, 19 November 1993.
32. *Ibid.*
33. T. Long in interview, 19 November 1993.
34. 'Use of Irish', 12 May 1946 (NAI, 4/31/2).
35. *Ibid.*
36. Kinnane to Justice, 6 April 1944 (NAI, 4/31/2).
37. Justice to Broy, 12 June 1936 (GM).
38. Kelly (1992), p. 178.

39. Fanning (1983), p. 134–5.
40. Vaughan and Fitzpatrick (1978), 1926 census figures.
41. Fanning (1983), p. 59.
42. O'Duffy (March 1930).
43. *Ibid.*
44. A number of guards who joined in the late 1930s and during the 1940s remember seeing the Sacred Heart picture on the walls of various stations; G. Allen in interview, 23 November 1993; T. Long in interview, 15 July 1993.
45. O'Malley (1988).
46. 'Garda pilgrimage to Rome', *Garda Review*, November 1928.
47. *Ibid.*, November, December 1928.
48. 'Catholic Emancipation centenary celebration', *Garda Review*, August 1929.
49. 'Garda Síochána pilgrimage to Lourdes', (NAI H 235/257).
50. Allen (March 1992).
51. 'General order no. 14', *Iris an Gharda*, 1 October 1923.
52. Dunne (1981), p.105.
53. 'PTAA', *Iris an Gharda*, 16 June 1924.
54. 'PTAA', *Garda Review*, June 1947, June 1948, June 1949.
55. 'PTAA', *Garda Review*, August 1949.
56. 'St Joseph's Young Priests Society', 24 June 1926 (GM)
57. 'St Joseph's Young Priests Society', *Garda Review*, January 1948.
58. Editorial, *Garda Review*, December 1928.
59. O'Duffy to Home Affairs, 31 December 1923 (NAI, H 235/13).
60. Hartigan diary, January–November 1928.
61. General register.
62. 'General orders', 1922–3 (GM).
63. Mary Shaw in interview, 16 March 1992; Michael Maguire, who joined the Garda Síochána in November 1922, in interview with Donncha Ó Dúlaing on Radio Éireann, 28 November 1993.

11: THE VOICE OF THE GARDAÍ

1. Mutiny enquiry.
2. 'General circulars', 1 January 1925 (GM).
3. T. Boland in interview, 30 November 1993.
4. Editorial, *Garda Review*, May, July 1929; 'Rep. body meeting', *Garda Review*, December 1929.
5. O'Duffy to Justice, 28 January 1930; Justice to O'Duffy, 3 March 1930 (NAI, 4/129/1/A).
6. 'Rep. body notes', *Garda Review*, December 1934.
7. 'Garda Síochána right to vote', 12 January 1943 (NAI, 4/129/1A).
8. 'Franchise', 1 February 1944 (NAI, S9297).
9. Justice to Local Government, May 1947 (NAI, 4/129/1/A); 'Franchise', 1947 (NAI, S9297B).
10. Conroy commission, p. 162.
11. 'Rep. body regulations', 20 September 1923 (NAI, S3310).
12. Practically every time the representative bodies met after 1926, their

recommendations were published in the *Garda Review*, followed a few months later by the commissioner's response and some time later by the reply of the Minister for Justice.

13. 'Rep. body regulations', 1927 (NAI, S3310).
14. 'Rep. body', 13 January 1924 (NAI, H235/166).
15. 'Commissioner meets rep. bodies', *Garda Review*, April 1929.
16. 'History of rep. body', *Garda Review*, May 1932.
17. 'Rep. body notes', *Garda Review*, January 1934.
18. 'Death of P. J. Gallagher', *Garda Review*, December 1957.
19. 'Rep. body notes', *Garda Review*, July 1936.
20. *Ibid.*, July 1937.
21. Finance to De Valera, 13 December 1937 (NAI, S9967A).
22. Editorial, *Garda Review*, January 1938.
23. *Ibid.*, November 1938.
24. 'Rep. body notes', *Garda Review*, January 1941.
25. W. J. McConville in interview, 1 December 1993; T. Long in interview, 1 December 1993.
26. T. Boland in interview, 19 January 1991.
27. O'Duffy to Executive Council, 18 February 1924; O'Duffy to Justice, 24 June 1924 (NAI, H 235/166).
28. M. Hegarty in interview, 4 December 1988.
29. 'New Minister of Justice', *Garda Review*, March 1928.
30. 'Rep. body notes', *Garda Review*, July 1936.
31. Editorial, *Garda Review*, June 1938.
32. Kinnane to Justice, 4 November 1946 (NAI, S 99676).
33. Editorial, *Garda Review*, August 1952.
34. O'Duffy to Justice, 24 June 1924 (NAI, H 235/166).
35. Editorial, *Garda Review*, May 1934.
36. *Ibid.*, June 1944.
37. Editorial, *Garda Review*, March 1948.
38. 'New Minister of Justice', *Garda Review*, March 1928.
39. *Garda Review*, March 1933.
40. T. Boland in interview, 19 January 1991; W. J. McConville in interview, 26 January 1991; M. Hegarty in interview, 4 December 1988.
41. 'Dáil debate, Garda Síochána allowances', *Garda Review*, June 1929.
42. *Ibid.*, June 1930.
43. M. Hegarty in interview, 4 December 1988; W. J. McConville in interview, 26 January 1991; A. Flood in interview, 16 February 1991; P. Byrne in interview, 16 February 1991.
44. Editorial, *Garda Review*, June 1929; 'Seanad debate', *Garda Review*, July 1929.
45. 'Rep. body notes', *Garda Review*, November 1932.
46. Editorial, *Garda Review*, June 1944.
47. *Guth an Gharda*, 3 July 1924.
48. 'Garda Síochána annual report', 1931 (NAI, H235/302).
49. Editorial, *Garda Review*, December 1925.
50. 'Inspections by commissioners', 7 June 1938 (GM).

12: PREMATURE DEPARTURE AND AGEING

1.   All statistics relating to departure are taken from the General register unless otherwise stated.
2.   Figures for attestation to and departure from the force, 1922–52, are exclusive of DMP members unless otherwise stated.
3.   In a minority of instances it is impossible to know whether some members had retired or were still serving in 1952, consequently departure statistics may suffer from a small margin of error.
4.   O'Duffy (January 1930).
5.   *Ibid.*; Broy to Justice, 6 May 1933 (NAI, 4/57); McNiffe (1987), pp. 12–13.
6.   This figure includes those who were given the option of resigning as an alternative to dismissal.
7.   Hugh McGonagle, a native of Donegal resigned from the force in 1926 in order to emigrate to America (recollections of P. McGonagle, Clonmellon, County Westmeath).
8.   The departure patterns of the force, which have been analysed already, include most of these 336 officers. However, they are now being examined as a separate entity.
9.   Officers' register — all statistics relating to officers are based on this.
10. 'Wastage returns, Garda Síochána, RUC', 1929 (NAI, 235/259).
11. 'Extension of service', 1948–51 (NAI, 4/79).
12. 'Garda Síochána (retirement) regulations', 1951 (NAI, S7739).
13. General register; 'Extension of service', 1948–51 (NAI, 4/79); Shaw papers; these figures are exclusive of DMP members.
14. 'Extension of service', 29 July 1949 (NAI, 4/79); these figures include former DMP men.
15. General register; 'Taca', 1939–40 (GM); 1950 enquiry.
16. These were mainly men who joined the DMP in the 1922–5 period.

14: CONCLUSION

1.   Griffin (1990), p. 78.
2.   *Ibid.*, p. 175.
3.   *Ibid.*, p. 41.
4.   *Ibid.*, p. 448.
5.   *Ibid.*, p. 807.
6.   N. White in interview, 13 January 1991; T. Boland in interview, 19 January 1991; W. J. McConville in interview, 26 January 1991; J. Heffron in interview, 2 February 1991; M. Shaw in interview, 16 March 1991.

SELECT BIBLIOGRAPHY

PRIMARY SOURCES

National Archives, Dublin

Department of the Taoiseach, S files
Department of Justice, H series
Department of Justice, 4 series

Garda Museum, Dublin

Garda Síochána register of (temporary) appointments.
Garda Síochána general register of appointments.
Garda Síochána officers' register.
Diary of John Hartigan.
Patrick Walsh papers.
Commissioner Staines' file.
Inspection books.
Inspections by commissioner.
Commissioner's attic box.
Among a plethora of unsorted files the following are the most important: RIC,
    Taca, Cadets, St Joseph's Young Priests Society.

Garda Síochána Routine Orders
Garda Síochána code, 1928.
Garda Síochána guide, 1934.
Garda Síochána directory.
Iris an Gharda.
Guth an Gharda.
Garda Review.
An Síothadóir.
Síochán.
Report of the committee of the police service of England, Wales and Scotland
    1919 (Desborough commission).
Report of the Vice-Regal commission on reorganisation and pay of the Irish
    police forces 1920 (Ross commission).

Commission of the Garda Síochána; report on conditions of service 1970 (Conroy commission).
Garda training committee 1985 (Walsh report).
O'Duffy, E., 'History of the Garda Síochána', *Garda Review*, March 1929.
O'Duffy, E., 'Recruitment of Garda Síochána', *Garda Review*, May 1929.
O'Duffy, E., 'Policemen in the making', *Garda Review*, June 1929.
O'Duffy, E., 'Coiste Siamsa,' *Garda Review*, October 1929.
O'Duffy, E., 'Garda bands', *Garda Review*, November 1929.
O'Duffy, E., 'History of the Garda Síochána', *Garda Review*, January 1930.
O'Duffy, E., 'Chaplain', *Garda Review*, March 1930.
O'Duffy, E., 'Promotion', *Garda Review*, June 1930.
O'Duffy, E., 'Rewards', *Garda Review*, December 1931.
O'Duffy, E., 'Scott medal', *Garda Review*, January 1932.

Acts of the Oireachtas

Garda Síochána (Temporary Provisions) Act, 1923.
The Garda Síochána Act, 1924
Police Forces Amalgamation Act, 1925.
Police Forces Amalgamation (Amendment) Act, 1926.
Garda Síochána Compensation Act, 1941.
Garda Síochána Compensation (Amendment) Act, 1945.

Regulations made by Minister for Justice

Garda Síochána (Promotion) Regulations, 1924, 1925, 1929, 1936, 1942, 1943, 1947, 1951.
Garda Síochána (Designations, Appointments and Discipline) Regulations, 1924.
Garda Síochána (Discipline) Regulations, 1926, 1942.
Garda Síochána (Appointments) Regulations, 1937, 1942, 1943, 1945, 1947, 1951.
Garda Síochána (Representative Bodies) Regulations, 1924, 1925, 1927.
Garda Síochána (Retirement) Regulations, 1934, 1941, 1951.

Orders made by Minister for Justice

Garda Síochána Pay Order, 1924, 1927, 1940, 1942, 1943, 1944, 1945, 1946, 1947, 1949, 1951.
Garda Síochána Allowances Order, 1924, 1926, 1929.
Garda Síochána Allowances (Consolidation) Order, 1943, 1947.
Garda Síochána Pensions Order, 1925, 1930.

Archives Department, University College Dublin
Desmond Fitzgerald papers.
Ernest Blythe papers.
Richard Mulcahy papers.
Hugh Kennedy papers.

Franciscan Institute of Celtic Studies, Dublin
Seán Mac Eoin papers.

Privately Held Collections
Shaw papers (in possession of the Shaw family, Portarlington, County Laois).
Registry of candidates (in possession of the Ryan family, Dublin).

Interviews
Gardaí:

Name	Year joined force	Year of interview
Gd Tom Boland	1922	1991
Ch sup W. J. McConville	1922	1991
Insp John Heffron	1923 (DMP)	1991
Gd Michael Hegarty	1923	1988
Det sgt Peter Byrne	1923	1991
Det gd Ned White	1924 (DMP)	1991
Dep comm Alfie Flood	1924	1991
Sgt Dick Hearns	1929	1990
Sup Tom Long	1939	1991
Sup Tom Ryan	1943	1991
Sgt Gregory Allen	1947	1993

Spouses of Gardaí:

Name	Husband's Rank	Year joined force	Year of interview
Mary Shaw	Sgt.	1922	1992
Beatrice Coogan	Dep. comm.	1922	1991
Margaret Delaney	Sgt.	1925	1991

Newspapers

Leitrim Advertiser, 1922.
Meath Chronicle, 1922.

SECONDARY SOURCES

Allen, Gregory, 'Irish language, a study in shared problems', *Garda Review*, October 1975.
Allen, Gregory, 'Unarmed force', *Garda Review*, December 1976, January 1977.
Allen, Gregory, 'Birth of the Dublin Metropolitan Police', *Irish Times*, 2 August 1978.
Allen, Gregory, 'Could gardaí help in Irish revival?' *Irish Independent*, 18 November 1978.
Allen, Gregory, 'Constable connections', *Garda Review*, February 1983.
Allen, Gregory, 'The Passionists and the policeman in Ireland', *Síochán*, September 1985.
Allen, Gregory, 'The guards' moral battle against booze', *Garda Review*, November 1990.
Allen, Gregory, 'An unarmed force in a troubled land', *Irish Times*, 27 February 1992.
Allen, Gregory, 'Pioneers and the Garda Síochána', *Síochán*, March 1992.
Brady, Conor, *Guardians of the Peace*, Dublin: Gill and Macmillan, 1974.
Brady, Conor, 'Police and Government in the Irish Free State, 1922–33', Unpublished MA thesis, Department of Political Science, University College Dublin, 1977.

Breathnach, Seamus, *The Irish Police: From Earliest Times to the Present Day* , Dublin: Anvil Books, 1974.

Brewer, John D., *The Royal Irish Constabulary: An Oral History*, Belfast: Institute of Irish Studies, The Queens University, Belfast, 1990.

Coiste Siamsa, *A Souvenir of 50 Historic Years of Sport in the Garda Síochána*, Dublin: Parkside Press, 1972.

Connaughton, Shane, *A Border Station*, London: Sphere Books Ltd., 1989.

Coogan, Tim Pat, *The I.R.A.*, London: Fontana, 1987.

Critchley, T. A., *A History of Police in England and Wales 900–1966*, London: Constable, 1967.

Dunne, John J., *The Pioneers*, Dublin: PTAA Publishers, 1981.

Edmonds, Sean, *The Gun, the Law and the Irish People*, Tralee: Anvil Books, 1971.

Fanning, Ronan, *Independent Ireland*, Dublin: Helicon, 1983.

Farrell, Brian, *Chairman or Chief?*, Dublin: Gill and Macmillan, 1971.

Fedorowich, Kent, 'The problems of disbandment: the Royal Irish Constabulary and imperial migration 1919–29', *Irish Historical Studies*, May 1996.

Griffin, Brian, 'The Irish Police: 1836–1914, A Social History', Unpublished PhD thesis, Loyola University, Chicago, 1990.

Kelly, Adrian, 'The Attempts to Revive the Irish language through the Education System 1922–1960s', unpublished MA thesis, St Patrick's College, Maynooth, 1992.

Kelly, Adrian, 'Compulsory Irish in the schools, 1922–1960s', *Stair*, 1993 (journal of the History Teachers' Association of Ireland).

Keogh, Dermot, *Twentieth-Century Ireland*, Dublin: Gill and Macmillan, 1994.

Kotsonouris, Mary, *Retreat from Revolution: The Dáil Courts, 1920–24*, Dublin: Irish Academic Press, 1994.

Lyons, F. S. L., *Ireland since the Famine*, London: Collins/Fontana, 1973.

McGahern, John, *The Barracks*, London: Quartet, 1977; first published 1963.

McGahern, John, *The Leavetaking*, London: Faber and Faber, 1974.

McLysaght, Edward, *Irish Life in the Seventeenth Century*, Cork: Cork University Press, 1950.

McNiffe, Liam, 'Tuberculosis in Ireland', *Stair*, 1987.

Martin, Patrick, 'The Broy Harriers', *Garda Review*, October 1975.

Neary, Bernard, *Lugs, The Life and Times of Jim Branigan*, Dublin: Lenhar Publications, 1985.

Neligan, David, *The Spy in the Castle*, London: MacGibbon and Kee, 1968.

O'Donnell, Seán, *St. Mary's Hurling Club, Clonmel: 1929–1989*, Clonmel, 1989.

O'Kelly, Denis J., *Salute to the Gardaí, A History of Struggle and Achievement 1922–58*, Dublin: Parkside Press, 1959.

O'Malley, T. C., 'The guards and Mount Argus', *Garda Review*, July–August 1988.

O'Toole, Fintan, 'The Ireland we hope to leave behind', *Irish Times*, 29 November 1990.

Palmer, Stanley H., *Police and Protest in England and Ireland 1780–1850*, Cambridge: Cambridge University Press, 1988.

Shaw, John, 'In the beginning', *Garda Review*, January 1976

Shea, Patrick, *Voices and the Sound of Drums*, Belfast: Blackstaff Press, 1981.

Ua Maoileoin, Pádraig, *De Réir Uimhreacha*, Dublin: Record Press, 1969.

Vaughan, W. E. and Fitzpatrick, A. J. (eds.), *Irish Historical Statistics, Population 1821–1971*, Dublin: Royal Irish Academy, 1978.

INDEX